Access Denied in the Information Age

Also by Stephen Lax

BEYOND THE HORIZON: Communications Technologies Past, Present and Future

Access Denied in the Information Age

Edited by

Stephen Lax
Lecturer in Communications Technology
University of Leeds

First published 2001 by
PALGRAVE
Houndmills, Basingstoke, Hampshire RG21 6XS and
175 Fifth Avenue, New York, N. Y. 10010
Companies and representatives throughout the world

PALGRAVE is the new global academic imprint of
St. Martin's Press LLC Scholarly and Reference Division and
Palgrave Publishers Ltd (formerly Macmillan Press Ltd).

ISBN 0–333–92019–8

This book is printed on paper suitable for recycling and
made from fully managed and sustained forest sources.

A catalogue record for this book is available
from the British Library.

Library of Congress Cataloging-in-Publication Data
Access denied in the information age / edited by Stephen Lax.
     p. cm.
Includes bibliographical references and index.
ISBN 0–333–92019–8 (cloth : alk. paper)
     1. Internet—Social aspects. 2. Internet access for library users. 3.
Communication, International. 4. Information technology—Social
aspects. 5. Information society. I. Lax, Stephen.
     ZA4201 .A22 2000
     303.48'33—dc21
                                                    00–055679

10   9   8   7   6   5   4   3   2   1
10   09 08 07 06 05 04 03 02 01

Printed and bound in Great Britain by
Antony Rowe Ltd, Chippenham, Wiltshire

Contents

List of Tables

List of Figures

Notes on the Contributors

Robin Brown is Senior Lecturer in Political Communications in the Institute of Communications Studies, University of Leeds. He is the author of *Globalization and the State* (forthcoming) and is currently completing a book *War and the State in Twentieth-Century Europe*.

William Dutton is Professor in the Annenberg School for Communication at the University of Southern California. He directed the UK's Programme on Information and Communication Technologies (PICT) during its last years, which provided the basis for his most recent book, *Society on the Line: Information Politics in the Digital Age* (1999).

Anita Elberse is a doctoral student and researcher within London Business School's Future Media research programme. She holds Master's degrees in Communication from the University of Amsterdam and from the Annenberg School for Communication, University of Southern California. Her research concentrates on the implications of technological developments for the media industry.

Gary Herman is an IT consultant and writer. He was Head of Membership Publications for the National Computing Centre from 1987 to 1991. Since 1993, he has been closely involved with the Labour Telematics Centre. He has written extensively on ICTs, including technical reports and articles for the computing press. He has worked on a number of DTI awareness campaigns since 1989, covering open systems, software engineering, and the information society.

Joe Holly is the Workers' Educational Association's National Programme Officer for developing and co-ordinating the use of information and telecommunications technology for learning and teaching. He is Director of the Labour Telematics Centre, which provides education and training to trade unionists on the use and impact of the new technologies, and Director of the Centre for Employment Initiatives, designing innovative training and education projects in response to increasing globalization of work.

Traci Hong is a doctoral student at the Annenberg School for Communication at the University of Southern California.

Gill Kirkup is Senior Lecturer in Educational Technology, Open University, at present editing a reader, *The Useful Cyborg: Representing Gender and Technoscience*. This is her second reader on gender and technology. The first (with L.S. Keller) *Inventing Women* (1992) was reprinted in 1998. She has written and published extensively on women and technology and on gender and distance education in journals and books.

Stephen Lax is Lecturer in Communications Technologies at the Institute of Communications Studies, University of Leeds. Author of *Beyond the Horizon: Communications Technologies Past, Present and Future* (1997), he co-ordinated the ESRC-funded seminar series 'Informed or Forewarned: the Social Implications of New Communications Technologies' (1996–98).

Sorin Matei is a doctoral student at the Annenberg School for Communication, USC. He holds an MA in International Relations from the Fletcher School of Diplomacy and Law, Tufts University. A former producer for the BBC World Service, his current research focuses on international communication and the social ecology of new media.

David E. Morrison is Professor of Communications Research at the Institute of Communications Studies, University of Leeds, where he is also Research Director. His most recent book is *The Search for a Method: Focus Groups and the Development of Mass Communication Research* (1998).

Michael Palmer is Professor of International Communications at UFR Communication, Sorbonne Nouvelle University, Paris. He has published extensively on the history of the media in France and Britain, and on international news agencies. His books include *Des Petits Journaux aux Grandes Agences* (1983) and, with Jeremy Tunstall, *Media Moguls* (1991).

Michael Svennevig is Research Director of the Research Centre for Future Communications, University of Leeds. He has held research posts at both the ITC and the BBC, and was Head of Media at Research

International. He is author of *Television across the Years: The British Public's View* (1998).

Deborah Trayhurn is Principal Lecturer in the School of Information Management, Leeds Metropolitan University.

Frank Webster is Professor of Sociology, University of Birmingham. He is author of *Theories of the Information Society* (1995), with Kevin Robins, *Times of the Technoculture: from the Information Society to the Virtual Life* (1999), and co-editor (with Gary Browning and Abigail Halcli) of *Understanding Contemporary Society: Theories of the Present* (2000).

Anthony Wilhelm is Program Director for Communications Policy and Practice at the Benton Foundation, Washington, DC. The focus of Dr Wilhelm's research and publishing has been on exploring ways to address the 'digital divide' in society through bold uses of new media, such as the internet and digital television, as well as through progressive public policy. He is the author of *Democracy and the Digital Divide* (2000) which analyses several key challenges in achieving a democratic public life in cyberspace.

Granville Williams teaches Journalism and Media Policy at the University of Huddersfield. He edits the journal *Free Press* for the Campaign for Press and Broadcasting Freedom, and is an adviser to the Media Channel (http:www.mediachannel.org) which seeks to present, from a global perspective, alternative news and views about the media.

Brian Winston is Professor and Head of School of Communication, Design and Media at the University of Westminster. He has been Chair of Cinema Studies at New York University and Founding Research Director of the Glasgow University Media Group. As a television professional he has worked on *World in Action* and has an Emmy for documentary scriptwriting. Recent books include *Claiming the Real* (1995) and *Media Technology and Society* (1998).

Introduction

Stephen Lax

It was to be expected that a new millennium should bring with it a flurry of observers claiming that we stand on the threshold of a new society. We have not been disappointed. The media excitement at the fantastic financial speculation on the high-tech and internet stock market is but one instance cited to support this claim. This new society is labelled variously the information society, the knowledge society, the knowledge economy or, as this book chooses for no particular reason, the 'information age'. The contributors to this book examine various features of today's world, and find little evidence of a new information society.

Yet it is the information age, we are assured, because the key commodity for the twenty-first century is information. The technological developments of the last two or three decades mean that information can be moved around the world at speeds qualitatively (as well as quantitatively) different from the transport of goods. The consequences are economic and political: the information industries need no longer be located within a confined geography, and thus may seek out labour wherever it is most profitably available; governments may need to adopt different approaches to their relationship with business, while at the same time deploying new technologies to make this new information more widely and equitably available.

The contributors to this volume take a somewhat different view of the current period. The technology of communications has undoubtedly developed rapidly over the last two or three decades, and with it, the ways in which it is used have also changed. Yet there is a huge conceptual leap to be made before it is possible to argue that this is leading to a new kind of society, one in which existing social relations and orders are turned upside down. The chapters here instead stress that

1

the new information and communication technologies (ICTs) should be surveyed from the perspective of the present rather than some mythical vantage point with views of the future. These technologies are, after all, being deployed and used in the context of a capitalist system which has now more-or-less completed its globalization project; there is nowhere left on earth which cannot now be considered a potential market or source of labour and profit (or, of course, both). Many transnational corporations have multibillion dollar turnovers which dwarf the gross national products of several nations – for example, 'One man, Bill Gates, has more money than 135 of the United Nations' 185 members. The Ford Motor Company has a greater sales total than the combined GDPs of Greece, Ireland and Luxembourg' (Leonard and Alakeson 2000: 20). In this society, inequalities of class, race and gender show little sign of disappearing, and so these inequalities impact upon the application of any new ICTs. To construct an argument that new technologies are able to remedy this situation is therefore a challenge, but one which has obvious political appeal. Hence political commentators across the spectrum have championed new technological solutions to social problems.

Much of the commentary (and there has been a plethora of publications celebrating 'cyber-politics', 'cyber-democracy' or other expressions of 'cyber-culture') shares the opinion that *information* is the base upon which future society will develop. Thus the fundamental inequality to be remedied in future will be in access to information. Given that the internet is readily accessible via a personal computer, and more recently has become available (though in limited form) on digital television systems or on mobile phones, promoting equality of opportunity in this information economy means making sure above all else that this technology is affordable and accessible. Such routes to access do not need to be hampered by some of the institutional barriers in the way that, for example, race or gender have proved obstacles in attaining the higher levels of success in the 'old' material/money economy. A truly meritocratic system will be delivered online.

Such an argument, of course, is simplistic, but while the above description might be something of a caricature, there are nevertheless many who claim that institutional barriers and questions of power no longer mean as much as they have done historically. Yet if one adopts this line of thinking, one would presumably have to argue that everyone currently has equal access to educational opportunity (we all go to school); or that everyone has equal democratic rights (we all vote and can write to our MPs). Clearly we do not. The issue of 'access' and new

ICTs involves more complex questions – the questions which are considered in this book.

Access denied

Certainly, the question of *physical access* to this new information equipment is a real one. Yet gaining access to the new technologies is only one part of the problem. It will lead, in turn, to a series of questions. How is the technology to be utilized? The information which is suddenly accessible provides for new knowledge, but of what value? If the information offered by new technology is not considered to be important or meaningful, why should people bother with it? Therefore, any celebration of the new information technology must ask whether it promotes an increase in real *knowledge*. As soon as the question of the nature of information is raised, we must ask who decides? What kind of information is available, and, importantly, what factors determine what we are able to do with our newly acquired knowledge? In other words, how are the relations of *power* in society changed by the growth of ICTs?

Access

The focus of much discussion is, of course, the internet, and access to this technology is certainly unequal. In contrast, little attention has been paid to a less unequally distributed technology – the pager (in the US) or the mobile telephone (in the UK). In Chapter 1, William Dutton, Anita Elberse, Traci Hong and Sorin Matei examine the use of the pager in the US, and, in particular, people's reactions when pagers across the US were blacked out by the failure in 1998 of the Galaxy IV satellite. Contrary to received wisdom expressed in the media (and elsewhere) that people now depend on these technologies and are in some way shackled (to work or family for instance) by them, Dutton et al. show that most people used the pager to make aspects of their lives easier, but coped happily without it. Rather than being taken over by technology, they conclude, people incorporate ICTs in ways which suit them.

Access to other technology such as computers (at home or at work) is, however, highly unequal, and is differentiated by class, gender and race. Economic factors (that is, the cost of the equipment) are a problem at the institutional as well as the personal level. Gary Herman and Joe Holly (Chapter 2) argue that trade unions should aim to make full use of ICTs to further their aims, but recognize that access (not only to the technology itself, but also the skills to employ it) is not always straightforward. In Chapter 3, Gill Kirkup looks at a fundamental issue of access, the gender inequality in use of the personal computer, and argues that, despite the reclamation of the keyboard asserted by cyberfeminism, gender relations in fact look much the same as before.

Knowledge

Information remains nothing unless it is meaningful. In other words, unless we acquire knowledge by exposure to information, we are not enriched by it. So it makes sense to consider the state of knowledge in a world where information may be readily exchanged. Frank Webster (Chapter 4) argues against those who pronounce the end of the 'traditional' university as a place where ideas (and information) are scrutinized and analyzed, where inquiry and knowledge are esteemed. Cataloguing the undeniable changes in higher education, Webster argues these are less a manifestation of a new kind of institution (the 'postmodern university') than the result of subjection to market principles and underfunding, and that the ideals and in many cases the practices of the traditional university prevail. Deborah Trayhurn (Chapter 5) reveals further evidence of continuity rather than change in higher education, in this case undesirably in the gender divide in computing and technology courses. In these subjects, where, following the 'information society' line, one might have expected that the gender divide would begin to be closed, she finds that, despite efforts over two decades, traditional gender roles remain as entrenched as ever.

One of the most high-profile objectives is the UK government's plans (mirrored in the US) to get every school and public library connected to the internet. Stephen Lax argues in his contribution (Chapter 6) that the stated aim, to provide more equal access to information, is unlikely to succeed since it fails to acknowledge the true nature of divisions within society. Instead he suggests it is likely, if anything, to widen that gap and, further, to sanction the privatization of public spaces and knowledge. David Morrison and Michael Svennevig (Chapter 7) draw on extensive empirical data to suggest that any claim that new ICTs are creating a transformation in people's attitudes, beliefs or lifestyles is misplaced. Adoption and use of any new technology tends to be for pragmatic rather than ideological reasons, and therefore does not tend to change the way people see the world.

In the final chapter in this section (Chapter 8), Michael Palmer looks at the use of advanced technologies in the knowledge production process itself. Granted access to quality control and internal reports of the Reuters news agency, Palmer investigates the ways in which it monitored the use of its own and its competitors' stories during the 1999 NATO bombing campaign in the former Yugoslavia. He reveals how the rapid feedback gathered round the clock by the agency's headquarters helped steer the way in which the conflict was reported.

Power

The third question to be asked of the social role of ICTs is whether they undermine existing structures in society. For it may be that, on one definition at least, universal access to ICTs could be provided through public access points (in libraries and community centres, for instance). Does this of itself empower the powerless, or disempower the powerful? To argue that ICTs herald a new kind of society, one which is more equal and meritocratic, one must answer 'yes' to this question. However, on Chapter 9, Brian Winston reminds us that the history of the internet is like the history of so many other technologies (communications or otherwise). The internet's origins in the military research establishments, followed by its migration to the academy and thence rapidly to the free market, tell a story similar to that of the telephone or radio, and therefore represent as fully as any previous development the consolidation of markets (in this case the information-based entertainment and e-commerce markets) which is characteristic of free market capitalism. Granville Williams (Chapter 10) illustrates this process by describing the ways in which mergers of media empires allow massive corporations to exert a grip on all areas of the media and communications world.

From the perspective of universal access, in Chapter 11 Anthony Wilhelm discusses the 'digital divide' in the US, and argues that those at the bottom of the ICT ladder have little hope of ascending without sustained social reform. He suggests that the corporate giants of the communications industry, whilst professing concern at the division between haves and have-nots, in practice have thus far made little progress in closing this gap. Those best placed to deliver access, the non-profit organizations, in turn receive minimal funding.

Finally, in reinforcing the theme of continuity rather than transformation, Robin Brown (Chapter 12) tackles the question of globalization. In parallel with the information society discourse, globalization is widely characterized as a fundamentally novel development which constructs a new political landscape. Brown argues that the identification of globalization as a technological phenomenon is in part responsible for this overstating of its impact, and one which underplays the role of traditional institutions such as nation-states and local cultures.

The chapters in this volume firmly locate the so-called information society within the development of late capitalism rather than a revolutionary change in societies and economies. As such, it demonstrates as clearly as ever its limitations and inability to provide for all. Yet this collection does not present a pessimistic outlook. By more clearly understanding the world in which these technologies are developing, by recognizing the continuities with the past rather than supposing some schism in the near future, it surely provides a greater opportunity to argue successfully for a more egalitarian and useful provision of new technologies. That must be the first stage in ensuring that access no longer be denied.

Note

Many of the chapters in this collection originated in a series of research seminars, 'Informed or Forewarned: the Social Implications of New Communications Technologies', at the Institute of Communications Studies, University of Leeds between 1996 and 1998. This series was funded by the UK Economic and Social Research Council. I thank all contributors to the seminars, though naturally only a small selection of papers is able to appear here. I would also very much like to thank Graeme Gooday, Pete Reffell, and numerous colleagues at the Institute of Communications Studies for their inspiration and assistance in the running of this series.

Reference

Leonard, Mark and Alakeson, Vidhaya (2000) *Going Public: Diplomacy for the Information Society*. London: Foreign Policy Centre.

Part I
Access

1

'Beepless in America': The Social Impact of the Galaxy IV Pager Blackout

William H. Dutton, Anita Elberse, Traci Hong and Sorin Matei

Introduction: information, access, and the pager

Popular conceptions of the 'information society' are useful in conveying the social significance of the revolution in information and communication technologies (ICTs). Nevertheless, the idea of an information society fails to provide insights about the role of ICTs in society, and can be misleading in focusing attention on too limited a view of information (Dutton 1999: 3–14).

The social dynamic of the revolution in ICTs is not about information, but about access. Technology has not made information a new resource – for it has always been crucial in enabling individuals to fulfil their social and economic roles. Rather, the revolution in ICTs has changed the way we gain access to information and more. That is, information is but one of at least four interrelated dimensions of access. In addition to shaping access to information, ICTs define how we get access to people, to services, and to technologies themselves, such as how people use the internet to gain access to computers around the world.

Moreover, advances in ICTs not only shape how people get access, they also shape and reshape the outcomes of this process: what information people get access to, and when, and where people obtain access – influencing what you know, who you know, what you consume, and what know-how you must possess. In all these respects, tele-access may be one of the most pivotal social and political implications tied to advances in ICTs.

The concept of tele-access

Most debates about access in the information and communication sectors focus on issues of inclusion and exclusion, as the title of this book suggests, raising concerns over inequalities in access to ICTs. Over the last decade, since the advent of liberalization and privatization in telecommunications, such as with the divestiture of AT&T in the US, access has been most commonly discussed in debates over universal service in telecommunications. Universal service arguments maintain that every household should have access to a basic telephone service at an affordable price. Deregulation has made universal service a principal concern of public interest advocates in telecommunications, particularly in North America, and technical innovations have expanded this debate to encompass other ICTs, such as the internet (Anderson et al. 1995).

Nevertheless, the question of universal access to ICT network infrastructures in particular can obscure other issues of access, such as the value of filtering information – for example, screening calls from telemarketers. Most generally, new media can expand, reduce, screen and change the content and flow of information; enlarge or contract the geography of access; restructure the architecture of networks; or change cost structures in ways that fundamentally reshape access. The answering machine has redistributed power between senders and receivers. The Violence-chip (V-chip) could provide parents with more control over their children's television viewing. Social and technical choices reshape tele-access in ways that incorporate but move beyond the digital divide.

From the perspective of tele-access, individual actors, whether households or global corporations, should focus on how social and technical choices are shaping their relative power to gain access to information, communication services and technology. And, on the other side of the equation, how are social and technical choices reshaping the power of other actors – friends, enemies, businesses, and governments – to control access to them?

In this way, all ICT innovations are political in that they influence communicative power – the relative ability of different actors to control tele-access (Garnham 1999). Information politics in the digital age is about the design and uses of ICTs that reconfigure tele-access (Dutton 1999a). ICTs are becoming digital switches, which determine: 'Who Says What In Which Channel To Whom With What Effect?' (Lasswell 1971: 84).

The pager and tele-access

The pager, like any other ICT, plays a role in shaping tele-access to information, people, services and technology (Table 1.1). The pager

Table 1.1   ICTs shape access to information, people, services and technologies: the pager as a case in point

Access to:	Kind of activities	The pager as an example
Information (ICTs affect what you read, hear, see; what you know)	Storing, retrieving, analyzing, printing, and transmitting facts, statistics, images, video, data, sounds, etc.	Immediate knowledge of a telephone number or message from person calling them, irrespective of their location.
People (ICTs shape who you know; with whom you communicate)	Communications – with individuals, groups, multitudes; one to one, one to many, many to many, one to millions	Changing whom an individual speaks with by phone, but also face-to-face, by permitting people to be less tied to a particular physical location.
Services (ICTs influence what you consume; who pays what to whom)	Conducting electronic transactions and obtaining electronic services from remote or nearby locations	Enabling a call for service to reach a provider, irrespective of location or activity, and thereby influencing who eventually provides a service.
Technologies (ICTs shape access to other ICTs)	Producing, using, and consuming ICT equipment, techniques, and know-how shapes access to other ICTs	The pager requires access to related electronic systems, such as satellite and phone, to function, and is itself enabled by converging ICTs.

Adapted from Dutton (1999a: Table 1.1, 5).

most obviously conveys information, whether a beep, a telephone number, or a voice message. But it also, and most intentionally, shapes access – electronic and physical – to people, services and other technologies.

To many, the politics of the pager has been one of centralized control and increasing disparity. This contrasts with a popular conception of emerging ICTs, such as the internet and Web, being tools for individual empowerment and equality. Thus when access to pagers across the US was denied in May 1998, the primary story was one of individuals being freed from an electronic tether.

Technology shaping technology, ownership and control of the pager

This deterministic image of the pager as a tool for centralized control is anchored in part in the history of this technology as well as the experiences of those covering the news and writing editorials about this medium. The history of the pager is complex, being a technology formed from the convergence of a variety of related technologies, including one- and two-way radio, wired 'intercoms', and newer digital media. Still the early history of the pager is linked to the management of employees within large service-oriented organizations, and has contributed to its identification with management and control functions within the workplace.

For example, as early as 1921, the Detroit Police Department began using one-way radio broadcasts in ways that might be seen as an early form of paging (BPC 1997). For decades since, radios were used to contact the police, who would then use a telephone, such as a public pay phone, to call back into their station. Thus, the early use of radio was analogous to the later use of pagers as a device to locate individuals within a distributed workforce.

Later, radio systems developed for military and defence communications enabled two-way conversations using analogue radio signals. Motorola developed the 'Handie-Talkie' and the 'Walkie-Talkie' for the US military (Stone 1997: 143). But these wireless systems strove to emulate telephony rather than a page – defined in the *Oxford English Dictionary* as 'the act of summoning a person by means of a page or by calling the name until he or she is found'.

In this sense, paging may use the radio spectrum and technologies, but its design was influenced more directly by another technological paradigm, particularly the use of wired electronic systems within buildings, such as an intercom. Hospitals pioneered the use of hard-wired intercoms, employing voice or visual number displays in hallways and rooms to communicate a code that would summon particular individuals or types of staff, such as a cardiac arrest team. Individuals often failed to see or hear their page, and audio pages were disruptive to patients. Charles F. Neergard has been credited with identifying as early as 1939 the need for a system to replace hospital intercom systems. Hospitals and hotels were among the first civilian institutions to employ more personal systems like a 'Radio Pocket System' to page individuals within a single building (Motorola 1957). As one example, hotels found paging systems, such as the 'Handie-Talkie', useful for reaching employees and executives, wherever they might be within the hotel (Motorola 1956).

As late as 1974, pagers had no display screen, limiting their utility outside of a specific building, or organizational setting, where all responses to one's 'beeper', as it was often called, would be directed to one central location, such as a switchboard operator at the facility. This is one reason, in addition to spectrum scarcity, why this ICT was often limited within a metropolitan area to emergency medical personnel, such as doctors 'on-call'.

With technical gains in the efficient use of radio frequencies, and the introduction in the 1980s of pagers that could display a telephone number, the pager became associated in the public's mind with a broader variety of uses. In the US, for example, in sharp contrast with its identification with doctors, the pager came to be seen as a tool of drug dealers, whose conspicuous use of the pager led to it being banned from many schools.

In the 1990s, however, technical advances, including satellite and digital systems, expanded access to and through the pager exponentially, enabling a far greater variety of pagers at a wider range of costs. The cost of the most basic beepers based on low-power radio signals became so affordable that a few restaurants began using them for signaling customers that their table was ready for them to be seated. Individuals across much of the economic spectrum could afford to use an alphanumeric pager. At the high end, paging companies have found an emerging market for two-way pagers, that can receive and respond to alphanumeric and voice messages from anywhere in the world via other pagers, e-mail, fax machines, or telephones.

Nevertheless, most pagers used at the time of the Galaxy IV blackout were simple alphanumeric pagers. These would beep or vibrate when a message was received, and display the telephone number or another numeric code left by the caller. For example, the numbers '07734' are sent to say 'hello', since they look like the word when the pager is turned upside down.

The falling costs and enhanced functionality of the pager contributed to its widespread diffusion in the 1990s, with the number of pagers in service tripling from 1992 to 1998. By 1992, over 15 million pagers were in use within the US (Geltzer & Company, Inc. 1997), expanding to over 27 million pagers by 1994, with about one-third used for 'social reasons', and about 50 per cent of new pager subscribers classified as non-business users. In the span of four years, by 1998, over 42 million, and as many as 50 million individuals in the US were using a pager, representing 24 to 29 per cent of the adult population. It was at this point that 90 per cent were cut off during the Galaxy IV blackout (*Wired* 1997; O'Conner 1998; *Mobile Satellite News* 1998). This short-lived telecommunications disaster provided a unique opportunity for research to explore the social impact attributed to missing the pager, and thereby illuminate the social role of this largely unexamined medium of communication.

Access denied: the Galaxy IV pager blackout[1]

In 1998, most paging companies relied on satellite transmission to provide national coverage. Moreover, nearly all paging companies relied on one specific satellite – Galaxy IV. The satellite was built by Hughes Electronics, but owned and operated by PanAmSat, a division of Hughes Electronics, which was in turn owned by the General Motors Corporation. The cost of building and putting this satellite into orbit has been estimated at $250 million. Since paging requires the use of very little bandwidth or few bits to transmit a telephone number, PanAmSat could provide transmission capacity to paging companies throughout the US over this one satellite. In fact, the capacity of Galaxy IV enabled its transponders to convey a wide array of other information and communication services beyond paging – including the transmission of television programming. Because the satellite had been extremely reliable up to this point in time, very few paging companies would make contingency plans, such as deploying a second satellite that could be automatically used as a back-up system. Galaxy IV was expected to remain operational until 2008.

However, on Tuesday, 19 May 1998, at 6 PM (EST), the 'attitude mechanism', an electronic device designed to keep the antennae of the Galaxy IV satellite pointed towards the Earth, failed. The automatic switch, which was supposed to activate the back-up attitude mechanism when the main device failed, also failed to trigger itself. Although the satellite remained in a geostationary orbital location 22 500 miles above the state of Kansas (at 99 degrees west longitude), the satellite could not keep its transmission bearing through its onboard guidance system, nor could it be controlled from the ground.

The malfunction of both the main and back-up mechanisms affected paging networks immediately and throughout the US. When Galaxy IV failed, most paging companies were forced to interrupt their services almost completely, for periods ranging from a few hours to a few days. As paging providers worked around the clock to restore service, the media scrambled to assess the impact of the blackout. Estimates of affected pager users fluctuated, but converged on the estimate of 90 per cent of the nearly 50 million pagers across the US (*Boston Globe* 1998).[2] Ultimately, most services were restored within 24 to 48 hours of the blackout, with major metropolitan areas being among the first to be back in service.

Paging services were restored by moving the traffic to a neighbouring satellite (Galaxy 3R) and then, after a few days, by moving a reserve satellite, Galaxy VI, into the slot occupied previously by Galaxy IV. PanAmSat kept Galaxy VI in reserve for this kind of event. During this period, the 25 000 antennae pointed to Galaxy IV, from all over the United States, had to be repositioned manually. This required thousands of individuals across the US to travel to the ground satellite antennae and physically aim them at the back-up satellite. This relatively low-technology fix worked, restoring service within a matter of days.

The breakdown of Galaxy IV was a unique event. Although the satellite industry is often affected by difficulties related to launching, once satellites are positioned in a geostationary orbit, they rarely malfunction. Galaxy IV had shown signs of erratic service before this information disaster, but was irretrievably lost by this malfunction. In addition to the loss of this $250 million satellite, PanAmSat estimated that service interruptions led to up to $10 million of other losses.

Social implications of the pager: the silence of social research

The malfunctioning of Galaxy IV generated a flood of media coverage, much of it speculating on the impact of the pager blackout. Among these accounts, the consensus view was that being 'beepless' had been a welcome break – a moment of freedom from the 'electronic tether' of the pager (O'Conner 1998; *Atlantic Constitution* 1998). A number of media reports claimed that the paging blackout provided pager users with more freedom because the silence of their pagers made them unavailable to their supervisors, customers, or even their families' stressful demands. As one journalist put it: 'Weren't most people secretly pleased last month when the malfunctioning Galaxy IV satellite stifled 50 million pagers, with all the serendipity of a snow day?' (*Circuits* 1998).

Technological and social perspectives

This expectation of freedom is based on an underlying assumption that the pager is used primarily as a technology of control. A substantial literature on technology and society has argued that technology generally, and ICTs in particular, support control because they are perceived to be driven by the needs of large organizations that employ them (Beniger 1986). Undoubtedly, organizations use ICTs like the pager to keep in touch with employees working at home or away from the office (Holmer-Nadesan 1997; Dutton 1999: 150–4). To some, the pager has become an 'electronic leash' (Lewis 1995: 1, 5), undermining the boundaries between work and home, and extending work 'anywhere, anytime' (ibid.: 1). The historical origins of the pager as an instrument for monitoring and controlling employees within organizations fits well with this perspective. At other times, this control viewpoint is anchored in a relatively more deterministic perspective on the social role of ICTs.[3]

However, there are countervailing views which suggest a different impact of the missing pager, seeing it as a loss and not a gain in freedom. In fact, the most conventional view of the new media emerging from the convergence of digital technologies, like the pager, is that they are technologies of freedom and equality (de Sola Pool 1983; Negroponte 1995) in that they create more opportunities for individuals to choose how and with whom they wish to communicate. The internet and World Wide Web have spurred more people to view ICTs as empowering of individuals, but somehow the pager still remains more defined in terms of a mechanism for organizational control.

An alternative to viewing the pager as either a technology of control, or freedom, and one which led us to be sceptical of more deterministic claims, is anchored in studies of the social shaping of technology (Williams and Edge 1996). These studies support the view that users are able to play a significant role in shaping technologies in ways that reinforce their own values and interests (Danziger et al. 1982; Woolgar 1996). This analysis suggests that, for example, households 'domesticate' communication technologies, like the PC, as they integrate them into their day-to-day lives in ways that fit into the values and interests of the household (Silverstone 1996).

A lack of empirical research

How the pager fits within these contending views of the social shaping and impact of ICTs is an obvious question, but one on which social science and communications researchers have been silent. The few studies that have been conducted are more general surveys of public adoption and attitudes toward new technologies, and at times include the pager among lists of other ICTs, such as the personal computer (PC).[4]

One reason for the lack of research might lie in the pager's early history, which limited this technology to largely intra-organizational business uses. The pager diffused among households and businesses rapidly, but this has happened largely in the last decade. During the pager's most rapid diffusion, from 1992 to 1998, the attention of social science research on ICTs was diverted to the internet and World Wide Web. An exception includes an emergence of a few studies of wireless and mobile communication, but these were focused on telephony (Katz 1996).

A problem with the few surveys conducted on the pager is that once such ICTs are integrated into one's life, it is difficult to discern their importance. This is the proverbial problem of a fish not being able to see it depends on water. For example, a 1996 sample survey of 1008 US adults asked respondents whether ICTs like the pager and PC made their lives easier or more complex (Sloan School of Management 1999). Surprisingly large proportions of the respondents felt that ICTs had little or no impact on their lives. For example, 40 per cent of respondents said the PC or computer had no impact on their lives. With respect to the pager, 38 per cent said pagers made their lives 'easier and more convenient', 8 per cent said they made their life more 'complex', but a majority (53 per cent) said pagers had 'no impact' on their life.

The Galaxy IV pager blackout: a multi-method approach[5]

Given the media's deterministic perspective on the role of the pager, along with the near-absence of research on this technology, we conceived and executed a study of the social role of the pager in the immediate aftermath of Galaxy IV's malfunction. In this sense, our study falls within a tradition of 'fire station' research, which is characterized by a rapid response by field researchers to naturally occurring events.[6] Our study used multiple methods to gain a valid perspective on the social role of the pager blackout. It was anchored in a telephone survey of households in the five-county Greater Los Angeles area, which encompasses the counties of Los Angeles, Orange, San Bernardino, Riverside, and Ventura. The study began two weeks after the pager blackout, and lasted one full week. Its methodology was a brief (5–10-minute) telephone interview with a probability sample of 751 households chosen on the basis of a randomly-generated set of residential telephone numbers for the area.[7] We completed interviews with 668 households and obtained 250 households with one or more pager users (Table 1.2).

In addition, the research team became participant-observers of the blackout, focusing on friends and co-workers with pagers and listening to their experiences. Finally, several of our group conducted semi-structured interviews with pager users, which were recorded to gain a qualitative sense of the reactions to the blackout.

Implications for freedom or control

One of the most telling results of our survey was the degree to which the users missed the pager. Most did not perceive it as an electronic

Table 1.2   Random dialling survey sample of Greater Los Angeles area households, June 1998

Characteristic of households	Number of households	Percentage of households
Completed telephone interview	668	89
Not home, refused to answer, invalid number	83	11
Total Number Households Called	751	100
One or more pagers in household	250	37
No pager in household	418	63
Total number of households interviewed	668	100
Aware of Galaxy IV pager blackout	226	90
Unaware of Galaxy IV blackout	24	10
Total number of households with pager	250	100
Reported problem paging during blackout	150	60
Reported no problem with their paging	100	40
Number of households with pager	250	100

tether. Instead, most users saw it as a tool that enabled them to have more freedom of access, electronically and physically. For example, we assessed the 'electronic tether' theme played out in the media by examining the attitudes expressed by pager owners who had themselves experienced problems with their pager or in contacting others with pagers. Of the pager owners who experienced problems during the blackout, an overwhelming majority (75 per cent) reported no greater sense of freedom (Figure 1.1). Only 15 per cent reported a somewhat greater sense of freedom and a mere 9 per cent (13 respondents) reported a great sense of freedom.

We do not wish to adopt a position that is directly opposite to the 'tether' view and to suggest that the pager is a technology of freedom rather than control. Clearly, it played both roles, but for different users. Rather, the different responses of users suggest that some individuals and organizations employ the pager in ways that can enhance organizational control, and others in ways that empower individuals in relation to organizations. Generally, we found that the pager played a far more significant role than we had anticipated in reconfiguring electronic and physical access to information, people, services, and technology – what we define as 'tele-access' (Dutton 1999a) – in ways that affected the relative power of different actors.

Time and again, our interviews uncovered the degree to which individual users and organizations used the pager actively to relocate themselves physically or electronically in ways that either enabled or restrained access to them. Some organizations do indeed use pagers to keep their staff on call, but this often means that the staff can be where they can most effectively work. Pagers were used to bring work into the home, but also to bring private affairs into the workplace – for example, one user whose pager enabled her to get personal calls at work without her callers going through the office secretary. Parents used the pager in ways that enabled them to be further away from their children, knowing that they could be instantly reached by childcarers and teachers. A cameraman specializing in commercial shoots was able to move about and not worry about missing a call that would mean losing a role in producing a new advertising campaign. As he said, if they cannot reach him immediately, the producers 'just go to the next person on their list'. Example after example illustrated the degree to which people had literally reconfigured the geography of their work and everyday life around access to a pager.

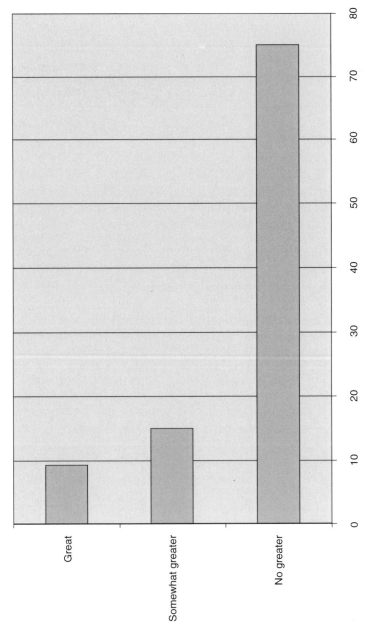

Figure 1.1 Perceived sense of freedom: percentage of all pager users who experienced problems

The social significance of the pager

The centrality of the pager to users was reflected in our survey in several additional ways. One particular theme that quickly arose from our study was the degree to which most individuals viewed the pager as signficiant to their lives – whether they liked or disliked this ICT.

First, the diffusion of the pager exceeded our expectations, as well as industry estimates of 19–25 per cent national penetration. Over one-third (37 per cent) of our 668 households surveyed indicated that one or more pagers were used by members of the household (Table 1.2). This equates to nearly 6 million residences within the Greater Los Angeles area. In addition, many of the households were (often self-identified) 'two-pager' households.[8] Los Angeles is an area built around freeways and the culture of the automobile and mobility. It is also relatively ideal for radio services, being located largely in a basin. While LA might therefore be expected to have higher than average levels of penetration, it nevertheless demonstrated the significance of the pager to this mobile, freeway-oriented population.

Secondly, the qualitative response to our survey was one of remarkable interest. Unusually for telephone-based surveys, our study had a response rate of nearly 90 per cent (Table 1.2). Even those without pagers were interested in the technology and the blackout, which was covered well by the mass media, and this coverage was central in informing people of the pager problem. In our survey, 90 per cent of the pager owners (226 of the 250) were aware of the blackout, and 92 per cent of these 226 were informed of the situation by the television, newspaper or radio.

One explanation for the significance accorded to this technology is a general tendency for 'people to exhibit strong feelings of deprivation' when denied access to media, such as TV (Berelson 1949; Wurtzel and Turner 1977; McQuail 1994). However, there were mixed reactions to missing the pager. Some felt deprived, some felt relieved. Nevertheless, our interviews repeatedly stressed the degree to which many individuals had organized their daily work or everyday life around the pager's availability.

Problems created by the blackout

Another indication of the pager's significance to access was the degree to which its absence created problems. All participants were asked whether they experienced any problems with their pager during the blackout. 150 respondents said they experienced problems while 55 individuals with pagers indicated that they experienced no problems.

However, another 21 respondents could not recollect the incidence or were not using their pager at that time.[9] For instance, one pager owner indicated that he had no idea there was a blackout, but was scolded later in the day by his wife for not answering her page. It was not until the next day, when he read of the blackout, that he was able to assign responsibility for missing his wife's page to this malfunction. Of the pager owners who experienced problems, the majority of them experienced problems with their own pager (67 per cent), followed by problems with both their own and other people's pagers (24 per cent), and finally by problems with only other people's pagers (9 per cent).

The fact that the blackout posed problems for most users is thus one further indication that users shaped the adoption and use of this ICT in ways that reinforced their needs and interests. That is, we did not gain a sense of relief from missing the pager – it created real problems. For example, among the 150 individuals who experienced problems with either their own pager or other's pagers during the blackout, 42 per cent reported their lives were changed for the worse by the blackout. This is not the reaction one would anticipate to a technology that is a status symbol with no impact on one's life, nor to one that is perceived to shackle the user.

Types of users: socializers, teleworkers, and integrators

We classified pager users in our study into three types, based on their response to a question in our survey about whether they used the pager primarily for work, primarily for contacting friends and family, or for both about equally. About one-third (34 per cent) of users said they used their pager primarily for work-related needs, and we therefore classified them as 'teleworkers'. Another third (33 per cent) said they used their pager primarily to maintain contact with their family and friends, and were therefore classified as 'socializers'. We classified a final third as 'integrators' because they reported using their pager for both work and contact with family and friends, rather than primarily for one or the other. This typology gained validity through the course of the study as it was meaningfully associated with backgrounds of users and their attitudes toward the pager. Moreover, our qualitative interviews reinforced the importance of the work versus personal contexts, even though there are many variations within each.

The utility of the pager

The majority of pager owners, across all types of users, expressed positive views toward the pager and its role in their lives. Sixty-three per cent of pager owners felt the pager was essential to their work and 83 per cent felt that the pager made their life easier. Almost everyone in the sample (96 per cent) liked the idea that people could reach them by paging, with 66 per cent saying they actually prefer this method of contact. Of all respondents interviewed, that is all 688 households with and without pagers, 67 per cent felt that society is better off with the pager. Among our 250 pager households, an even higher proportion (86 per cent) felt society is better off with the pager.

Table 1.3 shows the percentages of individuals in the three categories of primary pager usage who agreed with six attitudes statements. Almost all pager users, across all three types, liked 'the fact that people can reach them' by paging. Socializers, who use the pager primarily for speaking with family and friends, expressed this sentiment somewhat more often, but over 90 per cent of all types of respondents like the pager for this very reason (Table 1.3).

Socializers were most likely also to agree that pagers make their life easier. Integrators, the individuals who use the pager for the dual usage of work and personal communication needs, were somewhat less likely to express this view, but over a quarter of teleworkers tended to disagree with this statement (Table 1.3). Socializers and integrators were both more likely than teleworkers to agree that they prefer people to contact them through the pager. The teleworkers, who use the pager primarily for work, had a more mixed response, with only about half preferring to be contacted by pager. Teleworkers are more closely aligned with the integrators on whether the pager is essential to their work (Table 1.3). Over three-quarters of both types see the pager as essential. While this might be assumed, since both use the pager for work, nearly one-third of the socializers also say the pager is essential to their work, even though this is not their primary use of the pager.

About one-fifth of the users felt they 'depend too much on the pager' with teleworkers somewhat less likely to feel this way (Table 1.3). A larger proportion of integrators felt too dependent, with 26 per cent of this group saying they depended too much on a pager, but the socializers expressed this view almost as commonly (26 per cent). For a device that is sometimes portrayed as a status symbol or consumer fad, it is interesting to find that only 8 per cent of all pager owners felt the pager wasted their time. Equally surprising is the fact that within this small sub-population, the teleworkers are the most likely to agree with this statement. By contrast, 6 per cent of the socializers felt this way, and only 4 per cent of the integrators felt the pager wasted their time.

Table 1.3   Percentage agreeing with statements about the pager (N = 250 pager households)

| | Type of pager user | | | |
	Teleworker	Socializer	Integrator	All (total)
I like the fact that people can reach me by paging	92 (77)	99 (82)	98 (80)	96 (239)
A pager makes my life easier	73 (61)	93 (76)	84 (70)	83 (207)
I prefer people to contact me through my pager	51 (43)	74 (61)	74 (60)	66 (164)
Pagers are essential to my work	76 (64)	32 (27)	79 (65)	63 (156)
I depend too much on a pager	16 (13)	22 (18)	26 (21)	21 (52)
The pager wastes my time	14 (12)	6 (5)	4 (3)	8 (20)

Note: Numbers represent the percentage of agreement within that category. Values enclosed in parentheses indicate the actual number of respondents within category that agreed with the statement

Social shaping of the pager's role

To understand how the role of the pager might be shaped by an individual's social context and everyday life, we looked at the demographic profile of the three types of users in our survey (Table 1.4).[10] We found a clear pattern of demographic factors related to the social and economic role that the pager played in one's life. As Table 1.4 shows in more detail, teleworkers were generally older, white, male, with higher incomes and a higher level of education. Socializers tended to be younger, from racial and ethnic minorities, female, with lower incomes and less formal schooling.

Discussion

Pager users in the Greater Los Angeles area reacted to the Galaxy IV blackout in diverse ways, related in part to the different ways in which they used this ICT. But most users missed the pager, because they valued this relatively simple and inexpensive device, around which they had organized their lives to greater or lesser degrees. Moreover, the majority of non-pager owners felt that pagers (and similar technologies) were beneficial to society. Even among users who experienced serious problems during the period of the blackout, these positive attitudes toward the pager remained unshaken. It was viewed as something to be expected in a highly technological society – a satellite 'glitch'.

The 'electronic tether' theme played out in the media was not reflected in the sentiments of the pager users in our survey. Indeed, the majority of pager owners who directly experienced contact problems reported no greater sense of freedom. The important role that the pager plays in work – such as by enabling individuals to be reached by prospective customers – and in everyday life – by helping parents and individuals manage a geographically distributed lifestyle – suggests that the mobility enabled by the pager has reshaped access in ways that reinforce the values and interests of most users. In such ways, it is clear that pagers are not simply toys or status symbols, since they are reshaping tele-access in significant ways that generally empower users albeit some more than others.

Users can be grouped into three general types, based on their primary use of the pager. Teleworkers, socializers and integrators differed not only in the primary purposes for which the pager is used, but also in their social and economic backgrounds. While the value placed on the pager is equally high across all three groups of users, they value the pager for different reasons.

Table 1.4 Social and economic characteristics of each type of pager user

Demographic	Teleworker	Socializer	Integrator	Total (%)
Age				
16–20	2	76	23	21
21–30	22	34	44	27
31–40	40	16	44	22
41–50	62	12	26	17
51–60	68	18	14	9
>61	75	25	–	2
				100
Gender				
Female	28	41	31	47
Male	39	26	35	53
				100
Income				
<$20,000	18	39	43	15
$20,000–$50,000	24	35	42	38
>$50,000	55	22	23	47
				100
Race				
All minorities	16	43	41	46
White/Caucasian	48	26	26	54
				100

(cont'd)

Table 1.4 Social and economic characteristics of each type of pager user *(continued)*

Demographic	Teleworker	Socializer	Integrator	Total (%)
Education				
Some high school or less	9	75	16	13
High school graduate/trade school	18	42	40	24
Some college/college graduate	44	22	34	53
Some graduate work/graduate degree	54	23	23	10
				100

As simple, inexpensive, and widely diffused as the pager is, the social background and economic resources of households continues to shape how households integrate the pager into their lives. Even though the pager is more accessible to larger segments of the public, there is a pattern of older, white, male, and more affluent users integrating the pager primarily into their work, while younger, ethnic, female, and lower-income households are more likely to employ the pager primarily for domestic and social purposes. The integration of the pager into work and family life may be gaining prominence among many households, but these patterns of use remain in line with the way other ICTs have tended to reinforce other socioeconomic inequalities and, therefore, contribute and reflect the digital divide (Dutton 1999: 238–44).

Control over the pager has become more decentralized with its declining cost, greater ease of use, and increasing functionality. Users are able to employ the technology to serve a variety of uses and interests. Yet, some users are in a better position to benefit from this ICT within their work, while the occupational and domestic responsibilities of others limit the value of the pager within their work life. The fact that disparities can grow even as an ICT becomes more universally available was realized decades ago in studies of media effects. For example, while educational programming is accessible over television to nearly all American households, it is more often watched by children in more highly educated households, and more beneficial to children who already have greater verbal and analytical skills (Comstock et al. 1978). In such cases, even equitable access to information can widen disparities in knowledge gained.

This is one of the only social science investigations of the social role of paging technology. Carried out in the setting of a natural experiment, this case study has revealed the extent to which people have incorporated the device in their lives. Work in this field indicates that cultural, value and lifestyle factors play a major role in shaping the use of ICTs in the household and everyday life. Our research reinforces work on how households can domesticate technology in ways that reinforce existing values and interests in the household. Yet, this same process tends to constrain the use of ICTs in ways that may further exacerbate cumulative inequalities across socioeconomic groups – widening the gap between information 'haves' and 'have-nots'.

Since 1998, the pager has continued to diffuse. By 2000, 53 million pagers were in use in the US, reaching up to 20 per cent of American households (Geltzer & Company 2000). The critical role of the pager in shaping tele-access, along with its continued use in concert with the success of related ICTs such as wireless phones, should focus more social scientific attention on all kinds of wireless communications systems that support some of the same types of physical mobility. For example, in North America, the technology of the pager is rapidly converging with other wireless media, such as two-way pagers that receive and transmit voice messages, or wireless phones which embed a paging function within them, along with other services such as voice-mail. These converging technical advances are likely to enhance and reinforce the centrality of mobile ICTs in the work and everyday lives of households and organizations.

There is also a need to look more cross-nationally and comparatively to understand how institutional arrangements, public policy and national cultures have all influenced the diffusion and impacts of wireless media, like the pager. For example, the pager has not been as widespread in European nations, where wireless telephones diffused earlier than in North America. In North America, telephone costs in the early 1990s were perceived to be relatively low, while wireless telephony was perceived to be relatively expensive. The opposite perceptions shaped the widespread diffusion of wireless phones in European nations, such as Britain, where over one-third (37 per cent) of the population own a wireless phone, or Finland, where the figure approaches two-thirds (65 per cent) of the population (Cane 2000). While the world is entranced by the internet and Web, wireless media like the pager and mobile phone are reshaping tele-access, and reorganizing our work and everyday lives.

Note: The authors thank Pamela H. Dean, Mark Laterno, and Nuchpapa Mayteevinyoukij for help with the research reported here, and the Annenberg School for Communication at the University of Southern California for supporting this study.

Notes

1. This section draws on print and electronic news reports of the malfunction, along with interviews with industry representatives and reporters, following this story. Work of particular value included: Anon. (1998a, 1998b), *Circuits* (1998), LaPedus (1998), Mills (1998), and Zuckerman (1998).
2. Other services affected by this malfunction included several broadcast networks, such as: the mapping services of The Weather Channel, WB network, the CNN airport channel, Asia Radio Network USA, the Chinese Television Network, Telemundo, and some syndicated shows distributed by CBS, including *the Jerry Springer talk show, Martha Stewart Living*, and

Xena: Warrior Princess). NPR's 'All Things Considered' news program could not be delivered on May 19 to most Midwestern and Western local public radio stations. A large number of automated teller machines (ATMs) and automatic payment devices at gas stations were also disabled. These media, like the pagers, were affected for periods varying between half an hour to a few days.

3. An excellent presentation of the assumptions of a technologically deterministic perspective is provided by MacKenzie (1999).

4. There have been proprietary studies of the market for pagers, which are not in the public realm, but which also seldom investigate the social role of this technology.

5. An earlier report of our survey results was presented by Hong et al. (1999).

6. Other studies in this tradition within the communications field include a study of a 300-block area of New York City that was without telephone service for 23 days (Wurtzel and Turner 1977), and an earlier study that took advantage of a newspaper strike to investigate the social role of newspapers (Berelson 1949).

7. The telephone survey was administered by an independent survey firm, Davis Market Research Services, Calabasas, California.

8. The survey was designed to capture the number of pagers in each household, but this information was miscoded by the computer-aided interview system, and therefore, lost. However, it was a sizeable proportion.

9. One explanation for this relatively low incidence of problems is the degree to which a larger proportion of users in the Los Angeles area might rely on local systems that are tied to land lines, since the contours of the Los Angeles Basin creates an excellent area for reception of terrestrial services.

10. For determining whether differences were statistically significant across all the various demographic groups, a chi-square analysis was used.

References

Anderson, R.H., Bikson, T.K., Law, S.A., Mitchell, B.M. (1995) *Universal Access to E-Mail*. Santa Monica, CA: Rand.

Anonymous (1998a) 'Recovering the satellite Galaxy IV mishap shows fragility of communications', *The Hollywood Reporter*, 26 May.

Anonymous (1998b) 'Satellite malfunction cripples U.S. paging services', *Land Mobile Radio News*, 52, 22 May, 1998.

Atlantic Constitution (1998) 'Beepless in America: cosmic glitch caused a pause that refreshed our hectic lives', *The Atlantic Constitution*, 21 May, p. D1.

Beniger, J.N. (1986) *The Control Revolution*. Cambridge, MA: Harvard University Press.

Berelson, R. (1949) 'What missing the newspaper means', in P.F. Lazarsfeld and F.N. Stanton (eds), *Communications Research, 1948–49*. New York: Duell, Sloan and Pierce.

Bedford Park Communications (BPC) (1997) 'The history of paging', http://www.bedfordpark.com/beephist.html, March 1999.

Boston Globe (1998) 'Pager users cope after satellite zap', 21 May, p. A1.

Cane, A. (2000) 'Sales of mobile phones at record', *Financial Times*, 6 January.

Circuits (1998) 'Only disconnect (for a while, anyway)', 25 June, D1.

Comstock, G., Chaffee, S., Katzman, N., McCombs, M. and Roberts, D. (1978) *Television and Human Behavior*. New York: Columbia University Press.

Danziger, J.N., Dutton, W.H., Kling, R. and Kraemer, K.L. (1982) *Computers and Politics*. New York: Columbia University Press.

de Sola Pool, I. (1983) *Technologies of Freedom*. Cambridge, MA, and London: Belknap Press of Harvard University Press.

Dutton, W.H. (ed.) (1996) *Information and Communication Technologies – Visions and Realities*. Oxford: Oxford University Press.

Dutton, W.H. (1999a) *Society on the Line: Information Politics in the Digital Age*. Oxford: Oxford University Press.

Dutton, W.H. (1999b) 'The virtual organization: tele-access in business and industry', in G. DeSanctis, and J. Fulk (eds), *Shaping Organization Form: Communication, Connection and Community*. Thousand Oaks, CA: Sage Publications.

Fuller, B. (1998) 'The great pager panic of 1998', *Electronic Engineering Times*, 1 June.

Garnham, N. (1999) 'Information politics: the study of communicative power' in Dutton (1999a).

Geltzer & Company, Inc. (1997) 'U.S. paging industry facts and figures'. News release. Boynton Beach, FL: Paging Products Group.

Geltzer & Company, Inc. (2000) 'U.S. paging industry facts and figures'. News release. Boynton Beach, FL: Paging Products Group.

Holmer-Nadesan, Majia (1997). 'Dislocating (instrumental) organizational time', *Organization Studies*, 18(3) 491–510.

Hong, T., Matei, S. and Dutton, W.H. with Dean, P.H., Elberse, A., Laterno, M. and Mayteevingoukij, N. (1999) 'Missing the pager: the impact of the Galaxy IV satellite blackout', a paper presented to the Annual Meeting of the International Communication Association, San Francisco, California, May 1999.

Katz, J.E. (1996) 'The social consequences of wireless communications', in Institute for Information Studies, *The Emerging World of Wireless Communications: Annual Review*. Queenstown, MD: Institute for Information Studies.

LaPedus, M. (1998) 'Chip malfunction is blamed in failure of satellite system', *Electronic Buyer's News*, 25 May.

Lasswell, H.D. (1971) 'The Structure and Function of Communication in Society', in W. Schramm and D.F. Roberts, (eds), *The Process and Effects of Mass Communication* revised edition. Urbana, IL: University of Illinois Press.

Lewis, M. (1995) 'Nowhere to hide in a wired world', *The Arizona Republic*, 5 November.

MacKenzie, D. (1996) 'Technological determinism' in Dutton (ed.), *Information and communications Technologies*.

McQuail, D. (1994) *Mass Communication Theory*, third edition. London: Sage Publications.

Mills, M. (1998) 'Satellite glitch cuts off data flow', *Washington Post*, 21 May.

Mobile Satellite News (1998) 'Galaxy IV cloud may hold silver lining for mobile satellite operators', 10(11) 28 May.

Motorola (1956) 'Shoreham hotel staff now "radio-controlled"', *Motorola Newsgram*, November–December, 12–13.

Motorola (1957) 'Beeping Dr. Kildare', *Motorola Newsgram*, September–October, 15.

Negroponte, N. (1995) *Being Digital*. London: Hodder & Stoughton.

O'Conner, A.M. (1998) 'Outer space outage signals growing dependence on satellite customers', *Los Angeles Times*, 21 May, p. A1.

Siegel, S. and Castellan, N.J, Jr. (1988). *Nonparametric Statistics for the Behavioral Sciences*. New York: McGraw-Hill, Inc.

Silverstone, R. (1996) 'Future imperfect: information and communication technologies in everyday life' in Dutton (1996).

Sloan School of Management (1999) MIT Survey Sponsored by the Lemelson–MIT Awards Program (Cambridge, MA: Sloan School of Management, Massachusetts Institute of Technology). http://web.mit.edu/invent/www.index2.html, March 1999.

Stone, A. (1997) *How America Got On-Line*. Armonk, NY: M.E. Sharpe.

Williams, R., and Edge, D. (1996) 'The social shaping of technology' in Dutton (ed.), *Information and Communications Technologies*.

Wired (1997, December). The Wired/Merill Lynch Forum Digital Citizen Survey, 5. http://www.hotwired.com/special/citizen/survey/survey.html

Woolgar, S. (1996) 'Technologies as cultural artefacts' in Dutton (ed.), *Information and Communication, Technologies*.

Wurtzel, A.H. and Turner, C. (1977) 'Latent functions of the telephone: what missing the extensions means', In I. de Sola Pool (ed.), *The Social Impact of the Telephone*. Cambridge, MA and London: The MIT Press.

Zuckerman, L. (1998) 'Satellite failure is rare, and therefore unsettling', *The New York Times*, 21 May, D3.

2

Trade Unions and Access to the Internet

Joe Holly and Gary Herman

Introduction

Trade unions need the new communications technologies. These technologies create opportunities for unions at the same time as they produce challenges for all of us. The emergence of national information infrastructures and global networks has to inspire concern within trade unions about the impact of advanced multimedia communications on employment, the economy and society. Yet demand is being generated within those same unions for technological solutions to employment, economic and organizational problems. New concepts and new ways of working have changed the worlds of industry, business and politics – and must do so in the world of trade unionism, if unions are to survive.

The European response to these changes has tended to be reactionary for well-rehearsed historical and economic reasons. A century of wars, hot and cold, left Europe in the late twentieth century suspicious of ideologies and innovations, particularly when they threatened to destroy the continent's cultural diversity and the traditional pragmatism of its politics. The technologically driven Taylorism which characterises much of the rhetoric of downsizing and flexibility is alien to Europe in origin and character. At best, telematics has been seen as a social glue against the political and cultural fragmentation resulting from significant unemployment and the globalization of production and services. But information and communications technologies (ICTs) have driven much of the globalization of production, creating the demand for 'flexible' labour markets and new forms of social exclusion. The European Commission White Paper, *Growth, Competitiveness, Employment* (CEC 1993), the Bangemann Report (Bangemann 1994) and the European Council Action Plan (CEC 1994) established a framework for the development of ICTs in Europe which attempted to encourage their spread while mitigating the ill-effects of such a spread.

In the USA, by contrast, the heightened awareness of telecommunications and multimedia has combined with the internet to allow ICTs to be seen as a social and economic stimulant: educating children, strengthening production and trade and reinvigorating the political process. The contrast may be seen in the way in which trade union representatives were included from the outset in the US taskforce coordinating work on Al Gore's National Information Infrastructure (the NII or Information Superhighway). In Europe, it took a year of political lobbying before labour movement views were even canvassed.

In general, too little has been heard from European trade unions about their attitude to developments in ICTs. Trade unions are the set of social partners whose identity will perhaps be altered more profoundly and permanently than any other. Trade unions need to adopt more proactive strategies to overcome the obstacles, discussed below, which hamper them in achieving their democratic aims – nationally and internationally. The failure of trade unions in this respect contributes to the potential undermining of social and political democratization by these technologies.

The obstacles arise from the nature and development of the internet itself, from the specialist worlds of academic research and military strategy in its inception to its domination by commercial drives in its current manifestation. However, this is not to say that the internet cannot be used to further the aims of trade unions. It can, and should, be so used. It is important always to bear in mind that vested, non-union (and sometimes anti-union) interests have developed the internet. This has led to an imbalance of access to and use of ICTs whereby many are excluded and others have information provided which is distorted in various ways.

Globalization and the information society

The development of the information society has had a largely negative impact on the trade union movement. The use of ICTs, along with other new technologies, has diminished its influence in the industrialized countries and hindered growth in the industrializing world. Membership has declined as the old industries have declined and new, decentralized patterns of work grown. Yet the potential of new technologies for union recruitment, organization and campaigning remains great.

In the global economy, countries tend to underbid each other, particularly in terms of labour standards and 'flexibility'. The internal dynamic that has developed in the global labour market, assisted by the new technologies, has been of a downward spiral of tighter labour restrictions with deteriorating wages and conditions. The aim of trade unions is to halt this downward spiral by campaigning and organizing, and create an upward spiral through bargaining.

The trade unions have been slow to use or recognize the importance of telematics in any of the three broad categories of their activity – collective bargaining, providing mutual insurance and campaigning for legal change. However, trade unions and the labour movement worldwide are increasingly turning to telematics to improve the way in which they work. For example, the Liverpool Dockers' dispute, finally settled in 1999, relied for its strength and longevity over two years on the use of telematics to garner political, economic and industrial support worldwide. This was also true of the widespread industrial disputes of South Korean workers in the mid-1990s. Up-to-date, high-quality information directly related to bargaining, available at a speed not dreamt of a decade ago, is only one of the benefits that the technology can bring. The new information technologies have also been seen to provide considerable opportunities for strengthening social cohesion and citizenship.

Unions are beginning to understand and use the telematics, as described by John Edmonds, General Secretary of the GMB, in at least five ways (LTC 1993):

- To counter the information imbalance in bargaining.
- To understand and address industrial and social change.
- To gain benefits from working with supportive, union-friendly organizations (such as the Workers' Educational Association and the Campaign for Press and Broadcasting Freedom).
- To counter and reverse the tendency of information flows to follow and reinforce the given power structures.
- To underpin democratization both within unions and in the world in which they work.

The challenge is to understand and use the technologies and also to influence their development. ICTs can be used to counter the efforts of employers and governments, in the new global economy, to break n the trade union movement into the smallest possible units, in ny cases by law, while employers and governments operate in national and international networks. ICTs help to oppose this trend by allowing trade unions to cross false boundaries between individual manufacturing or service units. Indeed, even national boundaries should be no limit to union organization and action – although unions in the industrially advanced countries should be sensitive to possible accusations of cultural imperialism when engaging with their colleagues in the developing world.

Democracy and the internet

For the first time in history, electronic communications and transport technologies – the same technologies which are the driving forces of globalization – have created the material conditions for the trade union movement to contribute to democratic and human rights worldwide. What hinders them is not Luddism or the inability to understand the technologies. It is almost entirely the result of limited access.

Issues of democracy are evident in all aspects of trade union work. The use of ICTs and access to the internet highlight changing approaches to the working of that democracy. Old and new converts to the internet have argued that it can, both individually and collectively, provide inexhaustible sources of enrichment for private, working and public life. They see it as intrinsically liberating, allowing individuals to by-pass undemocratic structures of power and influence as people are able to communicate quickly and directly with each other without intermediaries. While previous communications technologies cohered around oganizational structures dominated by one-to-one (the telephone) or one-to-many (broadcasting) relations, the internet offers a working paradigm of many-to-many communication.

However, the democratizing potential of the internet and the use of ICTs can be questioned. The challenges which face trade unions organizing to use and exploit the technologies are considerable. These challenges are also those which face institutions and individuals more widely. Several obstacles stand in the way of the effective and economic use of the internet. In Britain, the issue of access has been recognized in debates and decisions relating to schools and education provision generally, especially in relation to the development of the National Grid for Learning (NGfL). Access is also the key issue for trade unions. Without full access, trade unions, their members and branches, cannot use the technology nor influence its effects in the workplace, in the community and in legislation. And 'full access' has implications for established ideas of universal service provision (USP) and for the rights of workers and unions to use corporate data networks for purposes relating to their employment.

Restrictions to access

Current debates on USP are informed by the dominant neo-liberal tendency within capitalism which seeks to decouple economic activity from the state. In this process, the advocates of neo-liberalism argue that so-called public interest obligations should be devolved to the market: the model is one in which citizens are transformed into consumers and the public sphere becomes privatized. In this version of the world, union members have no place *as union members* on the internet. Unions are part of the diminishing public sphere, and communications technology is no longer a social good (let alone a social necessity) but is rapidly becoming a simple commodity. According to the neo-liberal paradigm, if unions want to be represented on the internet, they must become buyers or sellers of internet services or content. This idea is becoming received political wisdom, despite being entirely contradictory to the view that all social partners must participate fully in the diffusion of new communications technologies if we are to achieve desirable social outcomes.

It is not good enough to for the advocates of social inclusion within a neo-liberal economic order to rely on simple funding models – typically, public-sector pump priming or private-sector subsidy. The major restrictions on access operate at a number of levels, all of which must be addressed as ongoing, not one-off, issues. Each level has ramifications for trade unions nationally and internationally and prevents the democratic use of ICTs both within unions and in society generally. Among these, three levels of access are especially pertinent to trade unions and can be summarized as:

- Information quality and quantity
- Technological infrastructure
- Availability of skills

The quantity and quality of information

There is a surfeit of information on the internet and the danger of 'information overload' is a very real one. Assessing the relevance of the available information has become a huge problem. Moreover, the quality of the information is often suspect. There are few ways of checking it and few of controlling it. Information is not knowledge and misinformation creates a lot of noise in knowledge creation. For trade unions, this may have a profound effect on the outcome of collective bargaining or campaigning on specific issues.

Those who see the internet purely in terms of its libertarian character fail to see the wood of relevance and truth for the glut of information trees. Accordingly, they risk breaking the essential connection between information and the ability to act on it effectively. The libertarian argument assumes that the totality of individual responses, like purchases in a competitive market, will make a difference which is essentially right and good. Unfortunately, like buyers in a market, internet users do not have perfect knowledge, and – regardless of the arcane mysteries of search techniques – it is in the interests of profit-seeking information suppliers and so-called 'content providers' to perpetuate that ignorance.

Furthermore, there are pressures which greatly influence the content and type of information available. Labour issues do not figure highly on the internet, as it attempts to transform itself into a mass medium. Commercial and deregulation pressures tend to 'commodify' information. The development and implementation of marketing models – successively, 'push' technologies, portals or Web site branding – tend to strengthen such trends, ensuring that the passive user is fed information to suit the ends of commercial content providers and not the requirements of public interest or its servants within the labour movement.

Technological infrastructure

Access to information logically follows, and is dependent on, access to the technological instruments by which information is delivered. We shall refer to this technological level as infrastructure – a usage which goes beyond the familiar focus on communications networks. Problems of access to the infrastructure manifest themselves in different ways.

First, although the price of computer hardware in relation to computing power is falling, the hardware itself is still relatively expensive. Second, once hardware is purchased, users find themselves on an upgrade escalator driven by technological change and increasing demands of the software. Users, therefore, have continuing financial demands to keep up. These two factors combine to put ICTs beyond the pockets of individual trade unionists and of union branches.

The cost of the technology has its dangers for internal union democracy as resources may only allow the concentration of the technology in central union offices. Unions may then follow the path of systems evolution first trodden by private corporations: moving from centralized accounting systems to centralized management information systems for the hierarchical control of the organization. The extension of private ownership of personal computers in Western countries may help to reverse the propensity to centralize, but the cost of computers in the industrializing world remains prohibitive. And, even in the industrialized countries there are large pockets of economic and social exclusion where costs of entry to the information society are prohibitively high.

Availability of skills

What is true of the hardware is also true of the skills required to maintain and support hardware and software, as well as the skills to use the applications software. These skills also need frequent updating with costly retraining and refreshing of knowledge. Moreover, as dependence grows on the technology, problems of back-up and security become greater. Investment in new organizational and technical skills is necessary, requiring even more expenditure.

For the less skilled user, logging on to the internet requires lengthy connection time, particularly if specific information is being sought in a database or online conferencing is taking place. Running costs may become very high. It is also important to ensure that the skills people obtain are those that maximize interactivity and participation in order to overcome the problem of passivity.

Ownership and control

These limits on access derive from the imperatives of those who own and control the infrastructure. There is increasing concentration of ownership and centralization of control within telecommunications, internet services and broadcasting, exemplified by the recent take-over of Netscape and CompuServe by America Online (AOL), Microsoft's investment in cable operations, Vodafone-Airtouch's take-over of Mannesmann (which itself recently bought Orange), and the merger between United Newspapers and Central TV in the UK (see chapter by Williams in this volume). This concentration of ownership raises complex issues of control over infrastructure and the content and type of information made available. Commercial and deregulation pressures tend to 'commodify' information and allocate a price to it. But the relationship between information and its transport creates a number of political, cultural and legal problems.

It is often argued that technologies – delivery platforms – do not matter. In the slogan of a year or two ago: 'content is king'. Yet while content may be the commercial driver, it is neither the most significant source of revenue nor the ultimate source of the political and cultural influence or power of the new media. The development of mass media in the past has always been played out as a battle between market and society, between private and public, between business and government. Without wishing to promote a technologically deterministic and politically fatalistic vision of the future, the evidence suggests that the uses of mass media follow from ownership of infrastructures of production and distribution. In this respect, the economic struggles between digital TV and digital telecommunications, and between terrestrial networks and satellite networks, are critical to our futures. In short, the aim of using new technologies to deliver content rather than to facilitate communication, which is becoming the major driver of technological and commercial developments in the converging media, is aided by the market dominance of particular technological platforms and structures of ownership. Nothing is written in stone, but the indications are that the internet (once the golden hope for democratizing interactivity) is being pushed down the e-commerce road towards the elaborated paradigm of passivity typified by Murdochian digital TV – buy what you want, when you want it, from wherever you want to. Such an outcome will further undermine our weakened sense of participation in civil society and marginalize the political role of trade unions to speak collectively for individual workers.

In market economies, it might be argued that trade unions and their members are consumers and consequently have a degree of power through discretionary purchasing. However, that power is dispersed and limited to those who have the means to purchase and to stay on the upgrade escalator. This runs counter to the libertarian view of the internet as an inherently democratizing medium, and ignores the effective control of private ownership. Moreover, the idea that consumer pressure can always replace the political demands of citizens or the economic demands of employees is patently absurd. Freedom of speech, freedom of assembly, or freedom from hunger simply have no market equivalents – they are obligations on a society, not consumer goods or services, and their scope is collective not individual.

Despite the unprecedented wealth and power of corporations, they still inhabit a world in which governance is necessary. In fact, the wealth and power of many corporations (and particularly the telecommunications operators) has only been made possible through the intervention of politics in the form of deregulation, market liberalization, trade agreements and standardization policies. Trade unions are increasingly seeing themselves as party to these processes, yet, for obvious reasons, they lag behind private companies and transnational corporations. They are unlikely to be as influential as the large telecommunications operators, broadcasting companies or software suppliers in determining the direction of technological change or the pattern of ownership. And yet the trade unions are part of a long-established, widespread and at times highly effective international movement which, with the advent of technological tools like e-mail and the World Wide Web, has become more active and more effective. The challenge for the trade unions is how to use the strengths of the labour movement and worker organizations to create and promulgate different visions of a technological future and the information society.

Using the technology

What strategies are available to trade unions and communities to exercise some control over the technology and to enhance its liberating potential? The Labour Telematics Centre (LTC) has argued since its foundation in 1993 that ICTs can be used to stimulate efforts for democracy and trade union rights. A predecessor of the LTC, International Labour Reports, used the internet effectively to gather information from international sources and support trade union and workers' movements worldwide through the 1980s and into the early 1990s.

Trade unions in both the industrialized and industrializing worlds are providing access to training and encouraging individual trade unionists to use and exploit ICTs. The LTC survey of trade unions worldwide, *Opportunity and Challenge* (LTC 1994), showed large in creases in the use of ICTs were anticipated between 1994 and 1997. Unfortunately, this survey has not been updated.[1] The LTC itself has not been unaffected by these changes. Whereas it once provided basic skills training, such training is now routinely available from individual trade unions and the TUC. In response, the LTC now focuses its activities on understanding the rapidly changing technology in its organizational, social, political and economic contexts through research, seminars and workshops.

Trade union engagement with ICTs and the internet has been more fitful than in commercial enterprises because they have less money for equipment and less money for the necessary specialists. In

Canada, the work of Marc Belanger has greatly influenced for the good trade union perspectives and take-up of ICTs. A number of extremely diverse groups run electronic mailing lists and maintain Web sites. Organizations such as Union-D, Labor-L, El-democracy, Labornet, Labournet, TUCNET, the ICFTU, Corporate Watch, and international trade secretariats like ICEM (for chemical, engineering and mineworkers), FIET (for white-collar workers) and the IFJ (for journalists) make an impact which, however, is small compared to the large corporations. Perhaps more importantly, they remain largely uncoordinated.

Trade unions must be especially clear as to the reasons and uses for acquiring information and communications technologies. The first reason is internal operational efficiency – that is, the effective and economic management of resources. This is a set of administrative and financial control tasks not dissimilar in important respects to those carried out by private corporations. The trade union movement should not put its effectiveness at risk by failing to adopt technologies which have improved productivity among employers.

However, in terms of the substantial furtherance of labour movement objectives, the second reason for adoption of ICTs relates to the needs of collective bargaining and campaigning. It is these activities which make the substantial difference between trade unions' and employers' uses of the technologies. Employers do not as a rule see their objectives as freedom, equality and democracy in an environment where the goal is to secure the economic, social and political well-being of their employees (LTC 1995).

Campaigning may be thought of as similar to the marketing activities of corporations. However, in trade unions there is a strong democratic and participative element not noticeable in advertising and sales promotions. The use of campaigning in industrial resistance and organizational communication to garner support, especially where it cuts across single-union structures, is a significant difference. In this context, access to ICTs is the crucial issue. In brief, the internal use of the technology is the same as other organizations; it is the presence and action of the membership that makes the real difference. Lack of access of the membership to ICTs hinders democracy within unions and weakens collective bargaining in relation to employers.

Communication rights

The restrictions on access to the technology raise the question of whether the development of the information society and its impact on the private, working and public lives of people requires democracy to be underpinned with 'communication rights' – for example, the right to communicate with fellow citizens privately and without interference using the internet. In order to exercise such rights it would be necessary in a democratic society to ensure access to the means of communication. In the information society, the attainment and maintenance of information is key to having a voice in decision-making. In a polity, to deny access to the means of expression, whether in the community, in the workplace or in society at large, is to deny the most basic requirement for a functioning democracy.

The internet should not become dominated by the demands of e-commerce; it must hold on to its ambition to increase participation in democratic society, no matter how difficult that might be in practice. It should play a role in all the institutions of democracy, including trade unions. The traditional activities of trade unions – collective bargaining and campaigning for legal change – provide a platform of experience and skills for significant action with regard to gaining access to the technologies and information.

In the collective bargaining context, trade unions should negotiate for access to and appropriate use of corporate email systems as a right – with privacy and confidentiality maintained. Where there is access to the internet, trade union access to e-mail systems and to relevant databases and other legitimate sources of information should follow. These rights could be similar to the agreements between employers and unions which allow the use of the employers' facilities for trade union activities.

In the case of campaigning, unions can go beyond the workplace to demand access. As guarantors of critical rights within a democratic society, unions should demand representation within the range of institutional access points, whether that means library terminals, PCs in community education centres or electronic village halls, or electronic kiosks in public spaces.

Perhaps the most basic of all communication rights is the right to be heard – a right which exists independently of any specific technology. It means the right to be involved in decision-making, the right to be represented within the media, and the right to free communication. It includes all the rights we have discussed above – access to technologies, access to skills, and access to infrastructures. At present, the right of unions to be heard has not yet been universally accepted, but information and communications technologies can amplify our voices and make it easier than ever before for people to listen.

Note

1. A number of organizations are trying to address this deficiency. See www.ilr.cornell.edu/library/reference/guides; www.labornet.org; and www.labourstart.org. The latter contains a global list of labour directories.

References

Bangemann (1994) *Europe and the Global Information Society: Recommendations to the European Council.* Report of the High Level Group on the Information Society. Brussels.

CEC (1993) *Growth, Competitiveness, Employment: the Challenges and Ways Forward into the 21st Century.* Known as the Delors White Paper COM(93). Luxembourg: European Commission.

CEC (1994) *Europe's Way To The Information Society: an Action Plan*, COM(94). Brussels: Council of the European Community.

LTC (1993) *Information Technology, Electronic Communication and the Labour Movement: Conference Report.* Manchester: Labour Telematics Centre.

LTC (1994) *The Opportunity and Challenge of Telematics.* Manchester: Labour Telematics Centre.

LTC (1995) *Working on the Infobahn: Teleworking and the Labour Movement. Conference Report.* Manchester: Labour Telematics Centre.

3
'Getting Our Hands on It': Gendered Inequality in Access to Information and Communications Technologies

Gill Kirkup

Introduction

The time of writing this chapter – Autumn 1999 – is an interesting one for anyone trying to understand the relationship between information and communication technologies (ICTs), especially global networked ICTs, and gender. After clear evidence that the internet has been a happy home for 'boys' of the white, high-income, mainly English-speaking variety, women (and others) appear to be getting their hands on it at last. The launch of a number of UK Web sites targeted specifically at women – www.handbag.com; www.zoom.co.uk; www.planet-grrl.com – has stimulated newspaper articles which argue: 'A year ago, there were almost no British Web sites for women. Now they are every-where' (Kinnes 1999: 56). In the same week the British pop music star Gary Glitter received a four-month prison sentence for being in posses-sion of a library of child pornography that he downloaded from the internet. For women: shopping for cosmetics and clothes, for men: shopping for pornography and sex. Is the internet showing itself to be simply another technology of Irigaray's 'specular economy' (Irigaray 1985), where trade in women's (and children's) bodies, virtual as well as corporeal, takes place? Are women (and others) really getting their hands on this technology, or simply being positioned as consumers as well as the consumed? Is the internet challenging either the material, or symbolic, gendered order?

In this chapter I will analyse empirical data that I have gathered, over a number of years, in my work at the UK Open University, on student use of computers. What is presented here is a material analysis of some aspects of internet use by a particular group of people. I will relate that data to debates in the literature on ICTs and gender to argue that they illustrate a continued, although changing gender inequality with respect to the access and use of computer technology. The evidence I present suggests that gender is having a stronger impact on the social and cultural production of the technology than the technology is having on deconstruction and reconstruction of gender, materially or symbolically. In the domestic environment in particular, the computer and the internet are reflecting and reproducing gendered social relations. Women are 'getting our hands on it', but less to challenge and subvert, more mundanely, in the situation I analyse, to continue the production of gender.

The gender/technology relationship

Feminist analysis of gender and technology in the 1970s and 1980s tended to be 'technophobic' and identify the operations of technoscience as a key force of oppression for women. For example, Cockburn, one of the most influential gender/technology theorists of the 1980s and early 1990s, described the historical construction of technology as a process in which men conspired in their own sex/class interests to exclude women from skills and power (Cockburn 1983, 1985) and in which the artefacts and systems of technology were implicated in the production of a gendered world (Cockburn and Ormrod 1993). Very few feminists, theorists or activists, have been enthusiasts for technology. Technology was inescapably linked to masculinity. Few could see its potential to challenge a gendered world. Technoscience, especially those aspects to do with the body, was perceived as dangerous, a source of disempowerment for women. *The Dialectic of Sex* (Firestone 1970) was the only exception to this. This book was a radical demand for a sexual and cultural revolution, based on an 'enlightened' use of technology. For Firestone, cybernetics, 'cybernation' and 'artificial' reproduction held the key to gender equality. She probably deserves the title of 'First Cyberfeminist' because her work prefigures postmodern writings on gender and technoscience. However, because Firestone saw female embodiment rather than gender as the problem, and technoscience the solution to transcend the limitations of the biological and the social, her work was seen as simplistic biological determinism, a trap that later proponents of the power of technology have tried to avoid.

Theorists of gender, as well as cultural analysts, have tended to coalesce around these opposing positions. Carol Stabile, a critic of both postmodern feminism and of what she sees as its opposite, a radical cultural feminism usually categorized as ecofeminism, described these positions as: 'reactionary essentialist formations (what I describe as *technophobia*) or equally problematic political strategies framed around fragmentary and destabilized theories of identity (*technomania*).' (Stabile 1994: 1).

It was not until Donna Haraway wrote her famous line, 'I'd rather be a cyborg than a goddess' (Haraway 1985) that feminist theory began to argue that an alliance of women with technology could lead to the end of gender as a system of inequality, especially an alliance with ICTs. Developments in technoscience are now seen as offering new ways of being embodied, of creating multiple identities and living them out, of negotiating power, of transcending oppressive prescribed categories, rather than transcending the body itself as in Firestone. The new analysis is concerned to situate the body at the centre of gender analysis (Balsamo 1997) and at the centre of knowledge production (Haraway 1988). The central figure of the 'cyborg' is a metaphor and a material thing, a creature which challenges the boundary between living things and 'made' things, between the produced and the reproduced. In the internet people are cyborg and can reconstitute gender as agents rather than victims. Recent work has attempted to offer models of the gender/technology relationship in which the two are mutually constituted, as material and discursive practices which constitute each other (Wakeford 1998).

However, in these discussions it sometimes seems as if the concept of 'gender', which has proved so useful as a tool for a materialist as well as cultural analysis, is slipping away. To counter this I find Harding's definition (1997) very useful in providing a framework in which to understand the different levels of the interaction between gender and ICTs. Harding describes four aspects to gender. At its most simplistic gender is a property of individuals, described in other feminist literature as what society makes out of sex. This is the ground of our gendered subjectivities. Gender is also a relation between groups, a property of material structures. This produces the gendered workplace, where women don't design the software, or control the company finances. The third aspect of gender is as a property of symbolic systems, where representational systems, language and imagery are gendered. This is the aspect that produces Lara Croft, digitized pornography and VNS Matrix. The final aspect is gender as a way of distributing scarce resources, so in the domestic and school environment men presume first call on access to computers. Adam (1998) has produced the most extensive discussion of the historical development of ICTs illustrating the operation of gender at all these levels, and from a European perspective. She concludes her book with a reservation which I share:

> Looking at feminist visions of the future through intelligent technologies, the situation reveals some tensions. Feminist AI projects may attempt to 'dismantle the master's house with the master's tools' but they must be wary of inadvertently building on neat extensions to his house by mistake. (Adam 1998: 180)

Gender is an instantiation of power, part of a complex process that is always in negotiation. The question is whether the mutual constitution of gender and ICTs are such that power is more equitably distributed, or whether the distribution of power is confirmed along the old gender/power lines.

The historical production of gendered ICTs

Claims for ICTs as tools to transform gender are countered by an analysis of the social construction of their history. They are a product of the development and convergence of other, older (gendered) media. Telephony, photography and film, broadcasting and computers have all contributed to the production of gender, and are experienced differently by men and women. Sometimes they have reinforced gender roles and structures, sometimes they have changed them, sometimes they have produced a challenge to previous gendered activity, but there is no doubt that they have been gendered (see Flichy 1995 on telephony, Spence and Holland (eds) 1991 on photography, Morley 1986 on television and Gray 1992 on video use).

My focus is on ICTs that people can use for their personal activities, which for most people will be those that they have in their homes. Technology is incorporated differently into the employment and the domestic environment. Domestic technologies and media have their own particular gender history (Wajcman 1991). Television, for example, has been a gendered medium in terms of its control. Research on TV watching in the mid-1980s (Morley 1986) showed men to be the ultimate arbiters of what is watched. They hold the remote control of the main family set (70 per cent of UK homes have more than one TV set (ITC 1997)). Men view attentively and in silence, while women engage in other activities and carry on conversations while watching. Although figures report more hours spent viewing by women, qualitative research suggests that this time is less attentive, and may be spent sitting with another family member while the woman herself does something else – for example, read. Not only do men and women watch different programmes (men prefer factual programmes and sport, women prefer fiction) they discuss their viewing with others in a different ways.

By the late 1990s, 87 per cent of UK homes had a VCR (ITC 1997). However, control over what is recorded and the operation of the VCR usually lie with the men and children in the family (Gray 1992). Even among Open University (OU) students, women were more likely than men to ask others in the household to record their OU course programmes: 16 per cent compared with 4 per cent of men.

Plans for digital interactive broadcasting suggest a convergence of television broadcasting technology and the internet in such a way that one device will be able to perform many functions – for example, receiving soap operas as well as allowing e-mail, and each function will be in symbiotic relationship with the other: viewers can watch a soap opera then engage in online chat about it or order related merchandise. Domestic ICTs will extend the functions of these older gendered media as well as enable new activities.

Women as users of domestic ICTs in the late 1990s

Understanding what is happening with respect to gendered access to and use of computers is particularly difficult at the moment, because globally access to the hardware and the networks is expanding dramatically in both the developed and much of the less developed world. There is an active trade in online reports on surveys of internet use. An extremely useful site which summarizes and makes links to surveys of internet use, and from which many of the references in this section are taken, is that of Nua Internet Surveys (NUA 1999). However, many of the surveys themselves use the internet to gather data, leaving non-users much less well researched.

Access to the internet remains less for women in all countries, although in the USA the gap between male and female access is closing. A large-scale survey of internet users by the Graphic Visualisation and Usability Center of Georgia Institute of Technology (GVU 1999) suggests that, in 1998, women were one third of users in the USA (35.8 per cent), 18 per cent of users in Europe, and 27 per cent of users in the rest of the world.

Women have certainly become internet shoppers in the USA and the trend appears to be continuing in Europe, but again the reported figures are contradictory. A survey by Harris Interactive estimates women to be 42 per cent of all internet shoppers, and the prediction is that this will grow with women becoming the majority of internet shoppers. Women are the majority of buyers for some products. NPD Online reports (NUA 1999a) that women make 58 per cent of online purchases of clothes, 65 per cent of toys, and 70 per cent of beauty products. In some social classes in the USA women have incorporated the internet into their (very gendered?) lifestyles. A survey (NUA 1999b) by women.com, a US internet portal for women, reported that 70 per cent of respondents felt that they could not 'imagine life without the internet'.

Although surveys of internet users are being carried out it seems constantly, apart from noting that over the years the figures of online users (both male and female) has increased, differences between the figures reported in different surveys carried out at similar times are still huge, which suggests an unreliability in much of the data collected. For example, Which?Online reported that women made up 43 per cent of British online users in September 1999 (NUA 1999c). In October 1999 a Commerce Net/Neilsen Media Study reported that 27 per cent of the total UK population were online, and women made up 38 per cent of users. The gender figures from younger age groups shows a different pattern, with more young women online. Fletcher research (NUA 1999d) reported that 61 per cent of users under the age of 18 are female, and they spend their time online differently from boys. Fifty per cent of boys spent their time downloading music and software, compared with 15 per cent of girls, and 50 per cent of boys went online to access entertainment information, compared with 25 per cent of girls. On the other hand, girls spent more time sending e-mail and using chat rooms. It is too soon to predict whether this behaviour will feed through to the behaviour of those same young men and women as they become adults, or whether patterns of use will correspond more closely to present adult patterns of use.

Computer ownership and internet access also reflects already existing inequalities of class and geography. Households in London and the South East are three times more likely to have internet access than Wales (6 per cent, 7 per cent and 2 per cent respectively (ONS 1997)). Nearly half of all professional households had a computer (48 per cent) compared with 17 per cent of homes of unskilled manual workers.

Professional households were four times more likely to have internet access (12 per cent) than skilled and semi-skilled manual workers (3 per cent), and six times more likely to have it than unskilled manual workers (2 per cent). It would be a fair presumption that many of these poorer households were headed by women. There is also a 'race gap' in developed countries. Hoffman (1998) reported that fewer than one third of black USA high-school and college students owned a computer, compared with 73 per cent of white students. Although the trends are of growth in internet use, by women and men, differences are emerging in the access and use of the medium which reflect those old power inequalities of gender, class and race.

ICT access and use: a case study of Open University students

Over a number of years, I have analysed large-scale surveys of the access and use of computers for UK Open University (OU) students. From the earliest analysis of data collected in the late 1980s, to the most recent data, I have observed an inequality of access for men and women students, and different gendered preferences for using computers (Kirkup 1993, 1996; Kirkup and von Prummer 1990, 1997). From the very first surveys there was a consistent gap of 10 per cent between the proportion of men students with access to a computer they could use for study purposes, and the proportion of women with the same access. Over time a variety of other indicators suggested that women's access was often to less powerful equipment and for less time.

OU students reflect a particular subgroup of the national UK population: they are overwhelmingly middle-aged (between 35 and 55) they tend to come from lower-middle-income jobs, and are more likely to come from the South and urban areas. What these surveys reflect is a snapshot of computer access and behaviour for this segment of the population in the periods surveyed.

The most recent data available is taken from a survey of undergraduate OU students in 1998. Four thousand were sampled and 2340 returns were received, 1220 of these (52 per cent) from women and 1120 from men. The respondents were studying different courses, with men more likely to be on maths, science and technology courses and women on social science and humanities courses. The data are not presented analysed by course, because I would argue we are interested here in the behaviour of a large population of men and women, and course choice is a gendered form of behaviour, that reflects similar interests in the population overall.

In the survey, 79 per cent of respondents had access to a computer that they could use for their OU studies, at home and/or at work. This is an extremely high figure and represents the fact that the OU encourages the use of computers, and makes their use obligatory on some courses. In terms of access to the technology itself, women have less access than men, both at home and work – 78 per cent of men but only 68 per cent of women had access at home, 38 per cent of men and 26 per cent of women had access at work, and 26 per cent of women and 16 per cent of men had no access.

However, the gender difference did not stop at access. When the sample are filtered so that only students *with* access are analysed, it becomes clear that the kind of access that men and women have is qualitatively different. This sample were asked if they had used the computer for networked access of any kind. Only 42 per cent of women with access to computers had used networked access but 60 per cent of men with access had done so.

Although national surveys (for example, Fletcher quoted by NUA) suggest that, in the UK, young women under the age of 18 are now more likely than boys to be using the internet for interpersonal communications, this pattern was not borne out in this group of older UK adults. Of the sample who had used computers for any kind of networked communications (383 women and 560 men), the pattern was for men to make more use of all networked communications activities than women. The sample were asked about their use at home and at work of e-mail, the World Wide Web and conference/ newsgroups, and how much they used it for work, personal and study purposes.

The use of technology at home showed the greatest gender inequality. Figure 3.1 shows that men were more likely to use e-mail for all purposes than were women. This is surprising since much of the literature about gender and communication styles would suggest that women would find the possibilities of personal communication very attractive once they had access to the technology, and this seems to be the case reported by Fletcher above. The sample has been filtered so that only the responses of those men and women with access to networked communications and who had actually used them, is examined. The higher use of e-mail at home by men for work purposes (32 per cent compared with 20 per cent women) and study purposes (41 per cent compared with 21 per cent) might make intuitive sense, but men's greater involvement in personal e-mail is surprising (52 per cent compared with 41 per cent women).

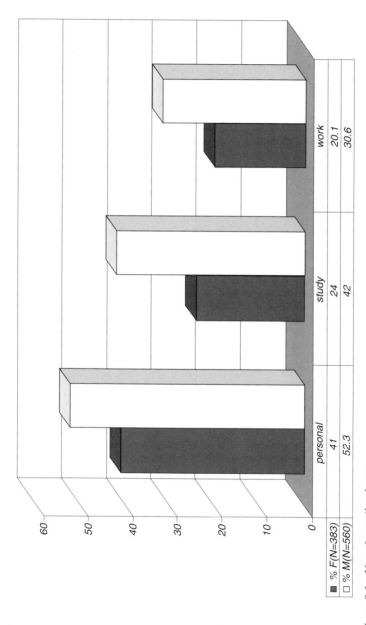

	personal	study	work
■ % F(N=383)	41	24	20.1
□ % M(N=560)	52.3	42	30.6

Figure 3.1   Use of e-mail at home

Figure 3.2 shows that conferencing and newsgroups were also used more at home by men. The fact that the greatest use of conferencing was reported to be for study purposes can be explained by the fact that the OU has an extensive conferencing system that students are encouraged to use to make contact with each other and their tutors. But twice as many of the men who use networked communications were engaged in conferencing for personal (non-study) activities (19 per cent compared with 9 per cent of women).

Figure 3.3 shows that men in the sample were using the Web at home more than women, for all the categories given. However, the figures for use at 'work' show much less gender difference. For OU students access at their place of work has been a reliable route for a significant minority of students. Yet that access has not been unproblematic. Some students reported being allowed access for study purposes only 'out of hours', but others have had much more restrictive rules. Some students reported that employers were so concerned about the possibility of files or systems being corrupted or their contents 'stolen' that it was a sacking offence to be to be found with floppy disks or CD-ROMs. (NUA reported (1999e) that 17 per cent of *Fortune* 1000 companies had installed monitoring or filtering software on their employees' PCs, and predicted that within two years 80 per cent of large US companies would be doing the same. They give an example of AT&T who are reported as monitoring the e-mail messages and Web site destination of their employees. Xerox is reported as sacking 40 people for 'inappropriate' internet use.)

The interesting issue for the OU sample is that for all categories of activity the gender difference for access at work is *less* than for the same activities done at home. In previous years surveys had found that women were more restricted in their work access than men, but for 1998 respondents there was no apparent difference in the quality of access, when they had it. However, it must be remembered that only 38 per cent of men and 28 per cent of women could get access at work for personal purposes. Figure 3.4 shows that a slightly larger, but not significantly so, proportion of men with network access used e-mail at work: 67 per cent compared with 63 per cent of women for work purposes, while 13 per cent of men used e-mail for study purposes, compared with 10 per cent of women. Almost similar proportions – roughly 22 per cent each – used e-mail for personal uses.

Figure 3.5 shows that use of the Web at work was also almost identical for men and women. Nineteen per cent of both men and women used it for personal reasons, 15 per cent of men and 13 per cent of

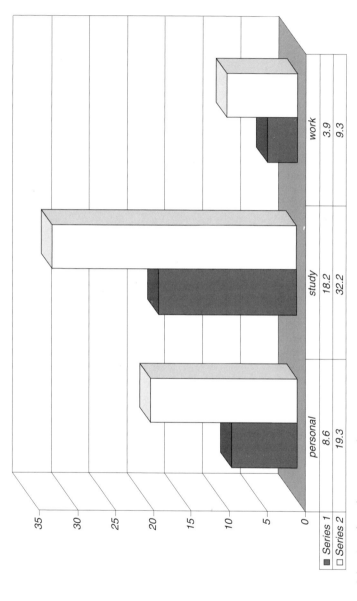

	personal	study	work
■ Series 1	8.6	18.2	3.9
□ Series 2	19.3	32.2	9.3

Figure 3.2 Use of conferencing at home

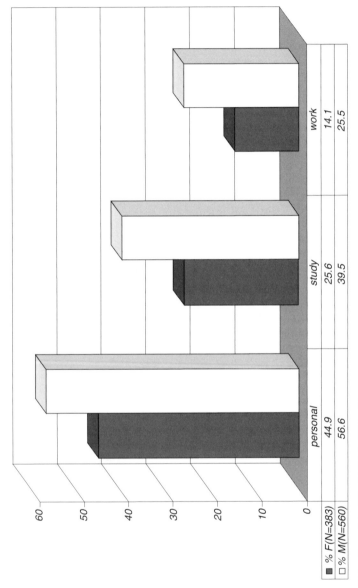

	personal	study	work
% F(N=383)	44.9	25.6	14.1
% M(N=560)	56.6	39.5	25.5

Figure 3.3 Use of the World Wide Web at home

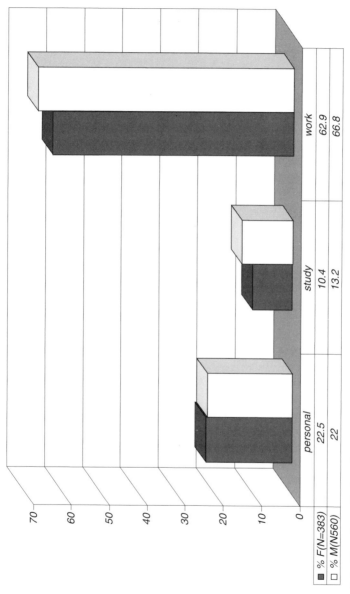

	personal	study	work
■ % F(N=383)	22.5	10.4	62.9
□ % M(N560)	22	13.2	66.8

Figure 3.4 Use of e-mail at work

58

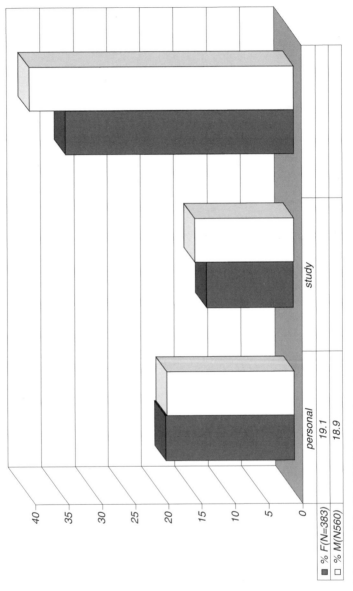

Figure 3.5   Use of the World Wide Web at work

women used it for study reasons and 39 per cent of men and 34 per cent of women were using it for work reasons. However, if these numbers are taken as a proportion of the whole sample the gender difference reappears. For example, only 6 per cent of all women respondents were using the Web at work for personal activities, compared with 9.5 per cent of all men.

Only computer conferencing and newsgroup use at work was much higher for men with than for women. Figure 3.6 shows that 19 per cent of men who used networking were using conferencing for work purposes compared with 9 per cent of women; 6 per cent of men were using it for personal activities compared with 2 per cent of women; and 5 per cent of men were using it for study activities compared with 4 per cent of women.

The indication from this data is that, within the domestic environment the computer is a heavily gendered technology, and women in the household are not the primary users, even when they are students on a part-time undergraduate course. This conclusion is supported by data from a previous survey. In 1996 a similar survey (a sample of 4000 undergraduates, a response of 2229) asked students who had computers at home about the frequency with which they and their partners used the computer – for any purpose. (We did not know who lived with a partner, so the responses can only be analysed on face value.) Figure 3.7 shows that men were much more likely to rate themselves as 'frequent' users (81 per cent), and women were twice as likely as men to rate themselves as 'infrequent' users. Figure 3.8 shows that women were twice as likely to rate their partners as frequent users than were men (59 per cent compared with 30 per cent). Men were most likely to place their partners in the 'almost never' category.

The picture is clearly one of a domestic technology in with both men and women see women as secondary users. This conclusion is further supported by the final figure in this chapter, Figure 3.9. These are responses again from the 1996 survey. Students were asked who provided the main impetus to buy the home computer. Male students overwhelmingly saw themselves as providing this impetus (79 per cent). Women, on the other hand, were almost equally likely to credit themselves, their partner or a joint decision. Only 2 per cent of men credited their partner with the main impetus, and they were also only half as likely as women to see it as a joint decision. Again this data only reflects perceptions; we cannot know the actual decision-making process, but the perception, overwhelmingly on the part of the men respondents, was that this was a technology they wanted and which

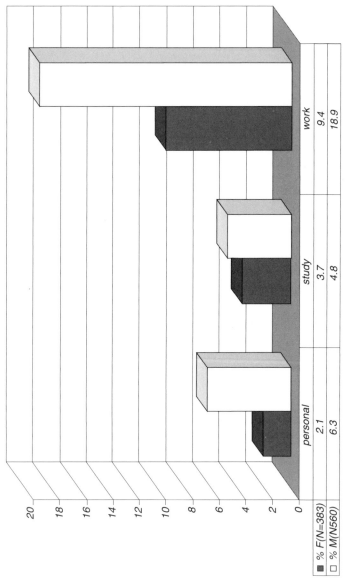

	personal	study	work
■ % F(N=383)	2.1	3.7	9.4
□ % M(N560)	6.3	4.8	18.9

Figure 3.6   Use of conferencing at work

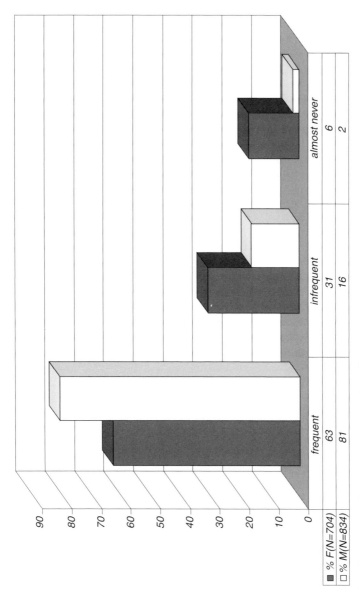

	frequent	infrequent	almost never
■ % F(N=704)	63	31	6
□ % M(N=834)	81	16	2

Figure 3.7 Frequency of home computer use by self

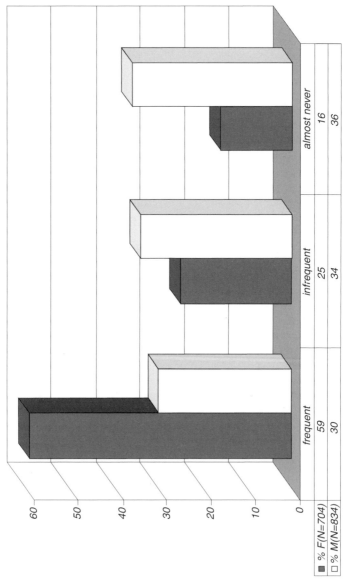

Figure 3.8 Frequency of home computer use by partner

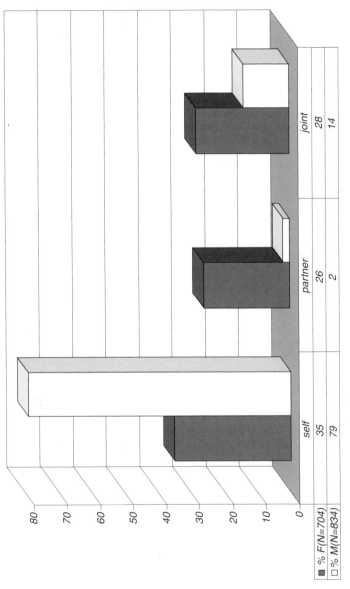

Figure 3.9 Source of main impetus to buy home computer

they brought into the household. Women continue to feel insecure in their knowledge of the newer ICTs which are sold for the domestic market, and as commercial pressure builds to purchase, the technology usually comes into the house championed by the male 'expert'.

At the time of the 1998 survey, digital TV was about to be launched. There had been a great deal of publicity, but no large-scale service was yet available. The sample were asked to choose a rating which best described how much they knew about this new medium from 'nothing' to 'a lot'. Women were overwhelmingly likely to say they knew 'nothing': 56 per cent, compared with 23 per cent of men. At the other end of the scale men were four times as likely to say they knew 'a lot' : 8 per cent, compared with 2 per cent of women, and three times as likely to say they knew 'quite a lot': 20 per cent, compared with 6 per cent of women. Men are again the enthusiastic early adopters of ICTs. They have much more confidence that they understand the medium (perhaps more confidence than understanding), but this confidence leads to their sense of self-efficacy with the technology.

The mutual constitution of gender and ICTs in the domestic sphere

The data discussed here demonstrate the mutual constitution of gender and technology in the domestic environment, but in a way that provides no challenge to the present gendering of either ICTs or of the environment in which they have entered. By and large, computers come into the home through the enthusiasm of the men there. In the gendered context of the heterosexual family relationship, both men and women expect the men to be the main enthusiasts, and most knowledgeable, about new technologies. This knowledge and the action which follows – the purchase of a computer – confirms the traditional gender identity of both men and women. Once in the home, men have primary call on the machine for leisure activities. This unequal relationship to the technology again reproduces gender difference.

The increase in women using the internet for shopping would in no way disturb this gendering of the technology, nor would the use of the internet for this kind of purpose produce a reconstitution of gender. The technology is incorporated into all those aspects of gender described by Harding (1997). Self-efficacy with a computer is part of gendered subjectivity; the way that men and women relate differently to the computer in their home becomes a property of their relationship. The computer and the activities it is used for are incorporated into different gendered symbolic systems. And finally, and most obviously, this expensive and scarce resource in the home is a primary device for male activity and secondarily for women. Domestic ICT developments continue, but, as mass commercial providers and portals dominate what can be done on the internet, the promise of cyberanarchy that Plant (1997) predicted, with the end of the specular economy and patriarchal order, has yet to be fulfilled.

References

Adam, Alison (1998) *Artificial Knowing: Gender and the Thinking Machine.* London: Routledge.

Balsamo, Anne (1997) *Technologies of the Gendered Body.* London: Duke University Press.

Cockburn, Cynthia (1983) *Brothers: Male Dominance and Technological Change* London: Pluto Press.

Cockburn, Cynthia (1985) *Machinery of Dominance: Men, Women and Technical Know-how.* London: Pluto Press.

Cockburn, Cynthia and Ormrod, Susan (1993) *Gender and Technology in the Making.* London: Sage.

Firestone, Shulamith (1970) *The Dialectic of Sex.* London: Jonathan Cape.

Flichy, Patrice (1995) *Dynamics of Modern Communication.* London: Sage.

Gray, Ann (1992) *Video Playtime: the Gendering of a Leisure Technology.* London: Routledge.

GVU (1999) 'Results of GVU's Tenth World Wide Web User Survey.' Georgia Institute of Technology. http://www.gvu.gatech.edu/user_surveys/survey-1998-10/

Haraway, Donna (1985) 'Manifesto for Cyborgs: science, technology, and socialist feminism in the 1980s', *Socialist Review*, 80 65–108.

Haraway, Donna (1998) 'Situated knowledge: the science question in feminism and the privilege of partial perspective', *Feminist Studies*, 14(3) 575–99.

Harding, Sandra (1997) 'Multicultural and global feminist philosophies of science: resources and challenges', in L.H. Neeson and J. Neeson (eds), *Feminism, Science and the Philosophy of Science* (Dordrecht and Boston: Kluwer Academic Publishers).

Hoffman, D. (1998) discussion of her research at http://rstl.com/racial.htm

Independent Television Commission (ITC) (1997) 'ITC publishes *Television: The Public's View 1996*', News Release 33/97.

Irigaray, Luce (1985) *This Sex That Is Not One.* Ithaca, NY: Cornell University Press.

Kinnes, Sally (1999) 'Domain of Women', *Sunday Times* 'Doors' supplement, 7 November, 55–7.

Kirkup, Gill (1993) 'Equal opportunities and computing at the Open University', in A. Tait (ed.), *Key Issues in Open and Distance Learning.* Harlow: Longman.

Kirkup, Gill (1996) 'The importance of gender', in R. Mills and A. Tait (eds), *Supporting the Learner in Open and Distance Learning*. London: Pitman.

Kirkup, Gill and von Prummer, Christine (1990) 'Support and connectedness: the needs of women distance students', *Journal of Distance Education*, 5(2) 9–31.

Kirkup, Gill and von Prummer, Christine (1997) 'Distance education for European women. The threats and opportunities of new educational forms and media', *European Journal of Women's Studies*, 4(1) 39–62.

Morley, David (1986) *Family Television*. London: Comedia.

NUA (1999a) 'NPD research: female shoppers to dominate this season', NUA Internet Surveys, 8 November. http://www.nua.ie/surveys/

NUA (1999b) 'Women leaders online: women can't imagine life without the web', NUA Internet Surveys, 11 November. http://www.nua.ie/surveys/

NUA (1999c) 'Which? Online: Study Looks at British Net Usage Patterns', NUA Internet Surveys, 16 September. http://www.nua.ie/surveys/

NUA (1999d) 'NOP research group: over 3 million youths online in Britain', NUA Internet Surveys, 6 July. http://www.nua.ie/surveys/

NUA (1999e) 'IDC Research: Filtering Now a Business Liability Issue', NUA, Internet Surveys, 14 October. http://www.nua.ie/surveys/

Office for National Statistics (ONS) (1997) 'British households are getting connected', News Release 335/97, 24 November.

Plant, Sadie (1997) *Zeros and Ones: Digital Women and the New Technoculture*. London: Fourth Estate.

Spence, Jo and Holland, P. (eds) (1991) *Family Snaps: the Meaning of Domestic Photography*. London: Virago.

Stabile, Carole. A. (1994) *Feminism and the Technological Fix*. Manchester: Manchester University Press.

Wajcman, Judy (1991) *Feminism Confronts Technology*. Cambridge: Polity Press.

Wakeford, Nina (1998) 'Gender and the landscapes of computing in an internet café', in Mike Crang, Phil Crang and Jon May (eds), *Virtual Geographies: Bodies, Space and Relations*. London: Routledge.

Part II
Knowledge

4
The Postmodern University? The Loss of Purpose in British Universities

Frank Webster

Introduction

There seems to be widespread agreement about empirical trends in British (and far beyond) higher education. I do not think, for instance, that the following would be very much disputed amongst commentators:

- There has been a sustained increase in student numbers since the early 1960s, and a dramatic leap since 1988, to such a degree that we speak now of a mass (as opposed to élite) system in which more than one in three school leavers goes on to university.
- There has been an associated decline in the unit of resource allocated to each student, such that universities nowadays are teaching many more students on much less income than hitherto (the measurement of this increase in productivity varies from between 25 per cent and 40 per cent over the past decade or so).
- The number of institutions carrying the title 'university' has also grown enormously: in 1960 there were only twenty or so universities in the UK, but today over one hundred organizations carry the word, a development radically assisted by the transformation in 1992 of the former polytechnics into universities.
- Academic tenure has been abandoned for those employed since the late 1980s, and new university staff have come more and more to be employed on part-time and temporary contracts. Relatedly, salaries have declined comparative to other professions and they have become more differentiated internally, most markedly at the senior levels.
- There has been a marked push towards making universities better connected to the outside world – a move signalled in terms such as vocationalism and practicality.

- Universities have become significantly more cosmopolitan, a trend evident in changes in student composition, overseas study programmes, as well as employment of foreign nationals.

One could continue listing such points about which there would be considerable accord, since no one disputes that higher education has been going through radical change over the last 25 years or so. But documenting what has taken place is not my main concern. I want, in what follows, to enter into a discussion which is characterized by sharp disagreement and disputation, not about empirical patterns, but about what they might amount to. I am concerned with how people consider changes in higher education in a conceptual sense. What do these conceptions tell us about the purposes, indeed the definition, of a university nowadays?

One interpretation, voiced often by politicians, business representatives, and even some vice-chancellors, is that this change is, in the round, something splendid. It has injected a dynamism – even an entrepreneurial spirit – into a higher education system which for long has suffered from being stale and stuffy, incapable of responding to new challenges and opportunities. In these terms new forms of funding, new contractual arrangements, and new courses represent positive developments. Commentators adopting this stance acknowledge that universities have certainly been shaken up by innovative managerial structures, and an influx of commercial practices has ruffled academic feathers, but given the long-term failure of the system to respond either to the needs of employers or to the vast majority of the nation's young people, then pressures towards greater 'value for money', 'accountability' and 'audit' are to the good.

A counter-argument, especially common amongst faculty of a certain age, is that universities are on the slide. The golden age of the 1950s and 1960s (Halsey 1992; cf. Bender 1997), when resources were plentiful, students a cloistered élite, and expansion routine, has long gone – and with it a diminishment of conditions of service, the quality of student–teacher interaction, even the civilities of intellectual endeavour. This does not, incidentally, have to be a conservative interpretation that yearns for days when the Exchequer footed the bill and universities were left to themselves to spend as they so willed. There are a good many radicals who, while welcoming the improvements in access for minority groups and those disadvantaged by class or gender, complain that what is offered is provided on the cheap.

However, what most interests me here is the analysis from another quarter. This view is one which responds to changes in higher education in a very different manner to either the boosters or complainers. It does not comfortably go along with the boosterism of those who celebrate the expansion of higher education, but nor does it accord with the glum outlook. Indeed, it sets off by most decisively rejecting the 'narratives of decline' which come from that diverse group of nostalgic elders, disaffected trade unionists, and disappointed reformers. Against these jeremiads especially, what is suggested is that what we have is a new type of institution coming into being – a postmodern university – which cannot be compared on any scale because it is so radically different to what has gone before. This position observes that both the doom-mongers and the optimists at some level share at least working ideas of the university: to one group it is being diminished while to another it is being improved, but both work with unproblematical conceptions of the university. This is possible only because both sides operate with tacit conceptions of the university – neither of them say clearly what it is, to them a university is what a university does – but at the least this allows them to take positions as regards the question 'How is the university performing compared to the past?' However, to proponents of the postmodern university what we have today cannot straightforwardly be compared with what went before because it is so radically different a phenomenon that it would be akin to comparing apples and pears. As Peter Scott, a key codifier of this position and surely the first postmodern vice-chancellor (he took over at Kingston University in 1997), puts it: 'mass higher education is not merely a bigger-and-better (or worse) version of élite higher education'; it is rather a 'rupture' with what went before (Scott 1998a: 29–30). That is, one cannot say whether things are better or worse regarding the university, since those in the past are so different (apples) to the new institutions we still call universities (pears).

In what follows I want to consider changes in higher education as they are perceived by those who suggest we are witnessing the emergence of the postmodern university. As will become clear, this suggestion is one which echoes a good deal of postmodern thinking in a more general sense. That is, it accords with the widespread view that, being in postmodern times, it is only to be expected that we have postmodern universities. After reviewing the arguments of those who see the coming of the postmodern university, I shall make a number of criticisms of their perspective, dissenting sharply from their interpretation while simultaneously suggesting that it is not only possible to distinguish defining features of a university, but also that it is time those factions which pronounce on the university's condition themselves make explicit just what it is that they are talking about. It does not help debate on the condition of the university when different sides do not make clear what it is that they mean by the word.

Passivity

I would comment further on this silence as to what constitutes a university. I do so by observing an oxymoron. This is that the marked lack of an idea of the university in the present period is itself allegedly indicative of the postmodern university. That is, it is this very lack of clarity about purposes, the absence of bold ideas of what the university is for, which is, paradoxically, said to be symptomatic of the postmodern university's coming into being, since a distinguishing feature of the latter is that it is at once everything and nothing, being made up of a multiplicity of roles, voices, places and patterns. Precisely because a motif of this new institution, to its adherents at least, is its very diversity, its lack of a core, its plurality of practices, then this suggests that we have, indeed, seen the coming into being of the postmodern university.

To charge that there is passivity about what constitutes a university must seem rather odd given my remark made above to the effect that both optimists and pessimists appear to share an idea of the university. To some commentators things have improved, while to others they have declined, so it would appear that there is a working idea in common usage. But there is no such thing! In reality, different actors contest one another without establishing any clear definition of the university in the first place. Look where one will today, all that one finds are a multitude of conceptions being brought in to play, seemingly guided only by the demands of particular circumstances.

To be sure, every university in the land publishes a 'mission statement' that acclaims its raison d'être, so one might presuppose that such institutions know what they are about. And so they do, but this has little to do with clarifying what constitutes a university. If one looks a little more closely, what one sees is that these mission statements are not at all about a conception of the university. Rather they are assertions of 'excellence' in all that they do, promises and claims made each with an eye to squeezing out more resources from whichever 'client' is most persuadable. In his book, *The University in Ruins* (1996), Bill Readings has a sharp eye for this, noting that claims of 'excellence' abound in university PR statements, but that, since these are devoid of any underpinning concept of the university, they serve to homogenize the most diverse of things. All are excellent, so long as they are capable of generating some resource or other. Thus universities today claim excellent accommodation, excellent teaching, excellent international relations, excellent union facilities, excellent sports facilities, excellent relations with the local community, excellent employment records for their students, excellent libraries, excellent car parking, excellent location ... excellence in everything (and nothing).

Compare such opportunistic publicity claims with earlier conceptions of the university – with, say, Cardinal Newman's notion of the university as a residential college in which students might be inducted into 'universal truths', or with Matthew Arnold's emphasis on their being centres of the 'best that is thought and known', or with Leavis's insistence that the university was a locus of moral sensibility which must resist 'mass civilization', or with Oakeshott's conviction that universities were charged with nurturing the 'intellectual capital' of civilization. In any comparison, what most strikes the reader is the absence today of a defining idea of the university, one which would insist upon priorities and principles. What we have instead is only opportunistic strategies to best ensure the prosperity of the institution.

Why such passivity in higher education today? At the outset one should acknowledge the dull compulsion of economics. The steady reduction of support to the universities has stalled careers, increased workloads, and generally induced a survivalist mode amongst many of those inside. Students look to get through without an excessive debt and to emerge with a good degree, staff hope that their contract will be maintained two years down the line, all employees fear a negative score in the Research Assessment or Teaching Quality exercises. There are good reasons here for keeping one's head down.

Equally important is a point made, in a somewhat different context, by Russell Jacoby (1987). This concerns the decline of public intellectuals, the weakening of a sense of engagement of intellectuals with what one might call the democratic conversations inside their societies. There was a time when many intellectuals addressed and wrote for what used to be called the 'intelligent public', a commitment which encouraged a plain style of writing and an engagement with urgent questions of the day. One thinks, in this light, of such as George Orwell, Arthur Koestler, A.J.P. Taylor, H.G. Wells, J.B. Priestley, Edward Thompson, Richard Hoggart and the like. However, since the 1960s, and congruent with the expansion of higher education, intellectuals have increasingly been institutionalized. As employees of the universities, they have been drawn to write for one another rather than for the wider public. This has encouraged the spread of an 'insider' language, a concern for writing for one's colleagues rather than for others, and a self-referential approach to intellectual work which excludes outsiders who have no access to the recondite subjects and specialist language in use. Examples abound: the Althusserian dominance of the early 1970s, Derridean deconstructionism, poststructuralist minutiae, the wave of postmodern theorizing in recent years.

Several things are worth noting here.

- In absolute terms there are today many more intellectuals than ever before, both in the UK and around the world, yet their influence on wider affairs appears to be negligible. Academics today can enjoy realtime contact with colleagues thousands of miles away, yet their influence on their own immediate societies is minimal.
- The language of these intellectuals is characteristically obscure, their articles read by no more than a few hundred specialists, their books by at most a few thousand, their most highly regarded practitioners being 'theorists' who are scarcely comprehensible by advanced undergraduates.
- A sizeable number of these intellectuals make a good deal of their own radicalism, yet theirs is too often a radicalism without teeth, since it neither confronts substantive positions in the polity, nor does it formulate positions with any clarity, nor does it take serious political risks.[1] So much of this radicalism is about lifestyle,[2] hence at once everywhere and without any practical consequences in terms of the political sphere and the mobilization of social forces. Fortunately for those who advocate their own radicalism in this way, it is done so in ways which in no way threaten their own sinecures at prestigious universities.

To make this observation is in no way to deny that are still today some public intellectuals. One thinks, for instance, of such as Michael Ignatieff, Tony Giddens and Terry Eagleton in this regard. But what is hard to deny is the *relative* decline of such thinkers, and with it a diminution of the confidence with which one might proclaim the purposes of the university.

Finally, and surely of most import, one needs to refer to the spread of postmodern thinking and practices. This seems to me to have had at least two major consequences. Firstly, postmodernism undermines the university from without. It does this by hitting hard at the old university claim to be a privileged source of knowledge about the world, the specific place in society where would be developed authoritative and expert knowledge. Postmodernism does this, for example, by asking what is so special about the university when so many people now have access to the internet (about 30 per cent of US households, quite a lot fewer elsewhere, but rising fast) which allows us to access no end of knowledge whenever we want, wherever we are, and from whomsoever interests us. Or again, what distinguishes a university when nowadays we have umpteen alternative sources of knowledge, on the net itself of course, but also in the plethora of think tanks such as Demos or the Heritage Foundation, or those research and development centres located inside corporations, often with hundreds of dedicated staff, or even those cultivators of intellectual endeavour such as the BBC, the *Independent*, or Channel Four. Finally, Michael Gibbons (1998) objects that universities no longer have a monopoly on the development of knowledge because they have over the years produced innumerable graduates who are equipped to reflect critically – and that this includes being sceptical of the claims by universities about the standing of their own research.

Postmodernity also undermines the university from within because what we find, in this vastly expanded and transformed institution, is that there is no longer any collective entity, so that the old conception – that a university is a community of scholars, doing different tasks, but united in commitment to a common pursuit of enlightenment – goes up in smoke. There is no 'inner life' in the postmodern university, and all imaginings of such, perhaps of a coterie of elderly dons in erudite disputation while gathered for pre-dinner sherry in Magdalen, belong only to the fantasy land of *Shadowlands*.[3] Quite to the contrary, all we come across in the postmodern university are conglomerates of differences (Bauman 1997), a bewilderingly complicated milieu in which physicists cannot (and do not even try) to speak to economists, and where nuclear physicists can make neither head nor tail of the work of theoretical physicists. Indeed, the same goes for every 'discipline', and the closer one looks the more one appreciates that conceptions of unified gatherings of scholars is an illusion. Instead, we have huge numbers of people, with radically different interests and agendas, united about nothing save perhaps the availability of car-parking facilities (as an exasperated Clark Kerr was said to declare while head of the University of California). Somewhat more soberly, Burton Clark makes the same point thus: 'Different worlds, small worlds. Institutional differentiation interacts with disciplinary differentiation in a bewildering fashion that steadily widens and deepens the matrix of differences that separate ... academics from each other.' (Clark 1997: 30–1).

Zygmunt Bauman (1987) adds to all this the observation that university faculty have been reduced to being merely another 'voice' in postmodern society, with no special claims to have access to legitimate knowledge. Where once university members might have been deferred to as legislators, they have now diminished into interpreters, whether the matter is science, literary taste or aesthetic judgement. It no longer matters much that you are called 'Professor', what you say is only one opinion amongst many others.

From a very different background to that of Bauman, management writer Peter Drucker says much the same thing when he announces that today 'there is no higher or lower knowledge. In the knowledge society knowledges are tools, and as such are dependent for their importance and position on the task to be performed' (Drucker 1994). This accords very well with Jean-François Lyotard's well-known argument (1984) that a principle of performativity (that is, use) predominates today, thereby undermining the former university justification that it pursued 'truth'. If science is no longer discovery-led, but is rather guided by the search for patents and inventions, and if management and engineering subjects have fully entered today's universities, then previous arguments for the university must be forfeited. Not the goal of Enlightenment, but the demands of performativity, are the new definers of knowledge.

But if the former defences of what might be included in the university are breached by performativity criteria, then the boundaries of exclusion from the university also collapse, and with them the former hierarchies, at the top of which were subjects such as Classics, Natural Science and Philosophy. If performativity alone is what matters, then why not degrees in Tourism, Golf Course Studies, Environmental Change, or even Leisure Studies? And if this is so, then what characterizes the university today other than its being a collection of differences, a diversity of knowledge activities pursued – and routinely abandoned – only because there is some performativity justification for their adoption?

This has been conceived as the transformation from a Mode 1 type of knowledge that is homogeneous, rooted in strong academic disciplines which are hierarchically organized, and transmitted to noviciates in an apprentice–master relationship, towards Mode 2 knowledges which are non-hierarchical, pluralistic, transdisciplinary, fast-changing and responsive to diverse needs such as students' experiences, industrial priorities, and social problems.[4] This plurality of knowledges must announce an end to common purposes of the university, there being no possibility of agreement on goals or even on methods of work. By extension, we must forego thinking about how to define what a university might be, instead simply accepting that there are an enormous number of very different institutions with radically different purposes and practices that might be called universities (for want of a better term).

The university is also being undermined because of the increasing difficulty of distinguishing it from growing sectors of industry. The suggestion here is that knowledge-rich corporations such as Microsoft and Zeneca, and even media organizations such as Channel 4, 'already possess many of the features of a university' (*Economist* 1997). These are brimming with highly educated employees, frequently people possessing doctoral degrees and working on cutting-edge projects in software production, advanced electronics, biotechnology or social investigation. Moreover, such companies have many connections with universities that blur previous distinctions, frequently in the form of joint deals, shared staff and even facilities. Thus the university can no longer be identified by virtue of its separation from the 'outside world', while simultaneously 'big companies ... are becoming more conscious of their role as creators, disseminators, and users of knowledge – a definition not altogether different from that of a university' (ibid.).

Relatedly, questioning the once privileged role of the university as regards research subverts its former distinctiveness. From within institutions, as well as from some figures in politics, serious questions are asked about the supposed interdependence and indivisibility of teaching and research that, in the view of some, characterizes a genuine university. As more and more students are to be offered places on degree programmes, then it may be asked whether it is really essential that all of their teachers are involved in research. It is commonly asserted that university work must involve research to teach undergraduates effectively. However, though it is unpalatable to many, the research evidence just does not support the assertion that research and teaching are necessarily mutually supportive (Astin 1993, 1999).

Correspondingly, voices have been raised to observe that there is no compelling reason to locate research inside universities. Already Research Assessment Exercises, and the distribution of funds on the basis of achieved ranks, mean that resources in UK higher education go for the most part to a cluster of around 15 institutions (and it has been estimated that 25 per cent of research funds in the UK go to just four universities – Oxford, Cambridge, University College, and Imperial College (*Guardian* 1999: 1)), so why not separate these from the rest? More radical still, it has been noted that 'research can be done in any suitably equipped institute' (Johnson 1994: 380) and that perhaps the best place for it is in centres such as the nuclear research institute at Harwell, rather than in universities, where other matters may be a hindrance. As the *Economist* (1997) puts it, 'an intelligent Martian might wonder why a university – autonomous, chaotic, distracted by all those students – should be an efficient place in which to sponsor economically worthwhile research'. Sir Douglas Hague, a recent head of the Economic and Social Research Council, argues from the perspective of the Martian, urging the marketization of universities since 'knowledge entrepreneurs' are better able to produce research (and even teaching) that is useful than the university 'dinosaurs' (Hague 1991).

Finally, what of the educational potential of new technologies? In the minds of some academics is fixed the idea, which draws heavily on Newman, of the university as a residential experience, but new technologies promise distance learning from one's own home, at one's convenience, accessing the best available informational sources, all at a fraction of the cost of attendance at a university. The 'virtual university' promises to undermine yet another foundation stone of the traditional university, leaving it unclear as to its justification or even to its location, as customized network facilities allow students to study how, when and what they judge appropriate. Thus Michael Prowse suggests, 'In due course, just-in-time electronic education, delivered to your living room by commercial companies, will undermine the most hallowed names in higher education' (Prowse 1995; cf. Gell and Cochrane 1996). As 'cybernaut' Sadie Plant enthuses, 'technology is bringing down the walls of the ivory tower' (Plant 1995). And, she might have added, leaving no justification for the university behind.

Combined, these factors mean that scarcely anyone wants to, or even can, speak for, still less define, the university today. At best perhaps are those postmodernists who will celebrate the heterogeneity, pluralism and 'multivocalism' that apparently thrives in higher education. But this is a celebration of everything and nothing, something which makes a virtue of abundance and nothing more. Old-fashioned intellectuals, Marxist or élitist (or perhaps both), are much disturbed by this, but even they seem to be silenced, either by economic uncertainty or the sheer cacophony that sounds off around them in higher education today. There are just so many voices, and so much differentiation, that to articulate unifying principles – and ones which may even suggest that some groups (of students and of subjects) do not belong inside a genuine university – is a daunting task. Moreover, the readiness with which complainants are quietened by the accusation of élitism is striking. How dare critics of the university, so often ensconced in the very institutions about which they deem to rail, speak out in defence of 'ivory towers' which have been closed to all but a tiny minority of highly privileged people up until the past few years? Indeed, there is something impressively democratic about the postmodern temper, noticeably in the way in which it promotes access and the rights of the individual to be heard. There being no authoritative discourse, it follows logically that everyone has a right of entry to the university so as to join in with whatever conversation is taking place. This certainly has an appealing generosity of spirit, though it leaves the university with no raison d'être.

One might have anticipated that such a conundrum would cause difficulty amongst postmodernists. But not so for Peter Scott. In his book *The Meanings of Mass Higher Education* (1995), Scott traces an affinity with the Post-Fordist Economy, Postmodern Times, and the Postmodern University. The affinity is that everything nowadays is shifting, is flexible, is impermanent and without fixity. Accordingly, everything about higher education is now 'fuzzy' (Scott's leitmotif), is 'fluid', 'non-linear' and 'complex'. Not surprisingly, Scott notices that the university itself is not at all a clear entity. In fact, what with 'franchising', 'branding', 'credit accumulation and transfer', 'partnerships' and all the rest (not to mention 'distance learning' or 'virtuality'), he notes that no one quite knows what the university is anymore. The Vice-Chancellor of Kingston University himself doesn't seem to have a clue. Nevertheless, appropriately postmodern in his laid-back insouciance, Scott (1998b) simply observes that 'although some writers still try to define what is special about the university ... most have given up. After all, we now have a British Aerospace Virtual University, and even a University for Industry', so what's the point of bothering about definitions? If a vice-chancellor can head a university without an idea of what it is that he is running, then why should anyone else worry?

Critique

While it is easy enough to recognize elements of the above description in today's universities, it seems to me a travesty to talk of a postmodern university having come into being. The rest of this essay will present reasons why this should be so.

I begin with an essay of the late Edward Shils, the doyen of conservative American academics. Shils observes that, while the university has been subject to major outside pressures – most notably an insistence that it be more 'practical' (of which more below) – the overwhelming majority of faculty remain committed to what he describes as 'autogenetic' values and practices (Shils 1997: 204). These constitute 'the defining functions of the university' (ibid.: 245), and involve a dual commitment to research and teaching that strives for 'truth'. Research – the search for original knowledge[5] – and teaching – the imparting of what is known and how it is known (something which presupposes a 'research spirit' even in teaching) – are herein inextricably connected. In addition, faculty are dedicated to the free investigation of phenomena,[6] without prior regard for issues of utility or profitability (ibid.: 247), in methodical, open and disciplined ways. This search for 'truth' prioritizes investigation, exploration, and an openness of academic activity in both the research and teaching activities.

Shils urges that a defence of the university be made on these lines in terms of 'civility'. By this he does not mean good manners, but rather that the university ought to impart, to all involved, whether student or faculty, a wider perspective than that of the self-interested or utilitarian. To Shils the qualities of self-interest and utilitarianism are the antithesis of 'civility', which implies a capacity for disinterestedness and detachment (cf. Filmer 1997) which are hallmarks of university practices (Shils 1997: 289–90).

How odd and anachronistic this must read to postmodernists: a defence of the university in terms of truth-seeking, detachment and disinterestedness. So orthodox is social constructivism nowadays that scarcely anyone may lay claim to being a truth-seeker without raising a snigger. Deconstructionists would make meat of Shils' élitist background: here is a man who spent the whole of his adult life inside the most privileged of academe's portals, commuting between Chicago and Peterhouse, Cambridge, in effect rationalizing his own biography.

Truth-seeking

Yet still I am drawn to Shils' argumentation for several reasons. First, he is not naïve about the challenge of 'truth-seeking'. To appreciate his position it is necessary to understand that the word 'truth' is used as a term of abuse (or at least of ridicule) by postmodernists, as if its proponents hold to some absolutist and philosophically gauche concept. But Edward Shils does not claim 'truth' as an absolute, but rather as an ideal, towards which everything approximates. As such he introduces a notion of the tentativeness of knowledge while resisting the drift into the relativism which bedevils postmodern thought and practice. The postmodern logic that runs: all knowledge is socially constructed, hence all knowledges are incommensurable, therefore all knowledges are equal, is roundly challenged by Shils in ways that find accord with the 'critical realist' assault on postmodern relativism (see, for example, Norris 2000). Consider Shils' conception of 'truth-seeking' in the following and one readily appreciates the sophistication of his position:

> The ascertainment of any truth is a difficult matter; the truth must be re-ascertained incessantly. These truths are changed continuously by new discoveries which may indeed be defined as the revision in the light of new observations and analyses of propositions previously held to be true. For these reasons, there must be elements of tentativeness and readiness in the attitudes towards any truths accepted at present. This readiness to revise is not tantamount to relativism. It does not mean that any proposition is just as true as any other proposition or that the truth of a proposition is dependent on the social position or political orientation of the person asserting or accepting it. It means that the propositions held at any moment are the best that could be achieved by the methods of observation and analysis which are acceptable in scientific and scholarly communities. The acceptance of these propositions, with these qualifications, implies an admission that these particular propositions will not so much be proven to be wrong as that they will be shown to require revision and replacement by propositions sustained by better observations and better interpretations. (Shils 1997: 4)

Furthermore, it should be recognized that Shils is sensitive to the socioeconomic contexts within which higher education now operates. He writes at length, for instance, of the unholy alliances entered into by university vice-chancellors, government officers and employment-oriented students, many of which combine to assault the ideals of the university. Yet still he insists that most faculty continue to subscribe to the goals of 'truth-seeking', openness, detachment and methodological rigour which distinguish the university from other 'knowledge businesses'. Here he finds agreement with a writer who has a quite different trajectory. Martha Nussbaum's *Cultivating Humanity* (1997) is a vigorous defence of liberal education, one which advocates inclusion in the curriculum of such things as Latin American fiction, feminism and cultural studies, as an important (and pre-eminently practical) means of developing critical social and self-awareness amongst students. Crucial to Nussbaum's position is a principle echoed in Shils: that knowledge is not relative, even if it is not absolute, and that the major purpose of a university is to develop tools for gaining more adequate knowledge, a task which requires openness to ideas and continuous self-examination. In Nussbaum's words: 'Reason has a special dignity that lifts it above the play of forces' (ibid.: 38). By extension, so too has the university.

It seems to me that this point of view remains vital inside the university. Evidence for it seems to me to be present in everyday university routines of debate, teaching and academic review and validation where argumentation frequently revolves around questions of evidence, intellectual independence and rigour. It sometimes seems that those who proclaim the end of academic authority have not participated in day-to-day university affairs. And this is not to suggest that what one will encounter are protestations of absolute truth; one will, however, come across manifold examples of people striving to sort the better argument from the weaker, to insist on a necessary distance from and dispassion about the subjects they study.

It is something one will also witness in the lower esteem of those matters which are demonstrably most 'worldly' and 'use-oriented'. This is by no means to say that the university will be divorced from the 'real world'. Quite to the contrary, much university activity will be deeply engaged with the affairs of the world. Yet, if it is to command intellectual respect, if it is to merit inclusion inside a university, it will necessarily exhibit what Max Weber famously called 'ethical neutrality' towards its subjects (Weber 1917). That is, courses in business and management, hotel catering and such-like strongly vocational programmes tend to be of lesser standing in the eyes of other university colleagues. This is not to say that courses in business cannot satisfy the criteria of a university. It is rather to say that, insofar as they are impelled towards offering a training in how to perform a particular role, rather than giving a detached assessment of the whys and wherefores of that role, then so are they compromised in the eyes of their peers.

To be sure, there is a tendency nowadays to mute observations within universities as regards this question. In part this stems from the economic presence of programmes such as business and management (which account for something like one in every five students in higher education today). It also surely owes something to the relativist ethos which is quick to decry any assertion that some subjects are more worthy of inclusion in a university than are others. One recognizes these forces, but it really must be insisted that the basis of judgements which relegate programmes where 'training' is the priority or where 'consultancies' are undertaken for reasons of financial gain is that there has been a corresponding offence made against university ideals. To say such things is frequently dismissed on the grounds that they represent an outdated snobbery, something which some authors even assert has harmed Britain's economic performance over the years (Barnett 1986; Weiner 1981; cf. Robins and Webster 1989). But they constitute no such thing. On the contrary, they evoke defining functions of the university itself.

Legitimacy

My second major objection to the suggestion that we have a postmodern university is allied to this justification for the university articulated by Shils and Nussbaum, but is a more substantive point. It centres on the credentializing function of the university and the legitimacy of this in the eyes of the public at large.

Postmodernists are surely right to identify challenges to the monopoly of universities over knowledge. As mentioned earlier, think tanks, R&D centres, the media, and even pressure groups such as Greenpeace and Friends of the Earth, are alternative sources of knowledge nowadays. Postmodernists' of course, interpret this as a diminution – or at least a levelling – of universities' credibility and this is consonant with the increased relativism of knowledges which has resulted in a lowering of the prestige of universities. One must respond at the outset to this in terms of historical accuracy. The university in Britain has never had a monopoly or even unchallenged dominance when it comes to knowledge. Indeed, it is probable that when Oxbridge alone represented the university then its knowledges were widely regarded as sectional and accordingly to be distrusted. After all, it was Thomas Hardy, scarcely a radical, who lambasted Oxford's pretensions to the higher learning in *Jude the Obscure* more than a century ago, and trade unions, and the labour movement more generally, have long since struggled to establish their alternative sources of knowledge precisely because orthodox universities were suspect (Ruskin College at Oxford, Fircroft in Birmingham and so on).

Nevertheless, the most important postmodern claim is that universities have decisively forfeited their authoritative standing more recently. In evidence is offered the explosive growth of institutions carrying the title, inside and outside of higher education itself. It isn't simply that Bolton Institute might now lay claim to the word; it is that entirely new institutions such as Unipart University, British Aerospace University, and the University for Industry unabashedly flaunt the word. The postmodern reasoning has it that, so many different places being capable of using the title, then the established meaning of the term must have disappeared.

But it must be objected that, whatever the claims made to the terminology, the legitimacy of the qualifications issued by these new (and not so new) organizations is signalled in what one might call their portability. That is, in their recognition across the wider society, such that a qualification from an institution may be esteemed wherever it is taken. And in this what is especially striking is the degree to which portability – and, by extension, legitimacy – is closely connected to the perception of a university's distance from narrow practicality or performativity. Conversely, the portability of qualifications is related to the awarding institution's commitment to established academic values of disinterestedness, free inquiry and critical thought. This is surely why qualifications from the likes of British Telecom and British Aerospace have little portability (outside of a narrow industrial sphere) and why the University for Industry will experience serious difficulties in getting any of the qualifications it may award generally accepted. No doubt interested parties will rail against public ignorance and 'anti-industrial' prejudices in this, but the likelihood remains that the general public will be wary in the extreme of 'universities' that are excessively tied to the 'operational' (cf. Barnett 1997) – and for the good reason that a genuine university must preserve a necessary autonomy from the utilitarian.

Hierarchy

My third objection is that the concept of a postmodern university, one which conjures up an institution which is at once internally heterogeneous and externally different from elsewhere, appears wilfully blind to empirical evidence of hierarchies of differences amongst universities. Now I willingly agree that judgements of difference are often very hard to make, and that they are also very harsh and even unjust. There will doubtless be readers of this essay who still smart over their 1996 Research Assessment Exercise score which they feel has been unfairly bestowed (and I have met some who admit the reverse – that they were fortunate to the attain the score they finished with). Others will feel similarly towards the Teaching Quality Assessment procedures. And still more will chafe against the harshest of all judgements, that of general reputation, which so frequently lauds the ancient institution and suspects the new. Nonetheless, it is truly astonishing to me that, for whatever reasons – ranging from democratic idealism, commitment towards inclusiveness, to a fear of being accused of snootiness – so many postmodern commentators on higher education turn a blind eye to the distinctively hierarchical and patterned character of universities.

This is also something which has major consequences for the social and economic valuation of degree qualifications. No one can, hand on heart, seriously suggest that all degrees from all institutions are of equal worth, not given the different qualities of students, staff and resources in the UK. For instance, the University of Durham ranks in the top ten in terms of its student intake's Advanced level scores, yet its graduates fall outside the top twenty when it comes to the proportion of first- and upper-second-class degrees awarded. Conversely, Oxford Brookes is about seventieth on A-level entries, yet climbs twenty points when it comes to graduate classifications (*THES* 1999). Few would suggest that teaching is either so bad at Durham or so good at Brookes. The most obvious and suasive explanation is that different standards are being applied. (See Chapman (1994) for evidence of this in Geography departments.) This being so, one cannot be surprised that members of the public are sceptical of the credo that all degrees are equal, and that they normally assess their worth on the basis of the standing of the institution which awarded the qualification. This is a pretty rough measure, but surely to be expected given the compelling evidence that standards vary between institutions. It need hardly be said that a degree from the two premier universities – Oxbridge – counts for a good deal more than those from most other universities (Purcell and Pitcher 1996). But it must be said that this is not because of some arbitrary prejudice on the part of those who so judge. When I hear, as one on occasion does, commentators talking in terms such as this – that it is only a matter of fancy that a degree from Birmingham should be more highly regarded than one from Wolverhampton – then I despair, because such talk is both unworldly and patronising of students.

Moreover, the refusal to acknowledge hierarchy – or to dismiss any claim for it as just one or another 'discourse', and thereby without substance – shamefully avoids addressing the issue of social justice. If one subscribes to the concept of a postmodern university, then unavoidably one celebrates the variety of universities and, amidst this enthusiasm, no one place is superior to any other since it is merely different. Well, comparisons are difficult, and at the level of individuals, courses and departments, there are important nuances to be recognized, but to conclude from this that hierarchies are no more than 'discourses' seems to me an abrogation of responsibility.

Let me baldly say why this is so. The best universities in Britain, certainly on aggregated measures, but also on just about every separate measure (staff–student ratios, staff qualifications, library expenditures, employment records, A-level points . . .), are the universities of Oxford and Cambridge. To be sure, some qualification is required to this overall truth, since for particular subjects Oxbridge's hegemony may be challenged. Nevertheless, the general truth remains, to which something else must be added. This is that, to gain entry to the undergraduate programmes at Oxbridge candidates score on average just under 30 points at A-level (that is, above two A and one B grades). In 1997 some three thousand candidates in England scored three grade As in their Advanced levels, yet only about half of these went on to Oxbridge. One may certainly exclude a proportion of these since they will have taken their superb results to other excellent institutions for the best of reasons, perhaps to medical school, or the Royal College of Art, or to the LSE. Yet it should be noted that fully half of Oxbridge's talented intakes come from a very narrow social segment of the population – the 20 per cent or so of all A-level candidates who are privately schooled (and, incidentally, of the remaining half most come from the professional middle class who have located themselves in the catchment areas of the better state schools).

The key issue here is why do so few of the many able and well-qualified candidates from the state education system, and from more modest social backgrounds, fail to get in – and often do not even apply – to the best of British universities? I cannot begin to suggest reform here, and that is not my purpose, since all I wish to do here is highlight the fact that subscribers to the conception of a postmodern university cannot, in logic, even admit that there is a cause for concern. Incapable of agreeing that there is a hierarchical structure to British universities, the postmodern account cannot respond to, or even acknowledge, issues of injustice.

Academic capitalism

It is not unusual for commentators to become excited by the 'flexibility, synergy and volatility' (Scott 1995: 70) of the postmodern university. But it is these very characteristics which, if unchallenged, would announce the end of the university as a meaningful term. If instead of an academic community we have mutual incomprehension, if research may be pursued satisfactorily outside academe, if utility is the primary criterion for inclusion in the curriculum, if effective teaching does not require the support of research, if courses can be studied without attendance ... if all we encounter is a plurality of differences, then, to say the least, the concept of the university is problematic (Delanty 1998).

However, we should challenge the protestations of pluralism that lie at the heart of claims that we now have a postmodern university. Quite to the contrary, the reality appears to be that universities across nations have been shaped decisively in a limited direction – namely one which makes universities most responsive to contemporary capitalism's needs and strictures. What has been called the neo-liberal consensus, which today is hegemonic around the globe, demands that marketization principles and practices permeate the entire social domain. This has meant that the relatively autonomous space that universities have occupied has markedly diminished, not as universities have become more plural, but rather as market forces have told more decisively on universities themselves to develop in directions favourable to commercial life.

Aspects of this include:

- The by now routine insistence from research councils that projects to be funded will be driven, not by intellectual curiosity, but by their contribution to improvements in competitiveness. In this way the state has thrown its weight strongly behind capitalist interests (Monbiot 1998; cf. DTI 1998).
- State policy, bolstered by industrial advice, that universities should strive to produce the 'human capital' that equips graduates to function effectively in the global commercial world. Phil Brown and Hugh Lauder (1995) refer to this as 'knowledge wars' where national governments have prioritized education as a means of gaining advantage in the global economy because the improved human capital will raise the nation's competitive edge.

To be sure, these two factors express a force which represents the interest of capitalism as a whole rather than that of specific segments of capital, and to this degree there remains a distance of the university from front-line commercial operations. Nonetheless, there is today a much greater degree of representation of business interest both on university governing boards as well as in the development of courses that have specific connections (for example, in partnership deals involving research programmes and in contracts entered into to deliver training courses for companies). Such measures ensure that universities are shaped to service capitalism, since anything not in the mainstream will find survival and sourcing problematic.

A further development has been the practice of regarding students as 'customers' who must be satisfied that their 'investment' in education gains a satisfactory return. Of course, responding to students' needs is not in itself a negative thing to do. Yet it can be – as it is more and more nowadays – when the university's 'customers' are perceived to be demanding that they are made more employable, or that their courses are demonstrably of practical use. Such demands easily come into conflict with alternative educational ideals, such as introducing students – regarded as noviciates in learning who are not always right – to alternative philosophies to those which are approved by the wider society.

Perhaps the most striking dimension of the consequences of commercial practices has been evident in the ways in which they have engendered change inside universities, privileging certain subject areas (such as business studies and biotechnology) and demoting others (such as music and aesthetics). This has gone so far that Sheila Slaughter and Larry Leslie (1997), in a comparative study of four advanced nations, adopt the concept 'academic capitalism' to describe a situation where faculty increasingly find themselves in hybrid public-sector and market contexts. That is, they are paid from public revenues for the most part, but called upon largely to service the commercial elements of the wider society. The effects have been remarkable, resulting in academics becoming much more competitive one with another, and becoming increasingly entrepreneurial as they seek out funding opportunities. In addition, the spread of what Slaughter and Leslie term 'entrepreneurial knowledge' is striking – *vide* the continuous expansion of business schools, contract research, and computer science courses over the last generation.

By the way, all of the above is not to allege that higher education has become indistinguishable from corporate capitalism. Slaughter and Leslie pointedly observe that the university's appeal, even if tarnished, remains that it allows for the relatively free exploration of 'theoretical' and 'basic' knowledge. That is, it provides space in which comparatively unrestricted investigations may be undertaken, and herein lies its appeal to many researchers who are employed outside the university in private concerns where they are still more seriously constrained by market factors than their university colleagues. With this, of course, we return to Edward Shils' depiction of the foundational criteria of the university.

Conclusion

Surveying current developments in higher education, one feels compelled to acknowledge that it is going through a period of rapid transformation. However, to contend that this represents a new phenomenon – the postmodern university – is to vastly overstate the extent and misread the direction of change. If under threat, there remain in place distinguishing features of the university, notably a commitment to 'truth' and its corollaries – free inquiry, academic rigour, detachment and disinterestedness. It cannot be suggested that these are transhistorical characteristics, but it should be recognized that they are deeply entrenched, and this with good reason, since they underpin what takes place inside the university. Further, higher education is being pressured to change, but this is not in the plural directions believed by postmodernists. Rather it is being brought further into line with market strictures, hence into concordance with academic capitalism. Before getting there, however, there are many points of resistance to be overcome.

Notes

1. Jacoby comments acidly on the 'radicalism' of deconstructionism, to the effect that it subverts everything while boosting the career of its proponents. Thus:

   At the end of the radical theorizing project is a surprise: a celebration of academic hierarchy, professions, and success. Never has so much criticism yielded so much affirmation. From Foucault the professor learned that power and institutions saturate everything ... [T]his means that university practices and malpractices are no better or worse than anything else. (1994: 182).

2. About, for instance, the 'subversive' reading of Charles Dickens as a 'phallocentric' author. Robert Hughes (1993) complains, again, of this sort of radicalism at a time, around 1989, when the world was undergoing some of the most significant political changes of the century.
3. A recent fellow of Magdalen, where *Shadowlands* was filmed, reports that tourists, walking in the grounds, have been heard to voice their disappoint-

ment in coming across bejeaned and T-shirted academics rather than those gowned, tweed-suited and pipe-smoking 'proper' dons as seen in the movies. Such postmodern delights!

4. Gibbons et al. (1994: 3) distinguish knowledges as follows:

> in Mode 1 problems are set and solved in a context governed by the, largely academic, interests of a specific community. By contrast, Mode 2 knowledge is carried out in a context of application. Mode 1 is disciplinary while Mode 2 is transdisciplinary. Mode 1 is characterized by homogeneity, Mode 2 by heterogeneity. Organizationally, Mode 1 is hierarchical and tends to preserve its form, while Mode 2 is more heterarchical and transient. Each employs a different type of quality control. In comparison with Mode 1, Mode 2 is more socially accountable and reflexive.

5. Nowadays, the word research requires some clarification. Shils takes it to mean contribution to original knowledge, an investigative, analytical and critical activity which is at the heart of university life. There may be some disjunction between this and the tendency, in the UK at least, towards a narrower definition which regards research as that which is income-generating for the university, though this may jeopardize the investigator's autonomy. Research, on Shils' definition, is catholic, considered to be any thorough, scholarly and investigative work that is freely pursued. Shils takes this to be a requisite of university life.

6. This argument was articulated by Parsons and Platt (1968). See also Parsons (1968). Oliver Fulton (1996) reported support for this 'calling', with disciplines and the collegium maintaining strong support amongst academics across four nations.

References

Astin, Alexander W. (1993) *What Matters in College: Four Critical Years Revisited.* San Francisco: Jossey-Bass.

Astin, Alexander W. (1999) 'How the liberal arts college affects students', *Daedalus*, 128(1) Winter 77–100.

Barnett, Corelli (1986) *The Audit of War: the Illusion and Reality of Britain as a Great Nation.* London: Macmillan.

Barnett, Ronald (1997) *Higher Education: a Critical Business.* Buckingham: Open University Press.

Bauman, Zygmunt (1987) *Legislators and Interpreters: On Modernity, Post-Modernity, and the Intellectuals.* Cambridge: Polity Press.

Bauman, Zygmunt (1997) 'Universities: old, new and different', in Anthony Smith and Frank Webster (eds), *The Postmodern University? Contested Visions of Higher Education in Society.* Buckingham: Open University Press.

Bender, Thomas (1997) 'Politics, intellect, and the American university, 1945–1995', *Daedalus*, 126(1) Winter 1–38.

Brown, Philip and Lauder, Hugh (1995) 'Post-Fordist possibilities: education, training and national development', in Leslie Bash and Andy Green (eds), *World Yearbook of Education 1995*. London: Kogan Page.

Chapman, K. (1994) 'Variability in degree results in geography in British universities', *Studies in Higher Education*, 19(1) 89–102.

Clark, Burton R. (1997) 'Small world, different worlds: the uniqueness and troubles of American academic professions', *Daedalus*, 126(4) Fall 21–42.

Delanty, Gerard (1998) 'The idea of the university in the global era: from knowledge as an end to the end of knowledge', *Social Epistemology*, 12(1) 3–25.

Drucker, Peter (1994) 'The age of social transformation', *Atlantic Monthly*, 274(5), November 53–80.

Department of Trade and Industry (DTI) (1998) *Our Competitive Future: Building the Knowledge-Driven Economy*. HMSO, December.

Economist (1997) 'Survey: Universities', 4 October.

Filmer, Paul (1997) 'Disinterestedness and the modern university', in Anthony Smith and Frank Webster (eds), *The Postmodern University? Contested Visions of Higher Education in Society*. Buckingham: Open University Press.

Fulton, Oliver (1996) 'Unity or fragmentation, convergence or diversity? The academic profession in mass higher education in comparative perspective.' Dilemmas of Mass Higher Education conference, Staffordshire University, 10–12 April.

Gell, Michael and Cochrane, Peter (1996) 'Learning and education in an information society', in William Dutton (ed.), *Information and Communication Technologies: Visions and Realities*. Oxford: Oxford University Press.

Gibbons, Michael (1998) 'A commonwealth perspective on the globalization of higher education', in Peter Scott (ed.), *The Globalization of Higher Education*. Buckingham: Open University Press.

Gibbons, Michael, Limoges, Camille, Nowotny, Helga, Schwartzman, Simon, Scott, Peter and Trow, Martin (1994) *The New Production of Knowledge: the Dynamics of Science and Research in Contemporary Societies*. London: Sage.

Guardian (1999) 'Entry to the super league', Education supplement, 13 July.

Hague, Sir Douglas (1991) *Beyond Universities: a New Republic of the Intellect*. London: Institute of Economic Affairs.

Halsey, A.H. (1992) *Decline of Donnish Dominion: the British Academic Professions in the Twentieth Century*. Oxford: Clarendon Press.

Hughes, Robert (1993) *Culture of Complaint: the Fraying of America*. New York: Oxford University Press.

Jacoby, Russell (1987) *The Last Intellectuals: American Culture in the Age of Academe*. New York: Basic Books.

Jacoby, Russell (1994) *Dogmatic Wisdom*. New York: Doubleday.

Johnson, Nevil (1994) 'Dons in decline: who will look after the cultural capital?', *20th Century British History*, 5: 370–85.

Lyotard, Jean-François (1979) *The Postmodern Condition: a Report on Knowledge*, trans. Geoff Bennington and Brian Massumi. Manchester: Manchester University Press, 1984.

Monbiot, George (1998) 'Integrity for sale', *Guardian*, 17 December

Norris, Chris (2000) 'Postmodernism: a user's guide', in Gary Browning, Abigail Halcli and Frank Webster (eds), *Understanding Contemporary Society: Theories of the Present*. London: Sage.

Nussbaum, Martha (1997) *Cultivating Humanity: a Classical Defense of Reform in Liberal Education.* Cambridge, MA: Harvard University Press.

Parsons, Talcott (1968) 'The academic system: a sociologist's view', *The Public Interest*, no. 13 (special issue), Fall.

Parsons, Talcott and Platt, Gerald M. (1968) 'Considerations on the American academic system', *Minerva*, VI(4) Summer 497–523.

Plant, Sadie (1995) *Wired*, April, p.7.

Prowse, Michael (1995) 'Endangered species', *Financial Times*, 20 November.

Purcell, K. and Pitcher, J. (1996) *Great Expectations: the New Diversity of Graduate Skills and Aspirations.* Manchester: Careers Services Unit.

Readings, Bill (1996) *The University in Ruins.* London: Harvard University Press.

Robins, Kevin and Webster, Frank (1989) *The Technical Fix: Education, Computers and Industry.* London: Macmillan.

Scott, Peter (1995) *The Meanings of Mass Higher Education.* Buckingham: Open University Press.

Scott, Peter (1998a) 'Mass higher education: a new civilisation?', in David Jary and Martin Parker (eds), *The New Higher Education: Issues and Directions for the Post-Dearing University.* Stoke: Staffordshire University Press.

Scott, Peter (1998b) 'Out of the ivory tower', *New Statesman*, 13 November.

Shils, Edward (1997) *The Calling of Education: the Academic Ethic and Other Essays on Higher Education*, edited by Steven Grosby. Chicago: University of Chicago Press.

Slaughter, Sheila and Leslie, Larry L. (1997) *Academic Capitalism: Politics, Policies and the Entrepreneurial University.* Baltimore, MD: Johns Hopkins University Press.

THES (1999) 23 April, pp. 32–3.

Weber, Max (1917) 'The meaning of "ethical neutrality"', in *The Methodology of the Social Sciences*, trans. and ed. by E.A. Shils and H.A. Finch. New York: Free Press, 1949.

Weiner, Martin (1981) *English Culture and the Decline of the Industrial Spirit 1850–1980.* Cambridge: Cambridge University Press.

5
Brickies or Bricoleurs? Gender in Computing and Design Courses

Deborah Trayhurn

Introduction: defining the 'problem'

In the UK attention has begun to focus on the success rates and number of *males* participating in various stages of formal education. Women's overall participation in UK higher education (HE) has exceeded males since 1994 (UCAS 1997) and yet courses in UK HE continue to demonstrate women's under-representation in the science, engineering and technology areas. Women continue to be under-represented in physics (Wertheim 1997), computing and, at the production end of the spectrum, on design courses. The numbers of places on UK HE physics courses has remained stable and women have formed a stable proportion of the physics students. There has been an expansion of approximately 500 per cent in the overall numbers of students studying computing in the UK (UCAS 1997), but despite such growth in this comparatively recent area of study, the percentage of women studying computing/IT courses has fallen. The numbers of women from the UK entering computer science courses in 1996 formed 18 per cent of the total number of students on these courses. This proportion fell to 11 per cent for the software engineering courses for the same group (UCAS 1997), indicating a varied interest in the continuum of courses, from those which are clearly engineering-focussed to those with an applied, business or management focus.

The decline in interest amongst women in taking IT courses in the UK is reflected elsewhere with the percentages of women taking computing/IT courses falling in 12 countries (including the US) between 1985 and 1990 and rising in only seven (Wright 1997). This is part of a longer trend, the numbers reducing from a high point in the 1980s by between 25 and 30 per cent over ten years. Closer examination of these numbers indicates that initiatives to encourage women to study computing/IT courses have succeeded only temporarily (UCAS 1997). These patterns of recruitment point to a continuation of gendered discourses within subject areas which prove to have been resilient to equal opportunities initiatives.

Attempts made in the UK to encourage women into physics have also faltered. Wertheim has contended that women have made least gains in this subject, but describes a tradition of intellectual transcendence arising to produce a 'priestly' cult of the subject, thus when women break into science, they become concentrated in the 'earthly' life science, and the 'heavenly mathematically based science ... remains ... the last arena of male hegemony' (Wertheim 1997: 237). In recent years, the discipline of geophysics has proved attractive to women entering UK HE, with some undergraduate courses reporting near gender parity. These courses frequently contain opportunities for environmental geophysics studies and so may present greater appeal for women seeking courses with clear relevance to perceived contemporary needs and concerns of society at large.

After over two decades of equal opportunities policies and feminist deconstruction of the polarities hard/soft or heavenly/earthly, the failure significantly to shift patterns of recruitment points to the resilience of the underlying structuring of disciplinary discourse. Women are clearly achieving in schools (Gipps and Murphy 1994) and are seeking and breaking into professions such as medicine and law (Siann 1997). In the language of Women into Science and Engineering (WISE) women have 'wised-up', but when they have done so they have not chosen IT or technical workshop-based subjects such as product design. Flis Henwood (1996) has analysed the discourse of WISE and found the underlying equal opportunities framework lacking; girls do not lack information, but are exercising different choices based on their perceptions of what disciplines offer. Gerda Siann (1997) has identified an 'I can, but I don't want to' trend among both males and females in relation to IT courses. She argues that, in comparison to other traditionally male-dominated professions, computing is relatively low status and less financially rewarding. In contrast to their male peers in computing, women appear to be adopting a more instrumental approach (Durndell, Siann and Glissov 1990). Women also value careers which allow for the exercise of social skill; and are often found undertaking roles such as technical communication, an overwhelmingly female occupation, engaged in communication and product development with focus on implementation with users (Gurak and Bayer 1994; Grundy 1996).

In her study of physics and English Kim Thomas (1990) similarly found that women were making positive choices in rejecting science. Physics is constructed as an instrumental, although 'pure' not applied, science. Physics alongside computing has failed to attract large numbers of women. The comparison with product design is significant, because unlike in computing (and physics) where there is a general problem of recruitment, design remains popular and competitive so that the lack of attraction Siann (1997) identified in IT does not apply. This suggests that instrumental motivations come to the fore when the intrinsic rewards are not as valued, since although recruitment in design remains buoyant, employment prospects in design are poor (Swanson 1994). It is important, therefore, to understand the positive choices that students are making. A study was made of those who make choices to follow courses 'against the grain' and the ways that they experience their courses to highlight the multifaceted relationship between gender and technology, and the related discourse of gender and design (Clegg et al. 1999). The study looked at the experiences of men and women on IT and design courses (Elkjaer 1992), the ways the students made course choices, and ways these were shaped by their perceptions of different disciplines. I intend to draw upon this study to comment particularly on disciplinary discourse and relate this to the computer science discipline, discussing issues beyond recruitment relevant to epistemological pluralism (Turkle and Papert 1990).

Overview of the case study

The case study (Clegg et al. 1999), was based in one UK HE institution and was designed to examine the stories of 53 first-year women and men who had chosen IT and design courses through semi-structured interviews. The range of IT and design courses available included: IT courses spanning Business Information Management, Business Information Systems, Computing, and Computing with Business; and for design, Product Design, Furniture Design, Interior Design, Graphic Design. No fashion or jewellery was taught and the Product Design course was less heavily technical than some others. The courses were typical of those found in UK HE institutions, with typical student composition (Siann 1997). Proportions of males to females on the design courses reflected the national Art and Design Admissions Register profile with women under-represented in Product Design. The computing course is not dominated by the formal methods of the research canon characterized by Karen Mahony and Brett Van Toen (1990), but is more industrially focused. The courses embrace a mixture of labora-tory-based computer work alongside lectures and seminars. The sample was made up of 26 design students (15 females and 11 males) and 27 IT students (11 females and 16 males).

Summary of study findings – disciplinary discourses

Overall findings indicated markedly different accounts in relation to the different disciplines and the students' experiences with materials. In design both women and men talked of 'always' having been engaged in some creative activity – drawing or making things. Their accounts were actively constructed as a personal narrative from child-hood in ways that suggested that pleasurable, visceral, hands-on exper-iences were central to the way they expressed themselves as a person. Yet for the female IT students experiences with computers began much later – with formal education, or use at work. The IT males told more varied stories, some of them were also able to construct a story from childhood based on computers as part of leisure. A woman graphics student described how doing art was important to her, indicating a passion about art and she constructed her story in a way which sug-gested that creativity was fundamental to her self-identity. She con-structed her key experiences in terms of creativity and imagination, confirming that in her understanding of design this was the key attribute. This centrality of the imagination emerged in interviews with the males as well indicating a dominant disciplinary discourse in design as personal creativity and as a core way that students identify themselves (Bonsiepe 1994). Product Design appeared the least expres-sive and most technical of the range of design courses. These distinc-tions were explicitly gendered in a number of the interviews.

The idea of 'always' having been involved and of that involvement expressing a core identity was absent in the IT interviewees. The closest approximation to the pattern found in design was among the males taking courses in Computing or Business Information Systems. Some of these males had been involved with computers from a young age and computers formed part of their leisure activities. These males felt that the exercise of computing skills came quite easily and naturally to them, the interest started young, they had 'always' had access to a computer, finding them 'fascinating'. However, the students described computing as an interest rather than part of their identity. Computing is not then a discourse of identity, its language is less visceral, more rationalistic; the pleasure described is the intellectual curiosity of knowing 'how things run'. Unlike the creativity of the designer, the image associated with involvement with computers from a number of interviews was oddball, male and unflattering. Home computer use was a male activity, carried out with male companions, with boys having privileged access in the classroom mediated through particular male teacher enthusiasts. This confirmed findings of a more general pattern (Durndell 1991; Durndell and Lightbody 1993) where women had experienced reduced access to a computer (Kirkup 1997). One girl had tended to use them for leisure pursuits with other girls at home, but later, in her mid-teens, she had also used them for 'typing' in a way that gave her keyboarding confidence in her school Business Administration course. Girls in this study experienced computing at an older age and in a way that confirmed limited access and the association of women and word-processing rather than games or programming (Kirkup 1997).

The women's accounts indicated that they had already had experiences in various types of work experience or through school which confirmed computing as a gendered discourse, supporting Bente Elkjaer's (1992) argument that girls experience computing in schools as 'guests' in the 'host' boys' space:

'I think the girls used to stick together as we got on better than with the lads. A lot of the lads were really into computers and made us feel a bit intimidated. Questions were asked in class and they obviously wanted to answer, and you felt a bit threatened by how much they know. There were a couple of lads that worked with us, but mostly the girls stuck together.' (quoted in Clegg et al. 1999: 48–9)

Recollections showed that the women in the study remembered school computing, as John Beynon (1993) describes, as places where dominant boys claim expertise.

The work that women in the study had done was mostly in routine administrative and business jobs. They had been end-users of IT, aware that if they remained in their roles their prospects were limited. These women had been successful in these roles, but in one student's case she sought a role where she would be challenged with some power to enable her to make change. She was persuaded to come into computing after experience with a powerful computing system which she described as brilliant in its control and scope. This woman Computing student described loving the course. The 'buzz' she described came from conceptualizing computing as a metaphor for complex organizations. She could draw on her own organizational experience and understanding. This suggests that there may be more than one discourse in computing. There is the dominant canon, characterized by Karen Mahony and Geert Van Toen (1990), dependent on formal methods and more likely to appeal to boys. There also appears to be an end-user discourse in which computing is intellectually framed by its relevance to real-world organizational systems. This second discursive framework seemed to appeal particularly to the women in the study. The females were just as enthusiastic as the men on the IT courses but tended to locate themselves within a different discourse. This suggests the relevance of Sherry Turkle and Seymour Papert's (1990) work identifying different epistemologies in computing. Underlying these disciplinary ways of talking there was also a set of conceptualizations of the 'technical' and its relationship to masculinity.

The 'technical'

For IT courses the computing laboratory is one of the ways in which masculinity can be sustained in public demonstration of technical 'mastery' and domination of technical spaces. The technical metaphors in product design emphasized the 'hands-on' and dirty aspects – in computing it was the 'machine' and the ability of boys to dominate the spaces in which the machines are housed. The men reported, almost as a matter of course, that where there had been access to computers at school the enthusiasts had been the boys, and that a male teacher, not necessarily an IT teacher, granted access. None of the women had had such privileged spatial access to computers in schools. This confirmed that it is not competency as such that is the issue. In terms of their own current assessment of their skills there seemed to be no differences between the men and the women on the IT courses. This is a finding born out in many studies, though some advance that women in their study 'tended to have better computing competencies than males' (Johnson and Johnson 1992: 33). Elkjaer's recasting of the notion of competence and incompetence as follows is helpful: 'But why is dominance in the public sphere of learning mistaken for competence and visa versa? I believe it reflects a collective repression, the purpose of which is to avoid acknowledging persons of the female sex as competent and to resist seeing the male sex as incompetent' (Elkjaer 1992: 36). This analysis stresses that it is the public demonstration of tools which is at stake in laboratories or workshops and not competency as such. Indeed as computers are increasingly used as tools throughout all HE courses, concern should be expressed over the possibility of the increase of the dominant discourse of competency in the way Elkjaer describes.

Instrumentality

There were differences between design and IT students in relation to perceived course outcomes and the likelihood of employment. IT students of both sexes were more instrumental in their approach while the design students stressed the expressive aspects of their studies. Those who believed they could succeed expressed themselves in highly individualistic terms based on creative vision and determination, with more males than females asserting this in the interviews.

For the women on the IT courses electing to study to degree level was a passport to a more interesting job, indicating an awareness of the ways gender affected choices. A number of them talked about their mother's limited choices. They also reflected on their own experiences of work (either full-time or filling in between school and university), which were overwhelmingly secretarial and administrative roles, with three in nursing, and one in hairdressing. These jobs are typically gendered and low paid. Their decisions to enter higher education were highly instrumental, in seeking jobs with enhanced job satisfaction not just more money. Equally important was getting a 'buzz' out of what they were doing, particularly for the women with a computing rather than business focus. The only reference to money in the interviews with the women was one woman in Computing who said it was not the prime motivation. More men mentioned money, even if in a light-hearted ironical way, and were clearly concerned to establish careers, making use of contacts they already had in computing.

One computing student described the pleasure he got in writing his own first programme as a child and stated, 'I'd like to design games but I wouldn't like to programme them' (Clegg et al. 1999: 53). This suggested that, for men too, instrumentality and the pleasure and intrinsic rewards of the job were a balance rather than an either/or. This particular quote also suggests that for some males the social interaction side of the work was important. There was further support for the view of a programmer role typically requiring a more reclusive, obsessive activity, when another male computing student stressed that he did not want to spend his time in front of a machine. This suggested that men who are attracted towards more industrially focused computing courses may share some of the desires for the exercise of social skills that Siann (1997) has identified as important for women. The study suggested that ideal-typical concepts such as instrumentality encompass a complex set of positions which, while influenced by gender, cannot be adequately described by a simple binary formula.

Case study discussion

The study gave some insights into the underlying mechanisms at work in the continued reproduction of gendered dualities in different disciplines. The students exercised choices about one course rather than another, and made statements about their perceptions of the dominant disciplinary discourse. Disciplinary cultures are sustained and transmitted through various symbols such as dress, styles of interaction and practices (Greed 1991). Careful attention to the detail of what is being said by those who are entering the professions gives insight into how gender is worked into the construction of disciplinary identities. There is ample evidence that girls can do, but what they choose to do is discursively constrained by gendered definitions of the technical. Both men and women in our study were aware of these constraints, whether or not they regarded them as legitimate.

Epistemological pluralism?

In this section attention is turned to the chilly climate (Hall and Sandler 1982) that students may find *within* the computing/IT classroom. It is clear that the limited numbers of women coming onto IT courses do not flow through to professional posts, but leak from the system in considerable numbers (WISET 1998). For educational practitioners of computing, working within an IT or computing framework, important questions of discipline content and pedagogical approaches have been raised (Grundy 1998; Adam 1997; Clegg and Trayhurn 2000). The dominant paradigm of computer science characterized by Karen Mahony and Brett Van Toen (1990) is centred upon formal methods for system and software production and is more likely to appeal to males. The UK approach to computer science is a technological one. Usability matters are frequently seen in context of a behavioural psychological approach. In adopting this approach social human–computer interaction problems typically are worked to solution through application of further technology, for example by using case tools or formal methods (CSTT 1997). 'Problems' are then clearly focussed, but with boundaries drawn which may limit examination of the context in which the problem is experienced (Star 1995) and practitioners be indifferent to the 'social complexities of computing' (Kling 1996a: 34). Kling argues for the inclusion of social analysis as an integral component of HE computer science courses' calling this a social or organizational informatics field essential to the development of all computer scientists (Kling 1996b).

Recent developments in UK HE, such as the work on benchmarking, offer an opportunity to reflect upon and develop the paradigms used. The Dearing report (1997) provided a basis for discussion of 'benchmarking' standards within and across disciplines. Benchmarks have been interpreted as a conceptual framework for the discipline, attending to coherence, identity, intellectual capability, techniques, skills, understanding and the level of intellectual demand and challenge to be experienced in study of the discipline in UK institutions (CPHC 1999). In the recent draft report presented to discuss proposals for computer science in the UK, the discipline is described as:

> the name given to the body of knowledge and techniques that are concerned with the design and exploitation of computer technology. It is a discipline that spans a multi-dimensional spectrum from deep and elegant mathematics to crafty programming, from abstraction to solder, from deep truth to elusive human factors, from scholars motivated purely by the desire for knowledge to practitioners making everyday life better. It combines the ethos of the scholar with that of the professional: the former probes the limits of computation, experimentally as well as theoretically, while the latter finds solutions to immediate problems of practice. (CPHC 1999)

It is not clear here whether there is clear intent to promote a paradigm beyond the technological. Arguments have been frequently advanced for the information systems developer to act within a social relativistic paradigm, recognizing plural, socially constructed realities incorporated into human factors. Advancing this model the developer (professional practitioner) would act as facilitator, enabling reflection, co-operation and experiential learning for all those involved with the system. Systems development would thus proceed from within, 'by improving human understanding and the rationality of human action through emancipation of suppressed interests and liberation from unwarranted natural and social constraints' (Hirscheim and Klein 1989).

Taking such an approach might recognize further, through pedagogical practices, the problem-solving approaches favoured by women who typically seek interdependence and relationship in problems, rather than using hierarchical, reductionist approaches (Gilligan 1982).

Concern to make the classroom or laboratory more accessible, has led Sue Rosser (1993) to argue for attention to a number of features, content and practice such as limiting the use of experiments which do not have clear problem-solving elements of social concern. This would include, for example, avoiding projects with obvious military purposes. She argues for consideration of problem-solving starting in more familiar contexts and transferring the knowledge and skills gained into more unfamiliar settings at a later date.

Turkle and Papert (1990) noted women's technical skills and different ways of approaching software development or programming using styles far from formal mathematics. They found certain women students having difficulties in producing software according to approaches specified and used the term 'bricolage' to represent the alternative 'inside-out' and more organic processes they adopted when building software. Turkle and Papert observed tensions produced in women trying to fit an individually restrictive overcoat of software production methods which had been presented on their courses, when these were not flexible in permitting students to choose and build their own tools and approaches to problem-solving. Epistemological pluralism produces better not worse computing for both men and women who are freer to experiment with styles outside the canon. The same argument can be adduced in system design.

Clegg et al. (1999) identified a discourse of end-users, with computer systems as complex models, which appears to approximate more closely to Turkle and Papert's 'bricoleur' student software developers in seeing things from the inside and as living systems. We know that women can do (Cifuentes and Lockwood 1996; Johnson and Johnson 1992), but further examination of software and system development methodologies presented is suggested when recognizing that they are choosing not to engage with the computer science discipline.

A study undertaken at the Open University found gendered preferences for particular systems methodologies among level 3 students. The course used three methodologies: Failures, Quantitative, and Checkland Soft Systems Analysis. Findings indicated that women in the sample group stated they were more likely to use the systems failure methodology in future, whereas men would promote use of the quantitative methodology (a synthesis of features from most widely used quantitative methodologies). When asked about the relevance of the methodologies to problem-solving in the *real* world, women responded favouring the Checkland Soft Systems Analysis methodology used on the course, and men again favoured the quantitative approach (GIST 1999). These findings suggest a need to consider further the methodologies used in systems development and the processes undertaken. The methodologies need to be effective in prompting and enabling collection of both quantitative *and* qualitative data. By implication sufficient stress on the analysis and design activities would be required, otherwise the problem boundary is not likely to be drawn widely enough to include participation and gain a rich set of observations to view alternative perceptions of reality (Gurak and Bayer 1994). In so doing explicit recognition of an end-user discourse may be achieved, and computer science and computers reclaimed for women (Perry and Greber 1990; Grundy 1998).

The computing science discipline appears to be unconcerned at the absence of women within the subject. If so then this fits Rosser's (1993) analysis of disciplines at phase 1. Frances Grundy (1998) reports typical comments about research into 'gender and computing' indicating that this is regarded as the province of social scientists, with no relevance to science subjects, including computing. She calls for computer scientists to consider large-scale changes to computing 'in all respects ... to involve women on the scale they have every right to expect' including 'radical changes to the syllabus' (Grundy 1998). In so doing we would be assuming that computer science is *not* genderless, nor objective or context-free. By implication we would recognize the paradigms deployed and their influences on computer scientists, the theories, methods, techniques, data collection and practices. By including gender as an issue or variable in experimental design, we may come close to the organizational informatics argued by Kling (1996b) and reach phase 6 (Rosser 1993). Computer Science would be redefined and reconstructed to include a more diverse society and with practitioners versed in observation (Greenbaum 1990) and social analysis.

Conclusion

Women were influential in the early days of computing, and there is an ongoing debate about women's relationships to the most advanced communication technologies (Plant 1997; Adam 1997). The limitations of the 'I can but I don't want to' argument is that it accepts that computing is anti- or a-social. Various successful models have been demonstrated which advance integrated curriculum content and practice (WISET 1998; CUWAT 1998). These example projects have drafted curriculum models and staff development activities where curriculum is recommended to take a wide-ranging 'holistic approach, including all players in a problem and considering the consequences of the proposed solution' (CUWAT 1998). In attending to these questions, we can challenge the dominant disciplinary discourses and puncture appeals to a hypostatized rationality or technological determinism. If we fail to do so we believe that we are failing all our students and, in particular, will not be able to provide the support our women students should expect.

References

Adam, Alison (1997) 'What should we do with cyberfeminism?', in R. Lander and A. Adam (eds), *Women in Computing*. Exeter: Intellect Books.

Beynon, John (1993) 'Computers, dominant boys and invisible girls: or, "Hannah, it's not a toaster, its a computer!" ', in J. Beynon and H. Mackay (eds), *Computers into Classrooms: More Questions Than Answers*. London: Falmer Press.

Bonsiepe, Gui (1994) 'A step towards the re-invention of graphic design', *Design Issues*, 10(1) 47–52.

Cifuentes, C. and Lockwood, C. (1996) 'Introduction of a case tool to teach structured analysis', *Computers in Education*, 27(3) 197.

Clegg, Sue and Mayfield, Wendy (1999) 'Gendered by design: how women's place in design is still defined by gender', *Design Issues*, 15(3) 3–16.

Clegg, Sue, Mayfield, Wendy, and Trayhurn, Deborah (1999) 'Disciplinary discourses: a case study of gender in information technology and design courses', *Gender and Education*, 11(1) 43–55.

Clegg, Sue and Trayhurn, Deborah (2000) 'Gender and computing: not the same old problem', *British Journal of Educational Research*, 26(1), 75–89.

CPHC (1999) *Benchmarking Proposals for Computer Science*. Personal electronic communication of national meeting to discuss draft paper, 23 November 1999.

CSTT (1997) *The New Knowledge Workers: an Agenda for Technology Education in European Universities*. Paper presented at the Euroconference 'European Management in the Face of Knowledge Driven Competition', Porto, Portugal, 19–21 September 1996, author unknown. http:// www. keele.ac.uk/depts/stt/staff/ob/pubs-OB2.htm. Accessed 4 November 1999.

CUWAT project (1998) *Changing the Curriculum: Changing the Balance*, Curriculum Women and Technology project report for EU Leonard da Vinci Programme (EU).

Dearing, Ron (1997) *Higher Education in the Learning Society*, National Committee of Inquiry into Higher Education. London: HMSO.

Durndell, A. (1991) 'The persistence of the gender gap in computing', *Computers and Education*, 16(4) 283–7.

Durndell, A. and Lightbody, P. (1993) 'Gender and computing: change over time?', *Computers and Education*, 21(4) 331–6.

Durndell, A., Siann, G. and Glissov, P. (1990) 'Gender differences and computing in course choice at entry in Higher Education', *British Journal Educational Research*, 16(2) 149–62.

Elkjaer, Bente (1992) 'Girls and information technology in Denmark – an account of a socially constructed problem', *Gender and Education*, 4(1/2) 25–40.

Gilligan, Carol (1982) *In a Different Voice*. Cambridge, MA: Harvard University Press.

Gipps, Caroline and Murphy, Patricia (1994) *A Fair Test? Assessment, Achievement and Equality*. Buckingham: Open University Press.

GIST (1999) *Getting to Grips with Gender and Systems*. Conference paper UK Systems Society 4–9 July 1999. Gender Issues in Systems Teaching Group, Open University.

Greed, Clara (1991) *Surveying Sisters: Women in a Traditional Male Profession*. London: Routledge.

Greenbaum, Joan (1990) 'The head and the heart: using gender analysis to study the social construction of computer systems', *Computers and Society*, 20(2) 9–17.

Grundy, Anna Frances (1996) *Women and Computers*. Exeter: Intellect Books.

Grundy, Anna Frances (1998) *Gender and Computing in the Computer Science Curriculum*. *Women into Computing Newsletter*, January 1998.

Gurak, Laura, J. and Bayer, Nancy L. (1994) 'Making gender visible: extending feminist critiques of technology to technical communication', *Technical Communication Quarterly*, 3(3) 257–70.

Hall, Roberta M and Sandler, Berenice R. (1982) *The Classroom Climate: a Chilly One for Women?* Washington, DC: Association of American Colleges.

Henwood, Flis (1996) 'WISE choices? Understanding occupational decision-making in a climate of equal opportunities for women in science and technology', *Gender and Education*, 8(2) 199–214.

Hirscheim, Rudy and Klein, Heinz (1989) 'Four paradigms of information systems development', *Communications of the ACM*, 32(10) 1199–1217.

Johnson, Julia and Johnson, Genevieve (1992) 'Student characteristics and computer programming competency: a correlational analysis', *Journal of Studies in Technical Careers*, 14(1) 33–46.

Kirkup, Gill (1997) 'Telematics and gender'. Paper given at Sheffield Hallam University, 23 April 1997.

Kling, Rob (1996a) 'Computer scientists as social analysts', in R. Kling (ed.), *Computerization and Controversy: Value Conflicts and Social Choices*, second edition. London: Academic Press.

Kling, Rob (1996b) 'The case for organizational informatics', in R. Kling (ed.), *Computerization and Controversy: Value Conflicts and Social Choices*, second edition. London: Academic Press.

Mahony, Karen and Van Toen, Brett (1990) 'Mathematical formalism as a means of occupational closure in computing – why "hard" computing tends to exclude women', *Gender and Education*, 2(3) 319–31.

Perry, Ruth and Greber, Lisa (1990) 'The computer cluster', *Signs: Journal of Women in Culture and Society*, 16(1) 1–28.

Plant, Sadie (1997) *Zeroes and Ones: Digital Women and the New Techno-culture*. London: Fourth Estate.

Rosser, Sue V. (1993) 'Female friendly science: including women in curricular content and pedagogy in science', *Journal of General Education*, 42(3) 191–220.

Siann, Gerda (1997) '"We can, we don't want to": factors influencing women's participation in computing', in R. Lander and A. Adam (eds), *Women in Computing*. Exeter: Intellect Books.

Star, Susan (ed.) (1995) *The Cultures of Computing*. Oxford: Blackwell.

Swanson, Gunnar (1994) 'Graphic education as a liberal art; design and knowledge in the "real world" ', *Design Issues*, 10(1) 53–63.

Tannen, Deborah (1991) *You Just Don't Understand*. London: Virago.

Thomas, Kim (1990) *Gender and Subject in Higher Education*. Buckingham: Society for Research into Higher Education.

Turkle, Sherry and Papert, Seymour (1990) 'Epistemological pluralism: styles and voices within the computer culture', *Signs: Journal of Women in Culture and Society*, 16(1) 128–57.

UCAS (1997) *Annual Report 1996 Entry*. Cheltenham: UCAS.

Wertheim, M. (1997) *Pythagoras' Trousers: God, Physics and the Gender Wars*. London: Fourth Estate.

WISET (1998) *Winning Women: Guides for Women into Science, Engineering and Technology in Higher Education*. Edinburgh: Scottish Higher Education Funding Council.

Wright, Rosemary (1997) 'Women in computing: a cross-national analysis', in R. Lander and A. Adam (eds), *Women in Computing*. Exeter: Intellect Books.

6
Information, Education and Inequality: Is New Technology the Solution?

Stephen Lax

The current UK government, like others around the world, has heavily promoted new information and communications technology (ICT) as the key to economic prosperity and individual betterment. It has funded a number of initiatives: promoting the use of new technologies for business transactions (e-commerce); 'leasing' recycled computers at low rates to poor families; and public ICT centres (e-libraries) where people can use (or learn to use) the technology. In October 1999 the Prime Minister himself, apparently embarrassed at his own lack of expertise, enrolled on a computer skills course in a north-eastern shopping centre. Perhaps the highest profile campaign among these government initiatives is the intention to connect all UK schools and public libraries to the internet by the year 2002.

The reasons claimed for this are familiar enough: the internet offers access to vast quantities of information, for school students' learning and for the public to access through libraries; schools and teachers will be able to share experience and advice on the latest educational tools on a national or even international scale; teachers and students will be able to contact 'experts' around the world on all sorts of topics; and the internet allows online ordering of goods and access to job opportunities. These claims, of course, overstate the case, suggesting that all that is needed to bring these systems into being is the provision of technology, but they nevertheless reveal a vision of how new ICTs are expected to transform society. We are told there are real gains to be had in the forthcoming 'knowledge economy' for those individuals who have the requisite ICT skills (unless you are *already* Prime Minister perhaps). For businesses, and the UK economy as a whole, future success depends upon stealing an electronic march over competitor businesses and nations.

While teachers and librarians would welcome investment in school and library technology, the expectations of the internet and related ICTs are unlikely to be fulfilled. The question of the possible effects of classroom computers in the education process has been addressed by others (for example, Selwyn 1999; Oppenheimer 1997; Kerr 1996). More fundamentally, I propose to argue that the idea that public access to ICTs and to the skills to use them will promote equality of opportunity is deeply flawed. Instead there is a greater likelihood that existing inequalities will continue or even be reinforced, and that the promotion of access to ICT equipment and its use will simply give the illusion of progress while deflecting attention from underlying social divisions.

The faith bestowed upon the technology is thus ideological in that it is part of the rhetoric of a classless society, or an information society in which, as the UK's Chancellor of the Exchequer put it, access to capital is no longer as important as access to knowledge (Brown 1996). The new communication technologies, and particularly the internet, are being offered as a kind of 'third way' technology, benefiting both individuals and businesses, blurring the distinction between 'public' and 'private'. At the same time as 'transform[ing] education, raising standards in schools' and 'freeing teachers to concentrate on teaching itself' (Central Office of Information (CoI) 1998: 7), ICTs in schools will familiarize pupils with new technology in preparation for employment (ibid.: 11). The implication of such an approach is that there need be no conflict between the private and the public interest and the government is unashamedly looking to the private sector to fund the provision of ICT in schools and libraries.

Information and communications technologies in schools

Before the 1997 general election, the Labour Party, then in opposition, made clear its belief in the importance of the internet: it introduced its policy document *Communicating Britain's Future* with the statement, 'We stand on the threshold of a revolution as profound as that brought about by the invention of the printing press' (Labour Party 1995: 3). It continued, 'The coming of the information society provides an unparalleled economic opportunity for Britain' (ibid.: 5). Noting its belief that 'it will be in education that the greatest potential uses for the new networks will emerge' (ibid.: 18), while commenting on the relatively poor provision of ICT in schools, it signalled its intention to prioritize schools and public institutions for improvements in technology. It commissioned the chairman of the Pearson media group, Sir Dennis Stevenson, to head an inquiry into the way forward for ICT implementation in schools. Reporting in March 1997, it found that ICT provision was patchy and outdated (Stevenson Committee 1997). This tallied with the Office of Telecommunications' Education Task Force report, which emphasized poor provision of ICT equipment in schools, particularly in the primary sector, and very low budgets within schools for ICT expenditure (Oftel 1997). The pre-election spotlight was focused clearly on ICTs in schools.

After the May 1997 general election, the Labour government set about promoting the introduction of ICTs, and particularly internet connection, in schools, libraries and other public places. In October 1997, the government chose the day of a visit to the UK by Microsoft chief Bill Gates to launch the idea of the National Grid for Learning, or NGfL. The development of a 'grid' of interconnected schools, libraries and museums would be a commercially driven, public–private partnership (DfEE 1997: 19). The government employed its arsenal of rhetorical devices to the full to demonstrate its determination to make the education system more 'modern'. Like the Conservative government before it, Labour couched the debate in terms of concern about falling standards in public education, particularly in schools, displaying no obvious hostility to the many educational reforms introduced by the Conservatives, and certainly no intention to reverse any of them.

From the start it was made clear that internet connection and ICT provision was not the sole responsibility of government. In opposition, Labour said it would 'seek to persuade' private businesses to donate or sponsor equipment, and negotiated with the former monopoly telecommunications company, BT, to provide free connection and fixed-cost internet access to schools and libraries. For BT, the carrot was a promise to lift the ban on its entry to the UK's cable TV market. Schools have been given ICT equipment by private businesses through various schemes (for example, supermarket vouchers or the recycling project run by the *Guardian* newspaper, and endorsed by Tony Blair). Since 1997, more schools have been connected to the internet, with 62 per cent of primary schools and 93 per cent of secondary schools having some sort of internet connection (DfEE 1999a: 18).

Technology and inequality

One of the expectations is that introducing ICT into schools will help to equalize access to learning opportunities by providing ready access to information to all school students, and access to teaching resources equally to all teachers (DfEE 1997: 14). Microsoft's Bill Gates suggests:

> virtual equity can be achieved much more easily than real-world equity. It would take a massive amount of money to give every grammar school in every poor area the same library resources as the schools in Beverley Hills. But when you put schools on- line, they all get the same access to information, wherever it might be stored. (1995: 294)

Of course, Gates is not the first to argue that ICTs will be able to make real the aspirations of education reformers the world over and provide equality of opportunity at relatively low cost. Parker and Dunn made the same case almost three decades ago: 'The greatest single potential of an information utility might be the opportunity to reduce the unit cost of education to the point where our society could afford to provide open and equal access to learning opportunities for all members throughout their lives' (1972: 1392).

The unstated but implied assumption is that the disadvantage suf- fered by those living in the poorer areas of the country – those who attend the poorest schools and whose libraries are worst resourced – has hitherto been an inevitable product of a competitive economy. It is just too expensive (financially and politically) to attempt to redress the balance. Now, the argument goes, that divide can finally be bridged with new technologies. This certainly offers a neat political solution, but is not as clear-cut as it might seem.

The success of the internet connection project, at least in terms of its ability to get schools connected, depends to a great extent on whether schools are able to attract private funding, either through donation of equipment or some sponsorship deal. It is clear that not all schools are equally attractive to private donors. In the absence of substantial private funding, schools are unlikely to be able to afford the connection of their whole computer network to the internet (even if the school has a local area network). Instead, in many cases connec- tion involves just one or two computers. The Department for Education and Employment (DfEE) 1999 survey of ICTs in schools found that two-thirds of secondary schools report some sort of network connec- tion to the internet, while just over half of the 62 per cent of primary schools which have internet access report some level of network connection (DfEE 1999a). Similarly, in 1997 the Research Machines survey of secondary schools noted that 46 per cent of its sample only had one computer connected to the internet, and 80 per cent three or fewer, but it anticipated that the rate of networked connection would increase in line with funding promised under the new NGfL (Research Machines 1998: 5). Yet during 1998/99, just one-third of the schools for which RM has provided access have connected their whole network (Research Machines 1999a: 5). In total, only 19 per cent of all primary and 27 per cent of all secondary school computers are connected to the internet. Without full networked connection throughout the school, the ability to integrate ICT across the curriculum is likely to be significantly hampered and the DfEE 1999 survey showed that the most frequent usage of ICT was in, predictably, information technology, business studies and art and design subjects, an even higher concentration than the previous year (DfEE 1999a: 22; DfEE 1998: 15).

Certainly then, the numbers of schools connected to the internet has increased since 1998, fourfold in the case of the primary sector. But the vision of computers in all classrooms linked together in an internal network and more widely to the internet is still a long way off, and most use of new funding appears to be to reinforce what might be considered 'traditional' IT subjects. Significantly, in 1999 ICT is now taught as a separate, stand-alone subject in *primary* schools (it has long been so taught in secondary schools), even in infant classes, a practice almost unheard of before (DfEE 1999a: 23) – computer literacy has truly become the 'fourth R' (Robins and Webster 1999: 187), a subject in itself rather than a general tool for the purpose of education. The reasons why schools are connecting only limited numbers of computers are not clear, though funding is likely to be a factor. Around half of primary and one-third of secondary schools which have connected to the internet have opted for the lower-cost modem route (rather than ISDN). The Education Departments' Superhighways Initiative monitored 25 ICT projects in schools and colleges. One of the group reports noted that after the externally funded pilot projects in schools were wound up, most would not continue in the absence of private sponsorship. The reason was clear:

Currently, the lowest quoted commercial costs for a basic managed service varied between the cost of one-and-a-half teachers' salaries per annum in the primary school, and four-and-a-half in the secondary schools. In the present climate, where schools are already facing the possibility of severe cuts in staffing, no school in the project was able to contemplate such additional expenditure without outside sponsorship. Since, clearly, not all schools could secure this, a nationally-funded initiative will be necessary if widespread connectivity is to be achieved. (EDSI 1997a: 21)

In the absence of a fully nationally funded system, the EDSI report warned:

Opportunities for different schools and colleges to gain access to several of these kinds of resource are, unfortunately, often unequal. In general, smaller schools with younger learners – especially in poorer or more sparsely populated areas – are likely to receive less funding per learner. The popularity of ICT may draw learners and private sector resources disproportionately towards the schools that are best placed to fund and further develop their existing ICT provision. If this seriously de-stabilises other schools nearby, the resources that should have gone into developing the ICT capabilities of those schools may instead have to provide basic emergency support. (EDSI 1997b: 46)

Thus some schools will find it difficult to establish internet connection, requiring a significant diversion of resources, whereas for those which are already well provided with equipment and networks, connection is likely to be more affordable.

Even without the inequalities imposed by the uneven distribution of internet equipment and connection, inequalities of usage would remain. The mere provision of computers and internet access in schools would not guarantee equality of opportunity. The degree to which a student is likely to benefit from using the internet at school or in a public access centre will depend on whether he or she has access to ICT elsewhere. In mid-1999 36 per cent of households had access to a computer at home – a figure which rises to 46 per cent for households with children. That access depends heavily on social background. The children of the wealthier and middle classes are more likely to have access to computers at home (futura.com 2000). Attewell and Battle's (1999) study of the relationship between home computer use and school reading and maths scores found a positive effect (after controlling for socioeconomic status): those with access to a home computer tended to score higher and the effect was more marked in higher-status households. Given inequalities in ICT access (in the UK as well as in the US) they conclude: 'It [home computing] may well widen educational inequality rather than narrow it' (1999: 10). That advantage has not diminished with more widespread school provision. Selwyn (1997) has argued that students with access to a computer at home have a more positive attitude to its use in general and are more likely to use one after their school careers.

As Attewell and Battle recognize, the complexity of social factors which conspire to maintain educational inequality cannot be undone by the application of technology. The amount of funding which will be required to connect all schools to the internet by 2002 is immense, given the low levels and quality of existing ICT equipment. Yet why should increasing ICT provision be the focus of so much attention if there seems to be no evidence that it will remove divisions in educational provision? There are also other areas of school education which would benefit from additional funding.

DfEE (1999b) figures for school expenditure between 1989/90 and 1998/99 show that, while total expenditure has remained more or less consistent as a proportion of GDP, capital spending has declined: despite increasing slowly since 1995/96, capital school spending remains around 3 per cent lower (in real terms) than ten years ago. Moreover, between 1989 and 1997, schools which adopted the newly-introduced Grant Maintained status were rewarded by very generous capital spending, further depriving the remaining schools. Thus, there is a backlog of repairs and investments, and this is felt most keenly in the inner city schools. Benn and Chitty (1997: 515) found that in 1994, 25 per cent of secondary schools and colleges were in need of 'major repairs or refurbishment to function effectively', and this figure rose to 35 per cent for inner city schools.

Schools themselves do not see ICTs as the most important issue. In 1998, Research Machines surveyed over 2000 primary schools. Asked to rank their essential needs for improving standards, the schools listed more human resources, increased budget, more staff training and greater curriculum flexibility as all of greater importance than more technology (Research Machines 1999b: 7). So while most people would agree that all schools should certainly be provided with the latest ICT equipment, including internet connection, if the intention is to make progress towards genuine equality of opportunity for all students, regardless of background, these new technologies are no more likely to provide this than any of the previous technological innovations. Instead, there might well be other priorities which would close some of the gaps in educational provision and achievement between the educationally-rich and educationally-poor, before worrying too much about the information-rich and the information-poor.

Information and communications technologies in libraries

Public libraries are currently less well provided for than schools with internet access. In 1997, only 5 per cent had a public terminal connected to the internet (Batt 1998: 17). Nevertheless, the commitment here too is that all libraries should be connected to the internet by 2002. According to the Library and Information Commission (LIC), the expectation is that this 'repositioning of the public library for the information age' (LIC 1998: 12) should provide access to cultural resources, and promote active citizenship and better government. As for the educational advantages, 'the UK will develop the skills base necessary for economic prosperity in the global information society and will enable more of its citizens to function fully in the emerging electronic information environment' (ibid.: 12). In other words, in an information economy, the public library will do for adults what schools are to do for children, illustrated by UK Culture Secretary Chris Smith's description of public libraries as universities on the street corner (DCMS 1999). Again, the expectation is that the private sector will play a key role in developing the network through public–private partnerships (CoI 1998: 14–15).

Public libraries serve a cross-section of their local communities. By far the most frequently used facility is book borrowing, despite the increased range of materials, such as videos and CDs, made available for loan over the last decade or two (Bohme and Spiller 1999: 18). The level of public expenditure on public libraries is modest, amounting to less than one per cent of all local authority spending (Audit Commission 1997: 4). However, even this expenditure has been cut by 9 per cent in the five years from 1992–93. There has been a year-on-year decline in the accessibility of public library services. The number of library 'service points' fell from 5448 to 4987 between 1988 and 1998, a decline of almost 9 per cent, and the opening hours of those which remain has reduced. The greatest decline has been among those libraries which were previously open longest: during this ten-year period, the number open for 60 or more hours per week fell by 42 per cent (leaving a total of 39 such libraries) and 23 per cent fewer were open between 45 and 59 hours per week. Of course, these are the libraries which were open at weekends and into the evenings – times when more people would be able to visit them. Correspondingly, a higher proportion (up 15 per cent) of public libraries are now open for only between ten and 29 hours per week, and this category now accounts for the largest number of libraries. This indicates a general reduction in opening hours across the board: the total service point opening hours per week in 1997–98 stood at 142 854 compared with 153 262 ten years earlier. Finally, a significant reduction (61 per cent) in the number of service points open for 10 or fewer hours per week represents the loss of many 'outpost' services such as those serving remote communities.

In general terms, then, public libraries have become less accessible; they have also become less public. Falling numbers of library visits (down 13 per cent over five years) and of book loans (21 per cent down over ten years) are not surprising given the reduction in number and opening hours of libraries. (All figures in this and the previous paragraph are taken from Creaser and Murphy 1999.)

It is against this depressing background that the government proposes to develop the New Library Network. Charged with developing its proposals for 'The People's Network', the Library and Information Commission reported in October 1998. It opened its report by recalling the original vision:

> A UK-wide information network made available through libraries and implemented on the basis of a high-specification central core could do more to broaden and encourage the spread of information and communication technology skills among the population ... than any other measure the government could introduce. (*New Library: The People's Network*, July 1997; quoted in LIC 1998: 1)

The report included proposals for generating content for the new network, identifying and providing training requirements for library staff, and for developing and implementing the network infrastructure. While the report makes no mention of the ongoing reductions in library opening hours or the decline in service point numbers, the new network should 'be accessible from elsewhere outside the opening hours of libraries ... [with] a scheduled availability of twenty-four hours a day, seven days a week' (LIC 1998: 45). Hence, access to the network and its content will be considerably enhanced for those privileged with computer access either at home or at work, while for the majority who are without this facility, a continuation of current trends will see access to information (in all its forms) through public libraries further curtailed.

The report also identifies ways in which the new network provision may be funded. In addition to encouraging private funding to establish the network, it suggests sources of revenue once the network is in place. It is considered 'likely' that libraries will charge fees for internet access, email and CD-ROM use (LIC 1998: 122) and even for word-processing (ibid.: 118). Further revenue could be generated by allowing companies to advertise on the network: the LIC assumes in its cost projections that a network user will encounter five advertisements during each session (ibid.: 122). So while access to content provided specifically for the new network (such as national and local government information, educational and cultural materials) would be free, this 'walled garden' would remain enclosed with its precisely targeted advertising, and would allow internet and CD-ROM access only on payment of additional charges. Targets for revenue income include £14 million from user fees and £2 million from advertising by 2002, by which time all libraries should be connected to the network. The Audit Commission's 1997 report *Due for Renewal* cautiously suggested that charging for the loan of books might be considered as a way of funding ICT developments (Audit Commission 1997: 57).

This does not suggest an information environment available freely to all. Of the few library authorities that currently offer internet access, three-quarters charge for that access (Batt 1998: 36); over half charge simply for access to a computer (ibid.: 37). Libraries are an important social resource. Sixty-four per cent of the population visited a public library in the twelve months of the BML survey (cited in Bohme and Spiller 1999), with three quarters of all households (ranging across all social groups) using libraries. In comparison with any measure of use of information technology, the public library represents a far more universally accessed 'information resource', with book lending, its principal activity, remaining a free service. Nevertheless, library users are still more likely to be from higher social groups: members of households from social groups A and B are more likely to be library members, to hold tickets for more than one library authority, and visit libraries more often (Bohme and Spiller 1999). People in social groups D and E are three times less likely than those in groups A and B to use a computer at all – in 1998, four out of five in groups D and E did not use a computer for any purpose (futura.com 2000), and they are therefore likely to lack the skills to use ICT or access the internet. It is unlikely therefore that the introduction of ICTs in this manner will go very far in opening up access and usage. In its promotion of ICT access and training, the government asserts that information about local and national government, about job opportunities and local services will become of key importance to the 'active citizen'; furthermore, this information will be delivered mainly, or even exclusively, through networks such as the New Library Network. The likelihood is that those most likely to benefit from such information are the already 'active', and that those who for whatever reason are excluded are likely to remain so (Lax 2000).

Compounding the problem of reduced numbers and opening hours, public libraries' expenditure on books, the number of additions, and the total bookstock have also all fallen significantly. Against this background, any claim to a truly egalitarian investment in public 'access to information' would surely recognize these problems as a priority rather than focusing upon the potentially more iniquitous deployment of a high-technology infrastructure, welcome though such a technological development might also be.

The technical fix, educational reform and private interest

The internet is not the first technology proposed as opening up new opportunities to solve social ills. The educational sector in general, and schools in particular, have repeatedly been seen as well placed to benefit from technological innovations. In *Teachers and Machines* (1986), Larry Cuban recalls how, in the past, film, radio and television have each been promoted as ways of enthusing students, cutting teaching costs, and opening up a world of information. Some of the similarities between then and now are striking: pre-dating Bill Gates by some 70 years, it was claimed in the 1920s that 'with radio the underprivileged school becomes the privileged one' (unattributed quote in Cuban 1986: 23).

In the history of UK education there have been a number of initiatives designed to address some of its problems, and which have seen the promotion of technology skills as playing a large part in their solution. Some of the more recent include the Technical and Vocational Education Initiative (TVEI), the City Technology Colleges (CTC) scheme, and specialist status schools. TVEI was launched in 1983 to enable schools to buy new technology training equipment, principally in the area of microelectronics. Aimed at 'non-academic' students, this was designed to emphasize a problem-solving approach to learning in a new technological area, one which was more appropriate to the perceived needs of industry, and one which would equip both students and the businesses into which they would be employed for the high-tech future. In the event, it was not considered a great success, most schools seeing the new funding as simply an additional source of revenue to be spent quite generally on new equipment (Benn and

Chitty 1997). The CTC initiative, begun in 1986, has been abandoned. The colleges were not to be part of the local education authority's provision but owned by private sponsors (who were expected to invest £8–10 million per college) who would employ all the staff. They were to take students from a wide range of backgrounds and emphasize technology training, again matching the expectations of industry. The government would pay the college owners a fee per pupil. The traditional school day was to be abandoned in favour of longer days with later finishes. Truly this would be a radical, technological route for education. Three hundred CTCs were planned; in the event, 15 exist, the scheme having collapsed largely through lack of enthusiasm and support from the industry funders (ibid.: 137). Finally the specialist status schools scheme allows schools to apply for specialist status in one area from sport, arts, languages and technology. Provided that they are able to raise £100 000 in private sponsorship, the government will give an equal amount, and additional recurrent funding. As might be expected, of the four options, technology is by far the most popular, followed by languages, sports and the arts. Nevertheless, despite the attraction of extra funding, of the more than 3500 schools which are eligible for this status, in October 1999 there were just 227 technology specialist schools.

These failed attempts to invoke technology as solutions to 'underachieving' schools are part of a process which suggests that a technical fix would make education more appropriate to contemporary needs (Robins and Webster 1989). Since the then Prime Minister James Callaghan's 1976 Ruskin Lecture, in which he argued that schools needed to focus more on the economic needs of the country, the tendency has been to ease out a liberal conception of education in favour of a more instrumental or functional system, with a greater emphasis on science and technology (Benn and Chitty 1997: 12). In particular, the 1988 Education Reform Act introduced changes which significantly shifted the focus of school education. The trend has been to a more centralized, bureaucratic system which has challenged, or replaced, the professional judgement of teachers and emphasized more than ever the role of industry in steering the curriculum. Increasingly, education and its practitioners have been seen as failing to adapt to the requirements of a changed society.

The changes included: the introduction of a highly-prescriptive *national* school curriculum; standardized assessment at ages 7, 11, 14 and 16; league tables of assessment results and, their obvious corollary, pupil selection at intake; removal of school budgets from local education authority control. The frustrations of teachers at the increased centralization and accompanying bureaucracy have been exacerbated by a highly politicized inspection regime, the Office for Standards in Education. The government which followed in 1997 has continued this centralization process with further reforms, including: emphasizing the supposed failings of teachers through new hierarchical classes of 'super teachers' and 'super heads'; further prescription through the literacy hour; and more directly involving private industry in running schools through the business-run Education Action Zones (Barnard 1999). This ethos has been extended to the public library with an increased emphasis on access to formal and semi-formal educational skill-based education (for example, the proposed University for Industry).

The drive to install ICTs and internet connection in every library and school in the UK thus continues a process of a more instrumental view of education in which government seeks to intervene and monitor, while welcoming the inclusion of private interests into the public education arena.

Public education/private provision

The introduction of systems and mechanisms more commonly found in the private sector (for example, performance-related pay, further prescription of working patterns) has reinforced the idea that the education was to take on a more functional, economic role. As well as encouraging schools to seek funding from private industry sources to implement their ICT development plans, the private sector is also being encouraged to fund the construction and repair of school buildings (*Independent* 1999). The notion that the private sector is preferable to the public for the provision of education finds its clearest expression through the aforementioned Education Action Zones.

The greater encroachment of the private sector in providing public education reinforces a functional role for education and allows the needs of industry to influence further the way that the curriculum develops. Some curriculum areas are more likely to attract private funding or sponsorship than others – a private business is more likely to donate computers than exercise books. By selectively resourcing particular curriculum areas at the expense of others, the perceived importance in both teachers' and pupils' eyes might well be influenced, and may even influence the success of these subjects over others. Private sponsors may go as far as to seek control, rather than mere influence. John Warwick of Capita Education Services argues that unless a private company providing schools' ICT services is given control over the curriculum, it is unlikely to be prepared to provide the service without guaranteed profit (quoted in Johnston 1999).

The blurring of the boundaries between public and private or commercial interest extends beyond the simple provision or sponsorship of new ICT developments. The proposals for the new library network include a national co-ordinating agency to 'promote the New Library Network as an advertising medium' (LIC 1998: 118). Growing commercial sponsorship of public spaces could soon mirror the approach of Channel One in the US, where the provision of 'free' TV and satellite-receiving equipment was conditional on all pupils watching a ten minute 'news' bulletin with two minutes of child-oriented commercial advertising (Apple 1998). Chris Whittle, Channel One's originator, is now a partner in the US-based Edison project, which is seeking to take over the running of some of the UK's schools (Jones 1999).

New technology for a new society?

Promoting technological solutions to complex problems has a number of advantages. The internet is new and exciting, and probably more appealing to potential private donor companies than what may be seen as the more mundane provision of books, repairs or even teachers. It is possible therefore for a government to give the impression of improving education at relatively little cost, without taking on the bigger questions of privilege and inequality in educational achievement.

However, this is not the main reason for the promotion of technology as a fast track to better education. Instead, the focus on ICTs is a response to a belief in the information society idea, the notion that everyone must become more technologically literate and adaptable in a new knowledge economy. Whether the view is that this new society is post-industrial, post-Fordist, or simply postmodern, the consensus is that if a 'new Britain' is to 'lead in the information age' (CoI 1998: 3), the emphasis must be on flexibility, re-skilling and transferable skills. Education, and new technology, therefore become key agents of this new society.

In this way, the promotion of the internet in schools and libraries reflects an ideological approach. Were it merely a means of persuading private companies to spend money on schools, it might not matter. But it is more than that. It is the product of a set of ideas that have found renewed currency in the last decade, centred on the notion that information is the key component of society, and therefore access to information leads to competitive advantage. For an individual, the issue is not whether or not one has a job, but whether one has access to *information about* job opportunities or educational provision. For the school pupil, access to *information about* a subject is the aim, or for her or his teacher, access to *information about* learning resources. By extension, it then becomes reasonable to suggest that equality of opportunity has truly been delivered, that there is no excuse for failure, and that the responsibility for success now rests with the individual teacher or pupil.

This view of society has been criticized for its pessimism in conceding that *genuine* solutions to social problems are unattainable (Marx 1994; Callinicos 1989), and for its failure to acknowledge continuities rather than change in society (Schiller 1996; Webster 1995). The two go together: a pessimism that submits to 'the end of history', and accepts that capitalist expansion and dominance is now secured for all time, will seek instead to construct a new means of explaining society which might permit the goal of equality to be achieved within a competitive market economy. By elevating the importance of information, redistribution of wealth (that is, information) is made technologically feasible. Such a view of society makes the role of technology of paramount importance (Robins and Webster 1999; Mackay et al. 1991). The government proposes to lease recycled computers at low cost to poor families 'in the same way as libraries loaned books in the last century' (White 1999), a scheme which is reminiscent of Newt Gingrich's plans to give laptop computers to the USA's poor instead of welfare payments. Yet the recipients are unlikely to be convinced of their new chances in the information society; for example, whereas the government cites the Craigmillar Community Information Service as an example of what is possible (CoI 1998: 4), a more detailed study of the same scheme reports that 'most respondents do not believe that a quick "fix" of new technology will solve the problems of the Craigmiller [sic] area', and 'in reality the majority of ordinary people currently have little chance of gaining direct participatory access to the networks served by CCIS' (Malina and Jankowski 1998).

The fetishization of information, and therefore of the technology which delivers it, is illustrated when corporate head Bill Gates is received on a UK visit by more ministers than some heads of state (Robins and Webster 1999: 187), or when Tony Blair writes with admiration: 'When you meet new technology entrepreneurs like Bill Gates, as I did a few days ago ...' (Blair 1999). Accepting the ideas of a globalized capitalism in an information society means reorienting the function of government – even diminishing its willingness to effect social change. The blurring of the boundary between public and private follows from this fetishism. Information becomes so important that it matters not how it is delivered, and the advertisements which will be carried on the 'people's network' will be merely a different form of information, even 'the people's advertisements'. For as long as these attempts at reinventing society persist, the new technological fix is likely to have as little effect as previous attempts. That would perhaps be a disappointment, though an inevitable one. However, people will see their public libraries closing their doors due to lack of funds; they will see their schools continuing to struggle to provide education in under-resourced classrooms. The idea that everyone will be equal in an information society or a knowledge economy will then be seen for the diversion that it is.

References

Apple, Michael W. (1998) 'Selling our children: Channel One and the politics of education', in Robert W. McChesney, Ellen Meiksins Wood and John Bellamy Foster (eds), *Capitalism and the Information Age: the Political Economy of the Global Communication Revolution*. New York: Monthly Review Press.

Attewell, Paul and Battle, Juan (1999) 'Home computers and school performance', *The Information Society* 15(1) 1–10.

Audit Commission (1997) *Due for Renewal: a Report on the Library Service*. London: Audit Commission.

Barnard, Nicolas (1999) 'Big push for next zone bids', *TES*, 15 January.

Batt, Chris (1998) *Information Technology in Public Libraries*, sixth edition. London: Library Association.

Benn, Caroline and Chitty, Clyde (1997) *Thirty Years On: Is Comprehensive Education Alive and Well or Struggling to Survive?* London: Penguin.

Blair, Tony (1999) 'Why the internet years are vital', *Guardian*, 25 October.

Bohme, Steve and Spiller, David (1999) *Perspectives of Public Library Use 2*. Loughborough: Library and Information Statistics Unit.

Brown, G. (1996) 'In the real world', *Guardian*, 2 August.

Callinicos, Alex (1989) *Against Postmodernism: a Marxist Critique*. Cambridge: Polity Press.

CoI (1998) *Our Information Age: the Government's Vision*. London: The Stationery Office.

Creaser, Claire and Murphy, Alison (1999) *LISU Annual Library Statistics 1999*. Loughborough: Library and Information Statistics Unit.

Cuban, Larry (1986) *Teachers and Machines: the Classroom Use of Technology Since 1920*. New York: Teachers College Press.

Department for Culture, Media and Sport (DCMS) (1999) News Release 161/99, 18 June.

DfEE (1997) *Connecting the Learning Society*. London: DfEE.
DfEE (1998) 'Survey of information and communications technology in schools 1998', *Statistical Bulletin*, 11/98. London: The Stationery Office.
DfEE (1999a) 'Survey of information and communications technology in schools 1999', *Statistical Bulletin*, 13/99. London: The Stationery Office.
DfEE (1999b) 'Education and training expenditure since 1989–90', *Statistical Bulletin*, 10/99. London: The Stationery Office.
EDSI (1997a) *Education Departments Superhighways Initiative: Group A Final Report Curriculum Projects in England and Wales*. London: DfEE.
EDSI (1997b) *Preparing for the Information Age: Synoptic Report of the Education Departments Superhighways Initiative*. London: DfEE.
futura.com (2000) Unpublished data from futura.com survey at University of Leeds (see chapter by Morrison and Svennevig in this volume).
Gates, Bill (1995) *The Road Ahead*. London: Penguin.
Independent (1999) 'Renovate crumbling school buildings', 10 November.
Johnston, Chris (1999) 'Great leap forward: the private finance initiative', *Times Education Supplement*, 15 October.
Jones, Adam (1999) 'Sums may not add up for school firm', *The Times*, 9 August.
Kerr, S. (1996) 'Visions of sugarplums: the future of technology, education, and the schools', in S. Kerr (ed.), *Technology and the Future of Schooling*. Chicago: National Society for the Study of Education.
Labour Party (1995) *Communicating Britain's Future*. London: The Labour Party.
Lax, Stephen (2000) 'The internet and democracy', in D. Gauntlett (ed.), *Web.Studies: Rewiring Media Studies For the Digital Age*. London: Arnold.
LIC (1998) *Building the New Library Network*. London: Library and Information Commission.
Mackay, Hughie, Young, Michael and Beynon, John (eds) (1991) *Understanding Technology in Education*. London: Falmer Press.
Malina, Anna and Jankowski, Nicholas W. (1998) 'Community-building in cyberspace', *Javnost – the Public*, 5(2) 35–48.
Marx, Leo (1994) 'The idea of "technology" and postmodern pessimism', in Merritt Roe Smith and Leo Marx (eds), *Does Technology Drive History? The Dilemma of Technological Determinism*. Cambridge, MA: MIT Press.
Oftel (1997) *Information Highways: Improving Access For Schools, Colleges and Public Access Points*. 'Recommendations of OFTEL's task force to the telecommunications industry.' London: Oftel.
Oppenheimer, T. (1997) 'The computer delusion', *Atlantic Monthly*, July, 45–62.
Parker, Edwin B. and Dunn, Donald A. (1972) 'Information technology: its social implications', *Science*, 176 1392–9.
Research Machines (1998) *The RM Report on the Internet in Secondary School Education*. Abingdon: Research Machines.
Research Machines (1999a) *The National Grid for Learning, One Year On*. Abingdon: Research Machines.
Research Machines (1999b) *The RM Report 1999: Computers in Literacy and Numeracy in Primary Schools*. Abingdon: Research Machines.
Robins, Kevin and Webster, Frank (1989) *The Technical Fix: Education, Computers and Industry*. Basingstoke: Macmillan.
Robins, Kevin and Webster, Frank (1999) *Times of the Technoculture: From the Information Society to the Virtual Life*. London: Routledge.

Schiller, Herbert I. (1996) *Information Inequality: the Deepening Social Crisis in America*. New York: Routledge.

Selwyn, N. (1999) 'Schooling the information society? The place of the information superhighway in education', *Information Communication and Society*, 2(2) 156–73.

Selwyn, N. (1997) 'The effect of using a computer at home on students' school use of IT', *Research in Education*, 58, 79–81.

Stevenson Committee (1997) *Information and Communications Technology in UK Schools: an Independent Inquiry*. London: Independent ICT in Schools Commission.

Webster, Frank (1995) *Theories of the Information Society*. London: Routledge.

White, Michael (1999) 'Chancellor unveils plan for computers for the poor', *Guardian*, 28 October.

7
The Process of Change: an Empirical Examination of the Uptake and Impact of Technology

David E. Morrison and Michael Svennevig

Political historians tend to be much given to an examination of terms when describing events, and none more so than the term 'revolution'. Were, for example, the events in Austria in the closing months of 1918 on the collapse of the Habsburg Monarchy and the founding of the First Republic a political revolution? The change in the political structure was fundamental, sudden and drastic enough to probably warrant such a title, but despite the far-reaching social reforms the private capitalistic ordering of the economy emerged from this tumultuous period unscathed: the established order was not fundamentally transformed (Leser 1966). We can learn from the political historian. To categorize Austria between the wars, to understand the unfolding of events, it is necessary to construct a language, especially for summary descriptive purposes, that adequately fits the detail of the situation. Once that is accomplished, and the descriptive category agreed upon by scholars working in the area, one has a working language with which to discuss and analyze events without always having to go back to first principles. The economic historian similarly tends to have a fine regard for the precision of language, and much dispute has taken place over the propriety of referring to the erstwhile industrial revolution of the eighteenth and nineteenth century as truly a revolution in the sense of sudden transformation of production. Was it no more than the continuation, albeit with considerable momentum, of patterns of production released by the earlier industrial 'revolution' of the sixteenth century (Braudel 1985: ch. 6)?

   With due reference to the historians' fine regard for language and terms, how is it that in discussing technological change the term revolution is thrown about with careless disregard for linguistic analytic precision (Briggs 1966)? To some extent the casual use of the term represents an economic and political hope rather than an empirical statement, while at the same time being accompanied by confusion over theoretical possibilities about worlds extrapolated from existing facts. What we see is the economic imperative of the business world to believe in that which it is selling. This hope for future business performance has then been taken up by politicians and applied to a political ambition; namely, the overcoming of intractable structural political problems. The hope, or even belief, is that through communications technology certain disadvantaged groups will be allowed to jump the circumstances of their history to achieve a social and economic life which past social engineering has manifestly failed to accomplish. Blinded by the sparks of sheer energy coursing through the communications infrastructure, the future takes on the dim glow of a world transformed. The feeling is generated that surely, somehow, all this hope, this energy, this financial investment, this communications cleverness, must lead to a radical transformation of communications between people, and by extension a transformation of how we live.

It would be foolish to consider that change in communications is not taking place – and quite rapid change at that – but it would be more foolish to mistake this change as truly revolutionary in terms of how we are going to live our lives. This misappropriation of language may be unfortunate, but it is not a crime. It is criminal, however, if through language we mistake what is occurring and therefore fail to act on social problems in the belief that such problems will be taken care of in the course of the unfolding of revolutionary practices, when those practices cannot bring about the hoped-for change. The term the 'communications revolutions', as we shall show, is a boast and not a fact.

To support our above statement, we first wish to clarify the components that we consider the term 'communications revolution' must contain to be justly awarded the status of revolution. Having accomplished that, we will then move on to examine whether or not, drawing on our empirical findings, the facts of change warrant the continued use of the term revolution. We will also consider whether, based on existing facts, it is prudent to consider that sometime in the future changes in the present will proceed to a revolution in the future. Is our age revolutionary, pre-revolutionary, or simply a heightened case of past change?

Definitions

Most usually, the concept of a revolution implies a dramatic break with the past either in terms of social political organization, or at the level of ideas – that is, in how we view the world. In addition to the idea of 'dramatic', conjuring the idea of sudden, revolution also implies a significant or radical change in social or intellectual performance. On this account we take it that a revolution must mean one or all of the following – a radical change in social organization; a radical change in how people view the world; and radical change in the way people lead their lives. It may be that one agrees that such a state of affairs does typify the times that we are living in, but even if this is accepted, it would not necessarily follow that what is being witnessed was a communications revolution – namely, that the revolution has been brought about by changes in communications. The argument is, however, that it is precisely the changes in the technology of communications that have, or are, producing radical transformations in the structure and organization of social life.

The development of communications technologies responsible for the supposed revolution is the product of scientific innovation dating back over two hundred years. What is new however, only thirty years old, is the combination of three items: the microchip, optical fibres, and the laser. As Robert Boyce points out, the microchip allowed the rapid processing of information represented in binary form, while the laser allowed information to be 'read' speedily, and optical fibres meant that it could be transmitted from one processor to another to a distant monitor (Boyce 1999: 2). In 1995, as Boyce further points out, world use of telephones for all transmissions was 60 billion minutes, with an expected rise in the year 2000 to 95 billion. As impressive as this is, such performance is overshadowed by the growth in internet use. In 1996, only five years after the internet became available to the public, the ITU estimated the existence of 60 million users, with an expected rise by the year 2001 to 300 million users. It is this growth, or expected growth of the use of the internet, allowing the connection of distant others, and connection to information that previously had to be physically 'visited', or gathered slowly and laboriously, that has led to the belief that this new movement in the organization of time and space must have radical impact on the organization of life sufficient to warrant the title revolution. The internet, as Boyce rightly notes, has come to be seen as the 'epitome of the communications revolution, and sometimes treated as a synonym for it' (ibid.: 2).

Unquestionably technological and social changes are linked, but to posit rapid movement in the former is not to extrapolate a consummate change in the other. Furthermore, technological change is uneven not simply in adoption between groups within the identifiable space associated with nation, but between areas of the world. If we look at Table 7.1 we see a remarkable disparity between language use and internet access or use. Internet use is far higher in the English-speaking world than it is in the non-English-speaking world, especially the non-European world. If we now look at national uptake between the USA and Europe (Table 7.2) again we witness disparity of use and uptake. We could advance explanations for the national differences in uptake seen in Table 7.2, but will resist doing so in favour of making some general points that are often overlooked by those claiming that a revolution is taking place; namely, that one cannot assume homogeneity between people, and that one cannot assume homogeneity within peoples. Our central point, however, is that to understand the uptake of technology one needs to know how technology fits, or might fit, within a culture and with peoples' lives. In short, one needs to know what the meaning of technology is for people, and then, and only then, will one be in a position to say what the meaning of technology is in terms of wider social performance that might then warrant the title, revolutionary.

Time and again in our focus group research, as part of the larger survey-based futura.com national panel study,[1] we were brought up against the facts of individuals' lives that suggested the existence and possession of objects that were supposed to transform domestic labour did nothing of the sort. Repeatedly we were told by household members that although the microwave was found useful, it had not been adopted by them in the manner or the original claims made for it by manufacturers – it had not replaced the hob or oven. Instead the microwave was used as a complement to the existing cooking facilities, speeding up the cooking process. Our proposition, therefore, is that one must be extremely cautious in using the term revolution, and not confuse the amplification of activity with absolute new performance. Even where performance might be considered new, one must still be cautious in attributing to it transformational power in the sense of

Table 7.1   Broadcast technology by linguistic group, 1998

	World population (%)	World internet users (%)	World internet hosts (%)
English speakers	8	58	52
Other European language	24	29	34
Non-European language	68	13	14

Source: EuroMarketing (1998). 1998 estimates.

Table 7.2 Technology take-up in Europe and the USA

	PCs per 1000 inhabitants	Internet users per 1000 inhabitants	% of households with Cable or Satellite
United States	362	79	72*
Denmark	304	57	67
Germany	233	31	86
Netherlands	232	58	97
Sweden	215	90	64
Finland	195	168	45
UK	193	43	25
Eire	170	2	56
Belgium	167	30	97
France	151	9	17
Austria	149	37	67
Luxembourg	133	56	94
Spain	94	13	12
Italy	92	10	4
Portugal	67	23	18
Greece	35	2	n/a

Source: PCs: ITU (1996 estimates), Internet users: ITU (1996 estimates); Cable/satellite households; SES/Astra (1997 estimates).
*ITU 1996 estimate

radically altering how people live. What is required in researching change produce by technical developments is the embedding of the technical in the social. Indeed, documenting the furthest reaches of new communications technology may be no more than documenting the lifestyles of certain groups. To be a member of the international business community flying the world is one lifestyle in which much new communications technology may make sense in that it supports that lifestyle – but such communication technology may make little sense to a building worker on a construction site. One must be cautious, therefore, in attributing causation to technology: technology has not created the lifestyles of those who have adopted the latest advances, but simply allowed the celebration of such lifestyles. If this is accepted then the political fear of the information-rich and the information-poor is much misplaced (Mosco 1996) in the sense that technology cannot do what political will has failed to do – eradicate differences in life chances. Our demand is that one must begin to examine this world empirically rather than make unsubstantiated claims of what the new communications technologies are doing, might do, or can do. What is required is an examination of people's lives to see what they are doing, what they would like to do, what they might do within the power opportunities of their lives, and, and more importantly, what they are likely to do based on the known facts of their existence.

Ideas and change

The story being told is of a world revolutionized by the potential of rapid communications: of an alteration in the distancing of time and space that will produce a fundamental change in human association (Giddens 1990). But even if every home became a shrine to technology, it is difficult to see what transformational difference this would make in terms of a leap in new ways of behaving, new patterns of association, or new ways in thinking about social reality.

When Max Weber discussed rationality and the changes wrought by industrialization, he did so in terms of forms of consciousness, explaining how the relationship between ideas and social organization was established through 'elective affinity' between certain beliefs and an economic ethos (Weber 1930). If we talk about the communications technological revolution in similar terms to Weber, then within which world is it taking place? In what way can it be said that the logic represented by technology – a scientific rationality – finds resonance in the beliefs held by most people which in some cosmological way makes sense of what is happening for them and to them, and facilitates the revolution itself? Of course, the role of Calvinism and the development of the work ethic that fostered capital accumulation and production, the subject of Weber's investigation, did not require everyone to participate in the 'project'. What mattered was that a critical few did – for others, the dynamic that was unleashed forced them into new sets of relationships and patterns of behaviour. Capitalism was not a sales pitch, or an exercise in marketing, but the worked-through complexities of historical developments that did not require the acquiescence of the individual as such. This is not the case with the so-called new communications revolution. It requires, to a greater or lesser degree, that people 'buy into' the project – if not, who will be communicating with whom?

For the type of changes messianically predicted one might expect that there ought to exist in the advanced contemporary world an elective affinity between beliefs – a scientific rationality and beliefs about the self that would make for ease of adoption of new communications technology – a combination of forces that would see the embracing of change driven by communications technology. In order to understand better the relationship of beliefs to participation in the 'technological revolution', we examined, in one wave of the futura.com survey, beliefs about such issues as alien abduction, the power of prayer, ghosts, telepathy, and the existence of unidentified flying objects (UFOs). In other words we looked for beliefs that do not sit easily with a scientific and rational view of the world.

A central question in the history of Western thought has involved the nature of rationality and the nature of belief consummate with social change. We might think here of Marxian notions of material base structuring thought, or ideas relating to elective affinity of ideas and practice. Although highly empirical from the outset, our study was nevertheless guided by some very large theoretical questions concerning ideational structure and social practice.

In accounting for change in social interaction due to changes in forms of communication brought about by technological developments – if indeed any radical change is taking place – what we wished to understand was the nature of the mental terrain upon which such change was framed. Just as science could not develop without a separation of the sacred from the profane – the opening of a space for empirical explanations of the world – to allow the development of a particular rationality, we wished to know whether or not a technological revolution at the popular level of uptake required the presence of a technological rationality. In other words, was a certain type of thinking necessary for the acceptance of the technical? Did how we look on the world, how we create the logic of meaning, have a bearing on who would, or would not, embrace technology? Expressed another way, was it necessary to have embraced the Enlightenment project for the full potential of technology to be unleashed and become a fact of existence at both a material and ideational level? Does how one positions oneself in terms of structuring reality figure in the configuration of technology as a social fact?

To begin to answer these questions, while aware that empirical investigation of the type we have adopted can only be suggestive and not conclusive, we wished, as stated, to examine for the existence of non-rational thinking. By this we mean thinking that sees the world as not been governed by causes that are open to empirical inspection. Or, to state this in a different way, do people see the world organized by forces that are beyond scientific reason?

What we see from Table 7.3 is that the idea that scientific development has led to scientific consciousness is wrong, or to be more precise, scientific consciousness does exist, but it is not all-pervasive. A variety of rationalities coexist in our society and, furthermore, coexist

Table 7.3   Beliefs

	Male (%)	Female (%)	All UK adults (%)
Telepathy			
Definitely/probably exists	45	55	50
Undecided	33	31	32
Definitely/probably does not exist	22	15	18
Clairvoyance			
Definitely/probably exists	49	61	55
Undecided	31	25	28
Definitely/probably does not exist	21	19	17
Ghosts			
Definitely/probably exists	42	48	44
Undecided	27	25	26
Definitely/probably does not exist	33	27	30
Read horoscopes?			
Yes, often/occasionally	36	56	46
Rarely/Never	64	44	54
Pay attention to horoscope warnings?			
Pay at least some attention	40	55	48
Ignore them	61	45	52
People born at different times have quite different personalities			
Always/often true	21	30	26
Sometimes true	40	45	42
Rarely/never true	40	36	32
Base:	3234	3896	7207

Source: futura.com *Wave*, 2 January 1997.

within the same individual. The individual does not look upon the world with one uniform belief system, but rather has a cobbled-together set of rationalities. In the focus group part of the futura.com study, in practically all the groups where belief in the paranormal was raised, accounts were given of having personally experienced ghosts or other metaphysical forms, or failing that, having known someone who had claimed such experiences. The descriptions given of these experiences were often very detailed and vivid, leaving no doubt that in the mind of the teller what had occurred was real. Table 7.3 shows the statistical distribution of beliefs in the paranormal – or non-scientific rationality – within the UK population.

As interesting as the figures in Table 7.3 are, we must, nevertheless, be careful in interpreting their meaning. It may be that they represent no more than a feeding-back of cultural myths, and the degree to which individuals accept such occurrences in any depth must be open to question. In other words, there exists in our culture a whole set of accounts about happenings that are drawn upon to make sense of that which cannot be made sense of by scientific reason, but this does not mean the abandonment of scientific rationality as such, or at least not in those areas where science has been shown (and accepted) as working.

The point about scientific rationality is that historically it has spread as science itself has extended its control to more and more areas of life. What one sees is the movement of a liberating army freeing up zones of the mystical in the name of the rational. But these advances have been partial. Whole areas of meaning have been left unattended by science in that it has nothing meaningful to say about certain areas of life – in particular, the nature of being. Occurrences undoubtedly occur that do not appear to belong to the material world, and hence are given non-material explanations or at best left 'unexplained'. What cannot be explained by the canons of everyday assumptions drawn from scientific rationality offer ready territory for fanciful constructions of sense.

There is another factor that requires consideration in examining rationality – namely, the inability of individuals to control fully their own lives – a whole raft of very important areas are subject to painful manipulation by others. Looking at Table 7.3 we see that women are more likely to believe in the value of clairvoyance than men, and more likely to believe in the predictive power of star-signs than men. It may be that women were simply more ready to 'confess' such beliefs whereas men, drawing perhaps on identification of the masculine with the notion of 'hard' explanation, were loath to admit to such uncertainty about how the world was organized. Perhaps, to be masculine is to be certain about matters and to see the world as capable of control. It is interesting in this context that women were no more likely than men to believe in the existence of ghosts. To believe in runes is of a different order than to believe in an afterlife – the former refers to the course of the world, whereas the latter refers to the nature of existence.

To believe in the paranormal is to accept a world beyond control which then produces behaviour of ritualistic nature, the carrying of talismen and so on, to guard against harm from that which cannot be safeguarded against by the power of understanding (science). Science is about control, even though in taming or controlling nature matter might be released that sets new problems of control.

One can characterize social thought from the Enlightenment onwards as coming increasingly under the influence of scientific rationality. This is not to say that all individuals have moved towards seeing the world equally through the lens of scientific logic, nor that a scientific logic has held total sway even in those individuals who have firmly embraced scientific rationality. Various logics can, and do, coexist. It is interesting, however, as Table 7.4 shows, those who can be considered active adopters of new communication technology, internet users, share very similar beliefs to non-adopters when it comes to what might be classed as the paranormal, that is, those realms of possible existence that escape a scientific logic of explanation. The survey moreover confirmed that a high percentage of individuals overall demonstrate a rationality that has not been truly imbued with the scientific. This does not mean that such individuals are non-scientific in the way they reason about the world, but rather that they are open to non-scientific rationales in their acceptance of meanings.

Table 7.4 demonstrates that it is not necessary to have a scientific or technocratic rationality in order to embrace technology. Nor is there any indication of a transforming rationality to one more suited to a major extension of communications technology. What this means, and we go back here to the point about the social acceptance of technology, is that technology is incorporated into people's lives on the pragmatic basis of its utility. In other words, communications technology does not find a ready space by virtue of its own logic – that somehow it is natural to communicate with the world in new forms, or that such communication is desirable. On this basis it is the world of work rather than the home where new communications technology will make its entry and sustain itself as a transformation force. In the

Table 7.4 Beliefs among internet users

% saying phenomenon 'definitely/probably exists':	Users	Non-users	All UK adults
UFOs	50	44	45
Telepathy	56	52	50
Ghosts	44	43	45
Power of Prayer to change events	30	33	30
Alien abduction	12	17	14
Base:	554	6653	7207

Source: futura.com *Wave*, 2 January 1997.

absence of any logic of elective affinity, or need for new advanced communications technology, it is highly unlikely that the home will ever become highly technocratized.

Globalization of the mind

If, as we have suggested, and hopefully shown, there is little evidence to suggest an intellectual platform for the ready uptake of technology – that is, an existing rationality by which to pave the way forward into the technological dream of a wired world – what evidence is there for the notion that new communications produces a psychic shrinking of the world – that interconnectedness leads to feelings of similarity between people with a shrinkage of space and time distanciation. What evidence is there, in other words, for a globalization of the mind as opposed to the globalization of capital?

Without doubt changes will occur, indeed are occurring, facilitated by new communications possibilities linked to an acceleration and globalization of capitalism, but the basic dynamic of capitalism will remain untouched. The new communicative forms released by the energy of the capitalist dynamic, the continued search for increased productive capacity, scarcely, however, transform the logic from which they come. The increased communications capacity will be put to work in support of existing structures, and at the political level will probably heighten existing inequalities of economic opportunity. Thus McLuhan's global village is not so much a village in the sense of a global community but a global market – an extension of an existing condition. What we see, and will increasingly see, is a functional amplification of communicative space. For example, e-mail is, in functional terms, essentially an amplification of the physical mail system. It makes life easier (or at least faster, which is not necessarily the same), but not radically different.

Holding to our notion of functional amplification, the difficulty is to determine when quantitative amplification might have qualitative consequences, or in the present case whether the sheer volume of cheaper, faster, and longer-range communication is such as to impact on social practices in ways different from previous similar communications. At this time we simply cannot say, for example, whether the substitution of e-mail for posted letters will change the relationship between individuals to institutions at large. Certainly the culture of e-mail communication allows easy entry into others' space, and particularly into the space of others who, for various political and status reasons, were previously seen as prohibited contacts. In this sense the 'world' is more accessible via e-mail than the letter, but whether one is any more likely to be listened to is still a question of power, not merely one of ease of communication. It is also the case that the internet allows conact on a friendship basis to 'unknown others' in a way perhaps the letter could not do. To have a cyber pen-friend, however, is not the transformational experience to be had by including people into one's negotiated physical space of existence. Having said that, it is a mark of modern society, indeed, one of its characteristic features, that the negotiated space of existence does include people who are not physically present, be it the business colleague at the end of the telephone whom one has never physically met, or the radio or television personality who is 'known', but never as a co-presence. The significance of this is an expansion of the horizons of existence and a re-configuring of trust (Thompson 1995). Nevertheless, such changes, no matter how much new communications has acted as a bridge between people, have not, and cannot, close the chasm of difference between people. The notion of globalization is best retained as a descriptive character of markets, not of culture. One may see symbolic representations of the market carried as personal statements in terms of consumption, but for the American country club member of a few years ago to sport a Harris Tweed jacket and drink Chivas Regal whisky did not make him an English gentleman, any more than the Reebok-wearing Korean youth in backstreet Seoul becomes member of some black group in the Bronx, always, of course, presuming that such attire was meant to project such meaning for those dressing in 'copied style'.

Culture that grows out of lived experience, cemented over time through the shared meanings of history fused with contemporary life, is an authentic expression of who one is, and draws power from the sense of difference. Indeed, the establishment of identity is grounded in a sense of who one is not. Thus, one might talk in McLuhanesque terms of a global village in the superficial sense of the export of products, and more so the export of entertainment, and see within in it the expressive dominance of American business methods and the American cultural industry. Even so, it is still worth noting that as strong as the penetration of American television products are in the world television market, indigenous products endure. For example, soap operas, with their supposed capture of real or proximate life, are almost always, for every country, more popular than imports mirroring or documenting distant life. Culture, in other words, is relatively impervious to outside penetration in the sense of undermining that which has developed organically.

Even before questioning whether or not increased communications has led to feelings of similarity between the peoples of varying countries, the map of Britain, is a stark reminder of the parochial nature of identity. Even in a geographical space as small as Britain, we can see from Table 7.5 that there is no uniform sense of identity. This is not to say that British citizens do not feel British – that is, do not have a collective sense of belonging – but it is to acknowledge that people from different regions within the British Isles view each other as different from themselves. London, for example, may be the capital of the country, the single most portrayed city on television, and the most reported on, but still only 39 per cent of the country perceive those living there as similar to themselves. Northern Ireland, with only one in four of the UK population viewing it as similar to their area of residence, really is the 'removed province'.

It is when we compare Table 7.5 with Table 7.6, which documents perceptions of other countries outside the British Isles that some remarkable, and perhaps surprising, features emerge. For example, more people in Britain consider people in New Zealand, and some other countries for that matter, as being more similar to themselves than they do some of their fellow countrymen. To a certain extent this can be explained by the respondents' sketchy knowledge of foreign

Table 7.5 Perceived differences between UK regions

% saying that people from area are similar to themselves	*Internet users*	*All UK adults*
The North of England	62	52
The North West	63	51
Yorkshire and Humberside	59	51
East Midlands	60	51
West Midlands	59	50
East Anglia	55	48
South East (excluding London)	54	44
South West	51	44
Central & Southern Scotland	48	40
Greater London	49	39
South Wales	45	35
Northern Scotland	38	33
North Wales	38	33
Northern Ireland	38	27
Base:	438	3630

Source: futura.com *Wave*, 3 October 1997.

Table 7.6   Perceived differences between UK and other countries

% saying that people from country are similar to themselves	Internet users	All UK adults
Canada	64	59
United States	66	57
Eire	66	56
New Zealand	59	54
Australia	58	52
Holland	55	45
Belgium	43	33
Germany	38	31
France	38	29
Sweden	38	28
Spain	36	27
Italy	32	23
Portugal	29	21
Finland	29	19
South Africa	22	15
Greece	18	14
Poland	14	11
Hungary	13	9
Denmark	7	5
Russia	8	5
Japan	6	5
India	4	4
China	4	3
Pakistan	3	3
Base:	438	3630

Source: futura.com *Wave*, 3 October 1997.

countries whose inhabitants they see as an undifferentiated whole. Thus, where language is a common factor, the assumption is that they must be similar to us, whereas people in say, Northern Ireland may speak the same language, but are not the same as us because they are 'known' to be different through first-hand contact. Of course, in countries such as New Zealand, Canada, Australia and the United States, Britain can be talked about as the 'mother country', or at least such countries are seen as historically having close ties via kinship and by extension culturally.

The point to establish from the above analysis is that an increase in communicative possibilities as a result of new communications technologies does not guarantee a transformation in association as suggested by ideas of globalization. Indeed, as we have suggested, to have close experience of groups is as likely as not to foster a sense of difference for the simple reason that other groups are different: culture as the worked-through expression of lives concretely lived does make for differences.

When Marx saw workers in Germany as having more in common with workers in England than the workers in the respective countries had with their own owners of industry, he was expressing this very point: worlds are constructed out of repetitive performances of daily life sedimented over time and given common symbolic expression by those sharing that world – the world is reflectively and reflexively built. Electronic communications cannot undo lived history.

Conclusion

We have argued, and supported by empirical findings from our study, that to call what is taking place a 'revolution', pushed by changes in communications technology, is not a revolution in the sense of a transformation of the way we live. The changes that are taking place are not fundamental changes, rather, they constitute a heightening of existing patterns of association. Where, for example, is the change in consciousness?, and where is the change in feelings of transnational communality? – two distinct indexes of the change that the new communications are supposed to have fostered, or will foster. Yet something is happening.

At this point we must distinguish between what might be termed a 'private world' and a 'system world' – that is between a world that is known and appreciated and a world that is neither known nor appreciated. If one must talk about a technological revolution, then it is one which is taking place in the realm of commerce and trade, not in the home. Of course, someone might become unemployed because of changes in some far distant financial market, and have no appreciation of how or why this happened or what role was played by communications. But what is new there? By the nineteenth century, in fact much earlier, the performance of the known world of the self was very much connected to the unknown world of the other. Thus, even in terms of movements in distant markets that affect the individual, the use of 'functional amplification' to describe that which is occurring is applicable not just to the domestic sphere, but also the economic sphere – there is little that is new, and what is new is built upon the old to heighten existing associations and performance.

It is the scale, however, of the investment in new technology, or venture capital, that is a remarkable feature of our current point in time. The South Sea Bubble adventure of 1720 in Britain, although a swindle, caused widespread alarm, coming as it did among many other such swindles, but the comparison with the venture capital being poured into new technology, the internet in particular, is difficult to avoid – the hopes and dream of a return on capital turning into a chimera. The extent of the investment is quite staggering. For example, Kirk Walden of Price Waterhouse Coopers notes that venture capital (VC) investment is now virtually synonymous with technology investment and each year the figures relating to investment are rising. Price Waterhouse Coopers' Money Tree Survey finds that VC investment for the third quarter of 1999 was 138 per cent higher than the amount for the same period in 1998. The figure for the third quarter of 1999 was just over $9 billion, meaning that the total amount of VC money invested by this time was over $21 billion. This represents a 50 per cent increase on the 1998 VC figure. Of the $21 billion invested in 1999, 86 per cent, or some $18 billion, was invested in technology companies and $10 billion of that went specifically to internet companies. Meanwhile, the number of internet companies receiving investment in 1999 was 473, up from 162 in 1998.

Such investment is not to be ignored, but the fact that the investment is in communications, and not automobile companies should not lead us to accept that life as we know it will be transformed – certainly not to the extent that the mass production of automobiles did early in the twentieth century. The respondents to our futura.com study did, however, recognize that whether they personally desired certain forms of technological combinations or not, they would be forced to accept them through uptake by large companies. Electronic banking was a case in point, barcoding in supermarkets another. Our respondents even recognized that although they themselves had little desire for much of the new communications technology, that once introduced they might grow, or learn, to appreciate the trumpeted benefits. Some respondents in our focus groups mentioned the resistance they felt on first confronting self-service petrol stations, but agreed that they had no desire to go back to the earlier form of petrol-pump attendant service. But these examples underscore our concept of functional amplification. Indeed, the much-heralded online shopping does not look new when the past is brought into view. The catalogue/mail order dynasties such as Sears Roebuck and Littlewoods made fortunes in the past, and no doubt the wired catalogue of the twenty-first century will make similar fortunes, but such a development is not a revolutionary leap forward in the ordering of domestic life.

The re-ordering of social life, should it come, will be driven by the adoption of technology by the business world, which then is forced, so to speak, on the private individual. In general what people adopt is what is functional to them, and as we stand at the moment what is being offered looks little different, apart from amplifying what is already in existence, from that which has been offered in the past.

Note

1. The futura.com study was established to begin to address empirically many of the questions laid out above. It has now been running for three years and is the largest of its type in Britain. Based on an original recruitment survey of over 6000 UK households, a panel was constructed that has now been revisited four times. In addition to examining uptake and attitudes towards technology, along with attitudes towards technology-related social issues, a series of focus groups and media clinics have been conducted to address questions not readily amenable to survey research.

References

Boyce, R. (1999) Introduction to R. Boyce (ed.), *The Communications Revolution at Work: the Social, Economic and Political Impacts of Technological Change.* London: McGill-Queens University Press.

Braudel, F. (1985) *Civilisation and Capitalism 15–18th Century Vol. 3: the Perspective of the World,* trans. Sian Reynolds. London: Fontana.

Briggs, A. (1996) *The Communications Revolution.* Leeds: Leeds University Press.

Giddens, A. (1990) *The Consequences of Modernity.* Cambridge: Polity Press.

Leser, N. (1966) 'Austro Marxism: a reappraisal', *Journal of Contemporary History,* 1(2) 117–33.

Mosco, V. (1996) *The Political Economy of Communication.* London: Sage.

Thompson, J. B. (1995) *The Media and Modernity: a Social Theory of the Media.* Cambridge: Polity Press.

Weber, M. (1930) *The Protestant Ethic and the Spirit of Capitalism,* trans. T. Parsons. London: Allen & Unwin.

8
The Value of the Ephemeral: Assessing News Output About Yugoslavia (1998–1999)

Michael Palmer

Producers and vendors of data streams and information flows seek to equate the sometimes competing demands of accuracy, speed, relevance, significance and impact. The 'modern' concept of news brokers and news agencies emerged in the mid-nineteenth century. Havas, Paris, in 1832–35, Associated Press, New York, in 1848, and Reuters, London, in 1851 were three of the major players then, as they are today (Agence France Presse succeeding Havas in 1944). The circulation of international news and the role of key news organizations have been studied from many perspectives. Here, we wish to explore issues relating to the information society and the professional concerns of news-agency editors who seek to reconcile the competing demands listed above; in so doing, they inform the debate about news, data, and information.

The need to reconcile and prioritize the different pressures that result from how professional news editors perceive these demands is a matter of fine judgement. Political, financial and technical factors impinge on news-editorial judgements that also take into account the services, resources, logistics and content of what the competition is offering. The complexity of the situation increases constantly: for example, a vendor distributes and packages not only its own material but also that of other information providers; electronic publishers like Reuters and Dow Jones may compete in some areas and cooperate in others. Here, we shall centre on quality control mechanisms within Reuters, relating mainly to perceptions of media and non-media usage of material concerning the biggest international news story of the first half of 1999: Yugoslavia/Kosovo. To single out one 'story' – one dominant news-agenda theme – in this way is obviously arbitrary. We are concerned with ubiquity; the provision and continual updating of material marked by a host of real-time, breaking news considerations. We wish to explore some of the thinking about performance that characterizes those 'in-house' who, in leading professional news organizations, assess 'product lines' and results – 'impacts', timings and the like. The history of Reuters, by Read (1992), is called *The Power of News*; a major study by the American historian of the media, Michael Schudson, uses the same title. Here, we wish merely to explore the synchrony of news as viewed by professionals who deploy resources and fine-tune production and control mechanisms accordingly. A 1996 Reuters Business information report, that quotes Francis Bacon – 'knowledge itself is power' – tackled the issue of the information overload. *Dying For Information* includes remarks like the following:

> More information has been produced in the last 30 years than in the previous 5000. A weekday edition of the *New York Times* has more information in it than the average 17th century man or woman would have come across in an entire lifetime. About 1000 books are published internationally every day, and the total of all printed knowledge doubles every five years.

Against this backdrop, we shall explore some of the ways in which Reuters monitored the host of material produced during the Kosovo crisis that, following months of Serb–KLO conflict, culminated in the March to June NATO bombing of Yugoslavia.

Yugoslavia: 'news in context' and 'hits' ... revisited

Reuters is an international news, information and data agency. Based in its London headquarters, a news quality control group monitors both the output of this and other agencies, and client usage of feeds from agencies and other purveyors of data, news and information. This chapter reviews recent control findings based on in-house reports. We thank Reuters and other agencies – AFP mainly – for granting access to the material used here.

The underlying issue addressed is the following: accuracy and exhaustivity at speed in factual reporting are often presented as the goal of many news and data agencies and other international news outlets. As, indeed, is the provision of services that satisfy customers – a satisfaction often measured in terms of impacts or client usage of agency material. These are overall goals; a tension – that some might call creative – exists between them.

Within Reuters, various protocols or measuring-rods enable the quality control unit to monitor both overall output and the by-the-minute, and indeed by-the-second, correlation between output and client usage. The aim is to provide a quasi-continuous commentary on how the news product is perceived by news professionals within the agency; their main motive is to dovetail assessments of the output with client needs and client perceptions about that output. Quality controllers comment and chastise, praising some and pinpointing defects to others. The overall aim is to point out failings in yesterday's performance so as to 'mieux encourager les autres' today, and to have happy customers throughout. One zealous quality controller put it thus: 'I don't want to meet a happy customer.'

Here we shall look first at what one might term the 'standing orders' governing assessment protocols and setting targets for news coverage worldwide, and second, at comments made by quality controllers monitoring coverage of a recent major international news story. The story chosen here relates to in-house assessments of production and client usage of copy on the conflict in Yugoslavia, centring in particular on Kosovo, both before the 1998 KLO–Serb flare-up and during the period of NATO bombing of Yugoslavia (March–June 1999). We shall centre on 'news quality group' assessments of the usage of Reuters and competing agency output in UK and European continental newspapers; this will mainly, but not exclusively, high-light the use of *English* language ouput – English being the most prevalent of the six major international languages of news-agency output – English (English-English, American-English), Arabic, Spanish, French, Chinese and German (the total number of languages in which Reuters produces services is about 25). A couple of scene-setting technical remarks are perhaps necessary. Reuters has various geographical divisions: we are mainly concerned here with Reuters Europe, Middle East and Africa (REMA), but we will also, on occasions, consider Reuters Americas (RAM). The goal – voiced by quality controllers ever since the unit or group was first set up (in its modern form) in the mid-1980s[1] – is to provide a seamless flow of copy at all times and to all destinations; the prose used must avoid 'speed bumps'. 'Seamless' means not only breaking news continually updated, but also includes re-writes and wrap-ups, so that the right balance of genres or types of copy are on-tap at all times. This balance relates to in-house and client perceptions of the appropriate range or mix of what one might term user-friendly and relevant material. This material ranges from breaking spot news to wrap-ups, from text to computer graphics, news-film and financial data, all of which must be delivered through the appropriate state-of-the-art digital technology – including more and more portals, sites and feeds (Reuters invested early in Yahoo!). 'Immediacy', observes one quality controller, 'nearly always provides the sharpest way to write and involve the reader'. The following story, issued in the world file on 11 April 1999, was criticized the next day by a controller:

> 'Yugoslavia–Albania–rations: Kosovo refugees are throwing away US-donated humanitarian rations by the thousands and have even burned some to keep warm, complaining that the food is inedible and has made people sick.'

'This was a good story', added the controller, '... but what is the food? Only in the 4th para. do we learn it's meatless, in 6th that three-bean casserole, legume stew and vegetarian goulash are foreign to their normal diet and in 11th that similar problems arose in Somalia.[2] Some signpost to that melded into the 2nd para would improve the story'.

News agencies monitor the share of media credits by agency, as they do timings of agency production on the same story. In October 1998, Reuters monitored agency material credited by a sample of 23 newspaper subscribers in the UK and Continental Europe. These included seven British dailies (five London-based, plus the *Yorkshire Post* and the *Scotsman*), three American dailies (printed and/or online versions of the *Washington Post, USA Today* and the *Wall Street Journal*), and twelve German, Spanish, Belgian, Swiss and French titles, the latter including *Libération, Le Figaro* and *La Tribune Desfossés*. Five agencies figured in the breakdown of the share of credits in October. Listed in alphabetical order, they are AFP, AP, Bloomberg, DJ and Reuters. Perhaps more meaningful is the number of news stories credited by the different media: in the period 20–30 October 1998, between them AFP and Reuters totalled 700 stories.

Thus do agencies and information vendors monitor their own performance and that of competitors. Consider the monitoring of the writing of leads – the all-important opening sentence or paragraph. The *Reuters Handbook for Journalists* (McDowell 1992) presents 'lead paragraphs' thus: 'These are the most important part of any story so it is worth taking time over them. Those first 20 or 30 words make or break the story. If they do not seize the reader's attention or imagination the story is dead'.[3]

We shall now examine some Yugoslav-related examples. Recall the situation in 29 January 1999, just before the peace conference held in Rambouillet, outside Paris, which would lead to the conclusion of an agreement, brokered by 'the major powers', that the Serb delegation, unlike the Kosovars, refused to sign. REMA editorial comment on 29 January reviews how RTRS and AP, in stories datelined London, 29 January, 'wrapped the story' – to wit, that the Contact Group was convening the Rambouillet conference:

> Here's how we wrapped the story compared with one of our competitors.
> RTRS: 'The major powers, losing patience with the conflict in Kosovo, on Friday summoned warring Serbs and ethnic Albanians to attend peace talks in France by February 6 and set a tight deadline for concluding the autonomy deal.'
> The AP wrap, by contrast, mentions 'NATO, the US and Europe' and doesn't mention France. It runs thus: 'Backed by a stiff NATO warning of possible military action, the United States and five European nations today called for a negotiated settlement by mid-February to end the violence in Kosovo.'

Too much should not be made of just one comparison of lead paragraphs in two agency stories. But there is a strand here to which we shall return. Factual reporting often stresses the importance of including in the opening words of a text the basic nuts and bolts – who or what did or said what to whom or what, when, where, possibly how, and possibly why – the famous '5 Ws'. Yet the lead – and indeed the headline of a story – does not just do this; it also carries inflexions that fashion perceptions. The AP lead mentions the US by name, but not the venue of the peace talks (France). This first example calls to mind a second picked up by quality control years earlier, when Yugoslavia was still in the process of becoming a major international news story of the decade. In March 1991, at a time of street demonstrations in Belgrade involving the opposition leader Vuk Draskovic, quality control compared two leads – from AP and RTRs – dated 13 March:

> AP: 'Thousands of anticommunist demonstrators continued their peaceful protest in Belgrade after national leaders failed to agree how to restore law and order in the marxist republic of Serbia.'
> RTRS: 'Yugoslavia appeared to move closer to a state of emergency on Wednesday after anticommunist demonstrators celebrated

apparent victory in Belgrade and the army considered measures to promote the country's security.'

Some media scholars might note the use of adjectives or descriptors used in the two stories. For example, if both leads refer to 'anticommunist demonstrators', only the AP story – geared primarily at US domestic media consumption – refers to 'the marxist' republic of Serbia. These are not points that the quality controller – familiarly known as a 'quack' – picks up. He or she is concerned with accuracy and impact, and with the timeliness of the story. The quack's comments included the following: 'Our interpretative spin and throw forward effort here was better than AP's feeble 'continued after' formula. Even so, apart from para. 2, it mightn't have been a bad idea to recycle more of the juice from Draskovic's rally.'

Let us return, at this stage, to what we earlier called 'standing orders'. These are periodically reactivated and updated in the form of memos posted on the Reuters intranet and elsewhere. In March 1998, the newsdesk operations of REMA were reorganized. The function of the newsdesk, at the interface between desk editors – many of whom are located in London – and the bureaux 'out in the field', was reaffirmed:

> The newsdesk now has the brief to co-ordinate newsgathering throughout REMA across the whole gamut of Reuters services – including both financial and general news. The news editors will work closely with specialist news editors on the various production desks ... London should be speaking with one voice to the bureaux ... At the same time, Newsdesk is the representative of the bureaux vis-à-vis the increasingly voracious appetites of the desk editors. It is the job of the central news editors to know what burdens a bureau is facing on any particular day.

Hence the need for concerted pre-planning, and the allocation of the logistics of news and editorial resources in order for the dovetailing of effort to provide seamless copy. The desk has to be proactive, and to ensure that the copy meets the needs of both specialist and non-specialist readers. The first must be provided with 'all the facts, figures and analysis he needs'. The second is known as 'Mr or Ms so-what?' and by including perspective and context and answering high-up the key 'so what?' question – why does this matter?, and to whom? – it should also serve the cross-market reader who may be less familiar with the background of a story.

In the March 1998 memo, three priorities were highlighted:

1. co-ordination between text and other services including pictures, RF(financial)TV, RTV and graphics ... 'so that all units of Reuters can benefit from the expertise of others'.
2. 'greater emphasis ... on real exclusives and genuine newsbeats. Being competitive on scheduled news events and producing well-written stories must be seen as a given. The value added for our clients is having the exclusive angle and the incisive analysis.' 'Good writing', 'added value', and 'market-moving news' are among the buzzwords of news-agency milieux in the 1990s.
3. the third priority we shall explore at some length: 'when news is increasingly a commodity, putting news in context right from the very first news break is another way in which Reuters can stand out from the crowd and make a difference'.

The rest of this chapter centres on 'news in context', and the production process to achieve this. Let us dwell for a second on the multiplicity of markets that the news agency 'feeds' or 'serves'. Clients include media of all kinds, including for instance both 'traditional print newspapers but also newspapers' online sites and services', governments and administrations, and business and financial circles and market-players. Reuters, as is well known, is the major long-estab-lished news and data agency serving all of these clients, especially – but by no means exclusively – the financial community. The latter are sometimes called – a simplifying, shorthand term – the 'core screen client base'. After the NATO bombing of Yugoslavia began, in late March 1999, it appears that the financial market-players, who include traders, money-dealers, arbitrageurs, and the like, took some time to appreciate the market-moving implications of Yugoslav developments. In the early weeks of the conflict, there were many news reports stress-ing that the conflict had signally less market impact than, say, the recent January 1999 launch of the euro. A month after the conflict had begun, in late April, REMA news editors suggested how the perceptions of the money markets were changing:

> Some in the markets underestimated the impact the crisis would have on their markets. Clearly they weren't trading in the drachma. [This alludes to the volatility of the currency of a Greece torn between official, government participation in the NATO effort, and a media-led public opinion strongly anti-NATO.] Given that the

Euro can now fall, or rise, up to half a cent on a report – sometimes erroneous – that the Serbs have launched an attack on northern Albania or that Yeltsin has decided to retarget missiles, we must address this problem of market participants having to crank up their knowledge on the whole Yugoslavia story fast.

We, more than any other agency, are there to help and get it right. These are our clients – paying thousands of dollars to have our screens on their desk.

Our heritage in Yugoslavia and the region [that is, Reuters' proven track-record and reputation over ten years of covering conflicts and wars in Yugoslavia] means we can and should offer a service of knowledge and reliability which is unrivalled. But it must also understand the needs of screen clients.

That means addressing the financial impact of the news we have on our own wire fast. Forex [foreign exchange] reporters need to read-in on the Yugoslavia story now as much as anyone else. They also need to remember and make sure that our copy reflects that we have more people in the region than anyone else and therefore they should 'trust Reuters'.

Partly based on the client feedback, but also based on good sense, we are trying to do more to address the market impact of the Kosovo crisis in a coordinated way – producing a daily item reflecting market reaction and also making sure that any market reaction of note finds its way into leads. Desks have a key role to play in this in making sure it is relevant.

The desk role is clear in 'glances'[4] – they must cover all top stories, whether battlefield or market. In the light of these considerations, Reuters editors noted that the NATO–Yugoslavia–Kosovo conflict was 'a perfect story', a 'general news story which has market impact'.

To the abundance of clients and client categories must be added the range of sources and of media outlets, as well as the range of modes of distribution of the information. A promotional piece of literature, the *Reuters Business Briefing*, dated 28 April 1999, highlights the range of media and other sources that it monitors and/or translates and which complement its own coverage of the Balkans. These include material in local languages and in English-language translations from local and national news agencies and other daily or weekly sources. These sources are woven into the seamless material, whose chief strength remains 'Reuters journalists from editorial offices in Skopje, Belgrade, Tirana, Sofia, Budapest, Sarajevo, Zagreb, Athens, Istanbul and Ankara', and in bureaux worldwide that report on the actions and reactions of other countries. This RBB is, indeed, a superb research tool, accessing Reuters' own material and that of a host of other sources – for example, material from the Russian agency Interfax, whose 'over 500 correspondents' help cover the 15 countries of the former Soviet Union, including Russia, the CIS and the Baltic states ('Product Information Bulletin', 13 April 1999). The network of an information vendor provides access to material other than its own.

The overall assessment criteria and goals stress that news is to be sought out. When so much material is soliciting attention, news editors must nonetheless be proactive in their own right. In January, the Reuters chief news editor posted on the intranet editorial performance targets for 1999. These included a target number of interviews. Such interview targets, first fixed in 1998, met with many plaudits from clients. News coverage had improved: 'We break news more often', Reuters' editor-in-chief remarked. Earlier we referred to statistics for October 1998 and the agencies credited by a sample number of media. The October 1998 figure for the number of interviews targeted for REMA was 427. Of course, predetermining the number of interviews from a given market area in no way militates against the use of journalistic 'nous' or 'savvy'. This is itself constantly monitored. The same REMA editors highlight week-by-week and month-by-month what they term 'best writing', 'initiative reporting', 'good writing' and so on. Let us consider some stories relating to Yugoslavia picked up by the REMA editors between March and May, examples of 'good writing, initiative reporting' and the like. One interesting feature is that many of these stories often run against the grain, refreshing a story, giving it a new twist, by developing a minor feature, or else by providing a rebuttal or complement to what is, at the time, what one might term the 'received news-worthy wisdom'. (This exercise is difficult: if news is a 'staple' – as the playwright, Ben Jonson called it in 1626 – it is, perforce, rapidly 'stale'. The international news agenda is constantly changing, and, indeed, the news priorities of different world areas are not necessarily the same at the same moment. Furthermore, perceptions, or the agreed 'wisdom' that colours interpretation, also change fast.[5])

On Wednesday, 14 April, in London, the British Defence Secretary, George Robertson, alleged that the Bosnian Serb general Ratko Mladic was commanding 'a gang of paramilitaries' in Kosovo. On the Thursday, a Reuters correspondent, Julijana Mojsilovic, conducted an impromptu interview with Mladic in 'a small restaurant in a Belgrade suburb'. Mladic's denial of Robertson's claims included strong soundbite quotes:

'These are my last public words. I don't want to be a sparring partner to international thugs who are constantly lying.' Providing context, the Reuters correspondent recalled: 'Mladic, the ex-commander of the Bosnia Serb army, has been indicted as a war criminal by the Hague War Crimes Tribunal on former Yugoslavia. International efforts to arrest him have not been successful.' This paragraph is followed by a further Mladic quote: 'I have not committed the crimes I was accused of. And we shall see if those who are now committing war crimes and genocide against Serb people will ever stand trial.'

Let us stay with Reuters-Belgrade for a minute. A few days earlier, REMA had already commended Julijana Mojsilovic for 'initiative reporting': she kept the Belgrade bureau up and filing after the (brief) expulsion of the bureau chief, Philippa Taylor, and other foreign staff (on the day following the beginning of NATO bombings, journalists who were nationals of NATO member-states were expelled from Belgrade). It was Mojsilovic who was again commended for keeping the story flowing through the tense, confusing early days of the conflict, and for her 'strong first-person pieces covering the crash of the US F-117 Stealth fighter/bomber' (4 April 1999).

Let us stay, indirectly, with Reuters coverage of Ratko Mladic a little longer. One of the other REMA accolades for reporting on Yugoslavia, in recent months (and years), fell on Kurt Schork.[6] Schork, an American, dubbed within Reuters 'our roving Balkans correspondent', covered the siege of Sarajevo between 1992 and 1996, building up the agency's office there from nothing, located in the Holiday Inn hotel. In his memoirs, the BBC TV news journalist Martin Bell – currently an independent MP – refers to Schork as 'the conscience-in-residence of the Sarajevo press corps' between 1992 and 1996. On one occasion his pointed questioning of Mladic at Sarajevo airport led to Mladic 'lunging towards him and shaking him by the throat' (Bell 1995: 51–2). On many occasions throughout the 1990s Schork was praised by Reuters' top editorial staff. In February 1999, for example, it was he who got the news-beat announcing that the KLO would attend the Rambouillet peace negotiations: 'intrepid as ever, Kurt tracked down the KLA general staff in the mountains to get the story, which earned RTRS credits on a number of news bulletins. It took the competition more than two hours to catch up'. We shall return to the difficulties of the Reuters bureau in Belgrade and Kosovo in March–June 1999.

Agency performance – and the search for competitive advantage – is measured in minutes and seconds, literally. Quality controllers number-crunch and list timings of various agencies' output on the same story.

They compare timings with other agencies, with CNN and other 'breaking news' outlets. For instance, on 25 March, datelined Belgrade, 13:14:49, Reuters carried the headline 'all journalists from NATO countries ordered to leave immediately – government'. Reuters quality controllers – 'the editorial performance management group' – minuted the equivalent Dow Jones headline – 'foreign journalists from NATO nations expelled by Yugoslavia' at 13:21:41. Let us consider two longer periods.

Reuters monitored 110 Kosovo timings from 18 February to 28 April 1999. It concluded: RTRS wins – 42; Dow Jones wins – 32; RTRS unmatched headlines – 26; Dow Jones unmatched headlines – 10. It repeated the exercise for the period 1 May to 28 July, during which period 122 Kosovo timings were monitored.

Covering an international story of the importance of Kosovo and the war in the Balkans stretches the resources of an international news organization. While pledging news-editorial resources to such a big story, it does not want to so overcommit itself that it risks underplaying other stories which markets, clients and end-users expect it to cover properly; nor must it exceed or overshoot news-editorial budget allocations. Within Reuters, quality controllers pointed to the danger of 'bulletinitis': giving too high, too urgent a priority to a particular story. Fine distinctions – news-judgement skills – are required. The situation is further complicated by the fact that the financial community – traders, arbitrageurs – 'move at the bat of an eyelid', acting on the basis of 'glances', and not necessarily 'clicking' on to the rest of the story. In mid-April, with the NATO air raids still apparently failing to cow the Serb leadership into submission, one controller argued thus:

> There was a time when flashes on the wire (as opposed to screens where markets allow more latitude) were reserved for news of supreme importance – wars, major deaths, plane crashes or earthquakes etc. Perhaps that was too strict, but have we gone way too far in the opposite direction?

And he began to campaign against what he terms a 'bulletin blitz'. He cited stories given 'bulletin' status, which he considered did not call for it: 'a genuine bulletin gives information'. For instance: 'UK's Blair says only way to help unrooted Kosovo Albanians is to continue air campaign' was judged 'typical claptrap of the last several days', not meriting bulletin status (20 April). Neither did: 'NATO's Clark says Yugoslavia must cease "aggression" at Albanian border' (17 April): ('routine claptrap'); nor again 'Turk PM Ecevit says too early to predict future coalition structure' (18 April) ('so what? and negative to boot').

REMA monitors the number of stories filed from different countries. We have looked at REMA headlines in the English-language news filed to one or more of the international services, focussing on the headlines for Yugoslavia during the period 22–28 March – the week the NATO bombings began, following the final, and unsuccessful, Richard Holbrooke negotiations with Slobodan Milosevic. The data relate to the stories datelined from Yugoslavia, and to what are called 'average retrievals' – that is, the number of times a given story was accessed; for sites with many users, one datafeed retrieval could represent a high number of users looking at any one story. Individual figures are meaningless; the sophistication which Reuters incorporates into the measurement procedure, by contrast, gives food for thought.

Here, therefore, are some of the data: 293 *stories* were filed from Yugoslavia, in the period 22–28 March 1999. The total number of 'retrieves' runs to 17 516. Data is available for the 'retrieved *headlines*' for Yugoslavia: only four headlines run to over 200 retrieves. They are:

24 March 13:44:51 'Wrapup: Nato on the move, sirens in Kosovo ...' (215 retrieves);
26 March 00:27:31 'Yugoslavia says shoots down two NATO planes' (275);
26 March 04:57:41 'After more Nato bombs, Belgrade opens car show' (218);
26 March 08:55:45 'Yugoslav army says inflicts heavy losses on NATO' (202).

It is noticeable that three of the four headlines relate to 'bad' or 'unexpected' news, from the viewpoint of the Western world. News that runs against the grain, that runs counter to expectations, is more 'newsworthy', has added value, and has greater impact.

Reference was made earlier to the 'so what?' question. The reader may well be asking 'so what?' after this presentation of some of the findings of quality control of output and performance in an international news agency. This is as much a story of a news organization's self-perceptions, and of its monitoring of how others see its output. News is indeed a commodity; its gathering, processing and distribution involve risks taken at speed. Journalists die to get a story – 'die' in both senses of the word (some journalists, not Reuters staff, died in covering the Kosovo conflict). Competition between agencies and other international news organizations (BBC World, CNN and so on) is continuous.

But there is often solidarity between journalists in the field, even when news executives back in the editorial headquarters press their respective teams to do all they can to beat the opposition. Of a given agency's many teams operating in the field, several do not have *that* many resources, which encourages multi-skilling and multimedia skills. For instance, Kurt Schork, based in Sarajevo, and operating out of the Bosnian capital in the period 1992–96, developed close ties and heated arguments with his photographer, cameraman and sound technician. They had different deadlines and requirements in covering stories. Multi-skilling means using a host of equipment, and producing a wide range of texts at speed, from a multiplicity of sources. But 'texts' and 'speed' are to be interpreted broadly: they may involve the news-editorial headquarters cross-linking text, pictures, graphics, video and audio clips.

This is where the dovetailing of the agency's resources comes in – both in the field, in operational headquarters and other news bureaux. To give but one example: Reuters news graphics based in London, monitoring the data on the NATO bombings, built up content that its Paris-based partner WaG assembled into a 'graphics spread'. This was published in *Le Figaro* on 27 April. While this, of course, is not 'breaking news' but 'recapitulatory, context-setting and stock-taking' information, its visual impact may itself generate new perceptions.

In late 1998, Reuters' Belgrade bureau had ten staff, including bureau chief Philippa Fletcher. During the March–June 1999 period, Ms Fletcher, although expelled on 24 March, succeeded after four days of lobbying in London, Budapest and Belgrade, in returning to Belgrade.[7] A stringer – an ethnic Albanian and former computing science professor – filed for about a month almost daily from Pristina, before escaping to Macedonia. Staff in Belgrade faced being called up by the Yugoslav army. Kurt Schork, out in the field on the morning before the bombing began, was warned not to return to Pristina: Serb gunmen were waiting for him (*Reuters World* 1999: 10–14).

Conclusion: access denied and access oversupplied – navigating between the two

Reuters news executives praised the efforts and performance of all involved in covering the Balkans war. There were slips and difficulties: Associated Press Television News often had more resources filming from the Yugoslav frontiers and in Belgrade. The impact of CNN was less than in the Gulf war. Serb authorities' control of TV images shown worldwide did not involve favouring a particular Western news organization like CNN, as did Iraqi authorities in Baghdad in 1990–91.

Throughout the late 1980s and the 1990s, Western media correspondents and academics had noted Milosevic's use of television in gaining, and maintaining, power (see, for example, Malcolm 1994, 1998; Silber and Little 1995; Glenny 1992). A major technological, socioeconomic and communications 'sea-change' had occurred between 1990–91 and 1998–99: the development of the internet and of intranets. Western observers noted how 'opposition', 'independent' and other sources in Yugoslavia used the internet to circumvent the official media and censorship. A Reuters journalist noted how the use of the internet to address the Yugoslav population, at the beginning of the NATO bombings, counted among the many 'firsts' of the Clinton presidency. Reuters itself warned journalists of the pitfalls of some of the information circulating on the World Wide Web. But it successfully developed strategies, beginning in the USA, whereby it became the most widely-used news source on the internet. Its news was more called up on Yahoo!, AOL, Infoseek and other major portals than that of two main branded news sites, CNN and MSNBC. Internet and intranet development bode well for established electronic publishers, online players and information vendors, however intense the competition from other established actors and new market entrants (Nibley 1998).

Those who posit, following Francis Bacon in the seventeenth century, that 'information is power' raise so many questions that news and data professionals, including established information vendors, are forever seeking to find answers, thereby ensuring that continued profits and survival will enable them to continue to do so. In 1626, the year Bacon died, the dramatist Ben Jonson produced a masque entitled *The Staple of News*, and news-as-commodity was lampooned from the very beginnings of the fledgling newspaper 'industry' in Britain. Today, news professionals themselves refer constantly to news as a commodity. Presentation, recycling and repackaging – of 'historical data, for example – themselves 'add value' to what the US journalist, Harold Kurtz, has called 'the fungible commodity of news' (1998: 14).

The value of the ephemeral is difficult to monitor; this is what we have tried to do. This requires taking into account: those who produce and file the copy from 'out in the field'; those who begin the news-editing process in the bureau to which the former report, or in the regional news centre; those who, within the regional headquarters, assess the product before it is despatched, transmitted, and put online; those who monitor the impact of the product, compared to that put out by competitors; and those who recycle the product, whose original shelf-life may have been only a few hours, for re-use as 'historical data'. Thus, apparently, does news gain in value.

Notes

1. The sophistication of quality control mechanisms increased greatly between the mid-1980s and the late 1990s.
2. A reference to the US military force sent to Somalia during an earlier phase of the Clinton Administration.
3. The in-house style-guide, 1995, contains the same entry. In 1999, a quality controller commented:

    the number of words or lines allowable in a first para is not set in stone and depends on the ease and flow of the sentence rather than on its length. Basically if the sentence goes over four lines but flows well, fits the flavour of the story and draws the reader in, it is legitimate. A five-line lead may work wonders while 16 words or a line and a half can be a klunky disaster. The right 'feel' for the language is part of the job.

4. The term 'glances' was defined in-house thus in January 1998 ('Glances' – guidelines on glance presentation/preparation, 16.1.1998: REMA editorial):

    'Glances' are 'the front page for many of our stories; they are among the most retrieved items and offer a chance for us to highlight the main stories, assist with navigation, and promote other parts of the service' – examples: 'Glance – Foreign exchange top stories at OOO GMT; Glance – World sports news' ... They must pack 'the most information into the tightest space but in a logical and clear way'.

5. Commenting on a Yugoslavia–USA–KLA story, dated 27 May, a quality controller noted: the story 'on the KLA growing bigger and better-trained should have included a line that only a few months ago the US labelled it a terrorist organization'.
6. On 24 May 2000, after this chapter was written, Kurt Schork was killed while reporting the conflict in Sierra Leone. Spanish APTN cameraman, Miguel Gil Moreno, was also killed. Tributes to both men appeared in the press around the world.
7. A report issued by the French organization, Reporters Sans Frontières, eight weeks after NATO bombing began, spoke of at least 80 journalists having been expelled since 24 March.

References

Bell, M. (1995) *In Harm's Way*. London: Hamish Hamilton.

Glenny, Misha (1992) *The Fall of Yugoslavia*. London: Penguin.

Kurtz, H. (1998) *Spin Cycle: Inside the Clinton Propaganda Machine*. London: Pan.

McDowell, I. (1992) *Reuters Handbook for Journalists*. Oxford: Butterworth-Heinemann.

Malcolm, Noel (1994) *Bosnia: a Short History*. London: Macmillan.

Malcolm, Noel (1998) *Kosovo: a Short History*. London: Macmillan.

Nibley, A. (1998) 'The internet gold rush: winners and losers', The Annual Reuters Lecture, University of Kent at Canterbury, 30 April.

Read, D. (1992) *The Power of News*. Oxford: Oxford University Press.

Reuters World (1999) 'Rising to the challenge of war in the Balkans', June.

Silber, L. and Little, A. (1995) *The Death of Yugoslavia*. London: Penguin.

Part III
Power

9
'Smell the Tulips': the Internet, Neo-liberalism and Millenarian Hype

Brian Winston

It was not until the 1920s that botanists solved the mystery of 'broken' tulips. The 'break' which caused a tulip bulb seemingly to blossom randomly with a second colour striping and feathering the bloom in a unique pattern is actually caused by a virus spread by aphids; but in the seventeenth century all that was known was that the outcome of a planting could not be predicted. The bulb might duplicate the flower whence it descended or it might flourish in unexpected ways – ways that could be given a value – values that could grow exponentially.

Although from the turn of the 1600s onwards 'broken' tulips were already commanding astonishing sums among the staid but wealthy burghers of the United Dutch Provinces, the phenomenon known as 'tulipmania' is deemed to be limited to the years between 1634 and 1637. It was then that the frenzy to bet on bulbs buried in the ground reached its climax. One went for 5400 guilders, say £200 000 of our money; a great auction realized some £6 million for 99 lots of buried plants (Pavord 1999: 6–7, 137–177).

This curious episode is not unique. The Dutch themselves got carried away again in 1734 over hyacinths, for example (ibid.: 171). These manias should be distinguished from more straightforward scams such as the South Sea Bubble, which involved an elaborate plan for the South Sea Company to take over the national debt and convert it into private capital. The venture had been founded in 1711, on the model of the East India Company, to trade, primarily in slaves, with Latin America and the Pacific. The Government was persuaded to privatize the national debt by having its debtors swap their stakes (mainly in the form of annuities) against South Sea Company stock. This proto-private–public funding partnership deal foundered when the stock rose tenfold in value on the back of the initial financial manoeuvre (rather than on trading) only to collapse again within months in 1720. It is the fact of value being created by manipulation rather than actual business (however frenzied) which makes the bubble different from tulipmania and from the contemporary frenzy for the digital.

As the millennium turns we can now, I believe, legitimately ask how close is the enthusiasm for the internet to tulipmania – a vast speculation against assets whose worth, though potentially real, largely remains stubbornly hidden. As with tulips, we are not here considering complete fantasy. The tulips were real just as the internet is real. The guilders paid for bulbs were real just as the specie spent on e-shares or the fortunes gained by IT entrepreneurs are real. But in both cases, it is the relationship between the two which is distorted to the point of complete, preposterous artificiality.

Some have suggested that survival of the plague which immediately preceded the tulip craze contributed to the lunacy of the incident; perhaps, in the same way, current mania is fed by a species of millenarian irrationality. Less exotically, there are other general parallels; for instance, in both cases we are dealing not with scarcity but abundance. There were a lot of tulips but only a few were held to be fantastically valuable. Similarly, digital technology eliminates the scarcity of everything from bandwidth to entrepreneurial possibilities (including minimal start-up costs), but it is generally held that only a few players hit – or can hope to hit – the jackpot in any given phase of development. Then there are economic conditions. Of the Dutch, an economic historian has written: 'An increasing currency, new economic and colonial possibilities, and a keen and energetic class of merchants together had created the optimistic atmosphere in which the blooms were said to grow' – and, similarly, the soil in which internet hyperbole flourishes (Postumus 1929: 171)?

We can think of this all-pervasive hype as being the equivalent of Kuhn's concept of 'normal science'; that is, activities designed to sustain an agreed scientific thesis or paradigm (Kuhn 1962: 24). In this case 'normal science' is the received opinion which sees the internet as a radically transformative development. The question I wish to ask is whether or not the weight of the Kuhnian-style 'anomalies', that is evidence contrary to and in conflict with the assumptions of the received opinion of such 'normal science', is now of sufficient weight to sustain a case so strongly that it is irrational to continue to ignore it; that, in fact, so to do is a species of e-mania.

The quotidian hype of the 'normal science' is ubiquitous. On the day I write this I find one book critic stating in the newspaper that 'digital ... is, as it were, faster than instantaneous' (Bayley 1999: 13). Much of the babble about new technology is as meaningless and technologically naïve as this. As he sits before his computer screen waiting endlessly for the system to download – and wait he must because even with compression the basic telephone network of the internet is still more than a century old in concept and struggling to become contemporary in its hardware – I suppose he muses on new meanings of 'instantaneous'.

The problem of such sloppy talk is not limited to the vagaries of journalists (or in this case design 'gurus' with a penchant for Coca-Cola bottles) but infects even the most intelligent of observers. Gordon Graham, the Regius Professor of Philosophy at Aberdeen, has published an inquiry into the internet which would be more thought-provoking were it better grounded in the economic and technical realities of the system it is investigating:

> A web page is a body of electronic impulses, or digital information, stored in a machine somewhere, a 'server' that has a specific physical location. However, thanks to the technology of hyperlinks, this digital information may be accessed from anywhere in the world and (given suitable software) the business of accessing it constructs the pictures, sounds, text and so on ... we need know nothing of these things to make, access and interact with text and images. Moreover, our ability to do so is virtually unlimited in space and time. Anyone anywhere at anytime, even with relatively limited means, can put things on and take things off the web. (Graham 1999: 69)

Here imprecision masks the inconsistencies and ignorances of received opinion. Is it really the case that one need 'know nothing of these things to make ... text and images' or does such language suggest a spurious accessibility? It should not be forgotten that the 'relatively limited means' needed include a telephone line (which is unavailable to about two-thirds of humankind, according to the ITU) and a computer (a species of consumer durable costing, in the West, on average at least two to three times as much as the next most expensive piece of electrical household equipment).

In the same way, the supposed unimportance of the location of the servers ('a machine somewhere', in Graham's phrase) has significant ideological implications. The physical system is commonly perceived to be without owners; cyberspace, unlike other spaces, is free. Is it then the people's cyberspace? Or is cyberspace not like the radio spectrum, the 'air-waves', which (in the words of the preamble of the US 1933 Communications Act) is 'deemed in perpetuity to the people' but is actually owned by great corporations? In fact is it not these same great corporations who actually own cyberspace? The servers which control the spine and the spine itself were handed over by US National Science Foundation (actually, in this context, the American taxpayers who had paid some $5 million for it to be built) to the private telecommunications giants Sprint, Ameritech and Pacific Bell in 1995. 'Somewhere' is actually the same place where the rest of the world's telecommunications and mass media infrastructure sits. 'Somewhere' safely belongs to the same old crowd (Winston and Walton 1996: 81).

This is why the largely unremarked privatization of the internet's central structure in 1995 so upset the more aware of those self-deluded technophiles who thought they were in a cyber-Eden. The cyber-radicals of the shadowy Internet Liberation Front, for example, announced:

> Once upon a time there was a wide area network called the Internet. A network unscathed by the capitalist Fortune 500 companies and the like. Then somebody decided to deregulate the Internet and hand it over to the 'big boys' in the telecommunications industry. ... The Internet Liberation Front is a small, underground organisation of computer security experts. We are capable of penetrating virtually any network linked to the Internet – any network. ... Just a friendly warning Corporate America ... (quoted in Winston and Walton 1996: 81)

Of course, the Internet Liberation Front has not actually undermined the 'somewhere'. It is there with servers situated, pace Professor Graham, in 'Mae West' and 'Mae East' (as the spine's terminals are known) on the American coasts.

Pretending otherwise is spuriously to suggest a lack of accountability and control. The net can be turned on and off (or fail) just like any other electrical or electronic network. Moreover, despite a common belief that its enormous size and its system of breaking messages into 'packages' make it unpoliceable, the same computing power that drives it can be also deployed to control it and its contents. The failure to do so on a systematic basis is often attributed to economics. It is held that the cost of control is too great, but there is another equally plausible explanation: that control is only sporadically effected can be seen as more a reflection of the limited threat the internet's typically safe middle-class Western user poses to the forces of law and order than it is a measure of the Web's innate anarchic power. Thus a media panic in the UK can hype the threat of uncensored paedophiliac cyberporn, and note that the police have only two officers assigned to the task of controlling it – yet will make no connection between these two facts (Cook et al. 1999: 3). A journalist can report that a search engine will throw up a mere 135 'kiddie-porn sites' but fail to understand how easy it is for the engine's owners to forbid such conjunctions of terms, dispelling the sites into the cyber-darkness (Arthur 1999: 3). Of course, the internet will still contain pornographic sites involving children just as back-street porn shops retail such images. It is the ease of electronic access that can be curtailed.

Panic demands for legislation (against the noise that it will be powerless because of the complexity of the technology) ignore that, in the summer of 1999, British courts extended the provisions of the Obscene Publications Act of 1959, which had already been redrawn to encompass computer-related pornography in 1994, to the internet by holding that transmission within Britain rendered contents liable wherever they originated. Downloading messages brought them within UK law (EJC 1999). At the same time, the UK government's Electronic Communications Bill extended police powers of internet surveillance to include a right to demand encryption 'keys' and to make it an offence to withhold them (Reeves 1999: 16). More could be easily not only enacted but also fully operationalized. Like all other policing issues, this is more a question of the political prioritizing of effort than it is of economics or technology.

This sort of hostile analysis of the hype, which insists on the primacy of a social, rather than a technical, focus, is often described as 'Luddite' or 'neo-Luddite', but it is not. Leaving aside the common slur implied by the use of this term on the Luddites (whom E.P. Thompson long ago pointed out were not so foolish as to object to the mechanical alleviation of their labour), putting normally unrelated facts together in order to combat received wisdom is mere realism (Thompson 1968: 600). Nor is it technophobic to do so. In fact, 'neo-Luddite' technophobia and the received wisdom of the technophilia deemed to be its opposite are but the two sides of the same technicist coin. For good or ill, both views suggest that we are powerless to control technical developments such as the internet. Mere realists reject technicism, arguing instead that the social context determines technical applications and can be controlled, or if not controlled, can be made (albeit with great difficulty) the site of struggle.

From this position, the occasional moments when the internet is used successfully to exploit society's contradictions – to aid and abet, say, a day of protest in the City of London or a revolutionary movement in Mexico – are nothing more than marginal glitches which need not be controlled. Should the system begin to fulfil the promise suggested for it by its more strident technophiliac boosters and reach significant numbers of impressionable people, then (the realist view suggests) it would suffer the fate of, say, the Polish telephone system under General Jaruzelski at the height of the state-communist counter-putsch to Solidarity in 1982 – it would simply be switched off. By 1995 America Online (AOL), soon to be the main internet service player, was already cutting off subscribers for 'net-abuse' – but only at the rate of six a day. As it is, the trade in pornography (estimated as constituting no less than 50 per cent of all non-academic internet use) is allowed to exist as one of the few real testaments to the effectiveness of e-commerce while the occasional kiddie-porn fan or paedophile ring is mopped up *pour encourager les autres*; and little else is done. Yet.

It seems probable that the bogus idea of the internet as a free and unfettered environment has its roots in the initial development of its forerunner, ARPANET, the Pentagon's distributed computing network established between key players in the military-industrial complex in the late 1960s to enable essential computers to survive nuclear attack. The perception is that such a network has no central control but, in fact, its initial purpose was exactly the opposite. It was designed to ensure that control could be exercised even in the most extreme situations of cataclysmic war. A distributed network is, in fact, not one without control but rather one with a moveable control. Each nodal point of ARPANET could run the whole thing; that was the prime design objective and, indeed, ARPANET's raison d'être.

Distribution is the first source of the phoney vision of freedom that was to become so prevalent three decades later; but there were also other factors in play in this initial phase of development which were to feed into the perception that a distributed-control network was actually an unpoliced and unpolicable one. The Pentagon, in effect, hid the entire military purpose of its new communication system behind a quite genuine computer science agenda. Just as the intercontinental ballistic missile programme had been disguised as a scientific space project in the 1950s, so the ARPANET's nuclear-war function was subsumed in the 1960s and 1970s by a genuine question: what can be accomplished if computers interact? So effective was this disguise that even some ARPANET pioneers convinced themselves that, despite their

Pentagon offices, they were not engaged in a military project (Hafner and Lyons 1996: 10). Nuclear attack was coded (in the phrase of pioneer Joseph Licklider) as a 'rare occasion' which might make it necessary for computer control to be dispersed whereas the possibly exponential power of computers as communicating tools would be 'a boon to human kind ... beyond measure' (Hafner and Lyons 1996: 38; Licklider and Taylor 1968: 110). This is why all but one of ARPANET's initial nine nodes were sited in universities in 1969/70. Computing was altogether a better public justification for the not-inconsiderable expenditures ARPANET was incurring. However, a decade later only sixteen of 62 ARPANET sites were on campuses. By this time the system, then costing $14 million a year to run, was buried in the military-industrial complex.

ARPANET used minicomputers to enable the inaugural academic/ military-industrial mainframes to interact. This was because those who controlled these big one-off, hand-made machines, each with its own operating system, were unwilling to sacrifice any of their computing power to this extra communication task. The first of the minis – $360 000 Honeywell DDP-516s in 'ruggedized' cases specially designed for battlefield use – was delivered to UCLA in September 1969. They were, in effect, proto-servers but were then designated Interface Message Processors (IMPs). The Pentagon's main ARPANET contractor, Bolt, Beranek and Newman (BBN), concentrated on linking these IMPs and building the spine – for example, charging the Department of Defense $640 000 (in late 1960s dollars) for writing the system's basic software. In effect, they were designing not an instantaneous network like the telephone system but rather a 'store-and-forward' system like the telegraph where the IMPs/servers function as telegraph offices and the messages, broken into packages, as words on a telegram. Electronics made the whole thing so fast as to give the appearance of instantaneity. BBN left the problems of creating the interface between each IMP and the mainframe it served to the mainframe operators to sort out as best they could. This was most significant.

The mainframe teams formed themselves into a Network Working Group (NWG) independent of BBN. The NWG rapidly created the L-O-G-I-N command and host-to-host protocols – Telnet, Network Control Protocol (NCP), File Transfer Protocol (FTP) – and the protocol for incoming data. They also quickly began using the network itself to do this work. This split between NWG (which became international as INWG in 1972) and BBN/Pentagon encouraged the notion, implicit in the common misunderstanding of a distributed system anyway, that nobody had overall control.

This sense was further enhanced by the failure of the authorities to take over such crucial work, despite the creation by the Pentagon of an Internet Configuration Control Board (ICCB). As far as members of the Network Working Group were concerned, the thrust of this initiative was clear: '"Time to roll up your toy academic network"' (quoted in Hafner and Lyons 1996: 247). But the Pentagon's power both before and after the fall of Saigon in 1975 was at a particularly low ebb, and academic distress at the arrival of the ICCB was bolstered by general campus hostility. For example, the Pentagon's attempts to use ARPANET to move illegal army intelligence files around was, predictably, leaked and, equally predictably, caused a scandal. In the event, the Pentagon's main contribution to the system (apart from owning it root and branch) was limited. Best known is its creation of the domain name system, agreed in 1986 – 'edu' for universities, 'com' for commerce, 'mil' for military and so on.

The distributed-network idea, the computer science agenda and, above all, the split between spine operator and users become central to the claim that the internet was in some fundamental sense unplanned and as a result is a particularly transformative technology – more transformative than the telegraph, telephone and television, more even than the railway. Actually, received wisdom held that the internet is most like the application of steam to aid human labour. By 1999, my paper was telling me that the internet is, according to no less an authority than the Chairman of General Electric, 'the single most important event in the US economy since the industrial revolution' (quoted in McCrum 1999: 11). Everybody seemed to agree – for example, Bruce Sterling in 1993:

> Originally, the Internet was a post-apocalypse command grid. And look at it now. No one really planned it this way. Its users made the Internet that way, because they had the courage to use the network to support their own values, to bend the technology to their own purposes. To serve their own liberty. (quoted in Winston and Walton 1996: 82)

Clearly this is now 'normal science', but in what sense can it be true? Is the internet really being as transformative as train and car have been? Is it more essential to the globalization of financial markets than satellites? Is it the crucial missing technological link in expanding television services? In creating interactivity? In transmitting text? In liberating humanity? And if it is not, or if (at best) it is but an enhancement of previous techniques, is not all this hype simply so much tulipmania?

That the received wisdom about the internet's transformative power might not be the end of the matter is grounded in an understanding of a number of anomalies. For example, it is widely believed that all these areas of IT activity are imposing a new overall spin on patterns of employment. However, the American government itself is making no such prediction. In the last decade of the millennium, the US Department of Labor believed the fastest growing area of total employment was in the ranks of retail persons operating outside of cyberspace. Next came nurses, cashiers and office clerks, truck drivers, waitresses and waiters and so on. Systems analysts, although doubling in number, still represented only 1.9 per cent of the workforce and were the only IT category in the top thirty job classifications – apart from the thirtieth one itself, computer engineers and scientists. Between them, these two categories were expected to grow from some 300 000 jobs to over 750 000 by 2005, but the bottom line is that all 'high info content' positions would even then only account for less than half of the overall predicted growth (Henwood 1995: 168–9). The number of jobs in the mall and flipping hamburgers continue to rise faster.

There is also a large question mark over the basic statistics on internet use. The figures have always been extremely amorphous and often self-contradictory. In 1995, there were supposed to be, for example, anything between 6.5 million PCs worldwide connected to the net; or perhaps there were 10.3 million in the US alone. Since there were then some 205 million personal computers worldwide, it was clear that at the outset of the period of major internet hype, whichever figure is taken, there was actually quite a reasonable take-up being claimed – even in usual unaudited mode of most of such statistics ('Communications' 1999: 832–6). Moreover, the main service providers were claiming only some 8.7 million subscribers worldwide. Nevertheless such hook-up figures were already being glossed into a 'user' statistic by simple dint of multiplying the connections by anything from five to seven. Seven was the constant used in the ARPANET mainframe phase when seven users per terminal was deemed to be the norm, but its relevance in the assessment of PC numbers has never been established. This ploy yielded the hyped 35–45 million figure being bandied about in the mid-decade.

The 35–45 million continued to rise by unexplained leaps and bounds. By the year 2000 it was projected to become some 280 million – or as many as a billion, in the heated opinion of some. Yet the other available figures still did not quite tally. Internet use was still lagging behind PC penetration. For example, 27 per cent of UK households had PCs, but only 11 per cent were connected. One survey suggested that even in high-income PC households, only one-third used a machine online and then for only 10 per cent of computing time (Cross 1999: 3). Some 20 years after the PC was introduced, only about half of all American homes had one. Moreover, 85 per cent of households earning less than $25 000 and 40 per cent of those with less than $50 000 had no PC (Freeman 1999: 3). This was the most computerized society on earth; and, again, one in ten of these PCs – nearly five million – were not connected to the internet (Veronhis et al. 1996: 317).

The same kind of worry can be applied to a consideration of the scale of internet service. AOL, by 1998 the dominant provider, albeit seriously embattled by competitors, claimed 15–16 million subscribers worldwide. To mesh less than 48 million American homes-with-computer and a percentage of the much smaller worldwide ISP number to the claimed 100 million-plus US internet users alone still requires a certain legerdemain (Caulkin 1998: 5).

It is the same with another basic measure – internet hosts. Hosts doubled every year between 1985 and 1999, but John Quarterman, whose Matrix Information and Directory Services (MIDS) has long been one of the net's few authoritative demographic sources, notes that there is now a slowdown in this growth rate. Between 1996 and 1998 the rate was 68 per cent a year. Between 1998 and 1999 it fell to 40 per cent both in the US and in Europe (Metcalfe 1999). This is the first time an internet levelling-off of any kind has been reported.

All of these astronomical numbers, whatever their provenance, are presumed by received opinion to illustrate the unprecedented nature of the growth of this technology. The anomaly here is, in fact, that they are not untoward. I should add that it is not part of the realist agenda, therefore, to dismiss the internet out of hand. It is useful (as some of the internet-based sources here cited indicate); but it ought to be put into perspective and it is perspective which suggests that the internet, even if all the user statistics are taken at face value, exhibits a far from exceptional rate of penetration.

The real success in the realm of communications devices in recent years is, of course, the cellular phone. Its impact is widely acknowledged, but dismissed as not being transformative. Gordon Graham, for instance, notes that there are 'more and less important inventions', clearly an observation to which one cannot object; but he goes on to claim that the mobile phone, for example, is but a refinement of the telephone and as such a good example of a 'less important invention'

(Graham 1999: 27). The number of cell phones in the US rose from 91 000 in the summer of 1985 to 4.3 million by 1990 to 28 million by 1995. The industry now claims 76 million subscribers (CITA 1999). And these figures – admittedly self-reported by the industry – represent at least twice the growth rate claimed for internet use.

To dismiss the mobile phone is, in effect, a further aspect of the internet-technicist's limited Eurocentric vision. By 1995, there were already about four-and-a-half times as many mobiles as there were PCs in the world – 893 million ('Communications' 1999: 832–7). So how unimportant was this? As a corrective to stalled traditional telephone provision, as a luxury for the affluent young, as a system for controlling outworkers of all kinds, the mobile surely represents a device of significance. But telephones are taken for granted in the West – 'less important'. So too are faxes. Yet these two are crucial communications technologies for the mass of humanity and to prove this (as it were) they have greater penetration than do computers and internet. Thus in 1995 of 217 states and territories reporting on their communications structures, 68, nearly a third – mostly in the Third and former Second World, reported faxes but no computers ('Communications' 1999: 832–6). But in the US and the UK that year PCs already outnumbered faxes (97 million to 16 million) and only about 4.5 per cent of the world's mobile phones were based within their borders. On the other hand, their citizens owned 47 per cent of the world's PCs. It is little wonder, then, that the internet becomes 'important' to the point of being transformative in these societies while other technologies are ignored; but the fact remains that the case for internet 'exceptionalism' (as it might be termed) must rest on grounds other than the speed and extent of the network's adoption.

It is also anomalous to see the internet as being too anarchic to fit within the basic structures of communications developments in the West. According to Herb Schiller, US official enthusiasm for the de-militarized internet fits into a pattern of support for specific telecommunications developments which would deliver, as a critical American foreign policy objective, an international communication system which was dominated by American technology and ownership: 'Under the "free-flow" principle, U.S. global strategy supported the rapid and fullest development of transport and information technologies, which underpinned the capability for the cultural domination that was being constructed' (Schiller 1995: 19).

During previous technological advances, the US had never managed to overcome the historical lead established by the British imperial cable network which was laid in the nineteenth century: 'The imperial rule of Great Britain in the nineteenth and early twentieth century had been facilitated greatly by control of the underwater message flows between the colonies and London' (Schiller 1995: 20). In this the UK was greatly aided by its control of gutta-percha, the best underwater insulator then available and a monopoly of one of its colonies, Malaya (Winston 1998: 274). So strong was this control issue for the US that the first transatlantic cable was opposed on these grounds in the 1860s: 'There were those who felt that in this submarine cable England was literally crawling under the sea to get some advantage of the United States' (quoted in Winston 1986: 259). This suspicion was to be converted into a policy objective of domination based on technological advantage, but a lack of patent advantage with the next technology, radio (as well as the difficulty of building a reliable world network because of atmospheric interference), meant that the US could not achieve this end with either wireless telegraphy or wireless telephony.

Next, satellites were perceived in the 1960s as the answer, for instance, by the Senate Space Committee: 'To construe space telecommunications too narrowly would overlook immediate and rich potential as an instrument of US foreign policy' (Oslund 1977: 161; Winston 1986: 283). They were also seen at that time by the Europeans as a threat:

> The fundamental question is above all more political than economic in nature: do the European governments consider it necessary and desirable to devote the necessary resources to programmes in order to secure an independent long-term capability and not to remain tributaries of American facilities or dependent on global systems in which the United States has a preponderant influence? (Snow 1976: 137)

European governments and their state-owned post and telecommunications entities did consider independence desirable and, led by the British and the French, pushed the parallel development in intercontinental cables based on MASER amplifier technology. This allowed them to resist the domination of Comsat, the American government's privatized agency dedicated to the exploitation of communication satellites. In the time thus bought, the Europeans also developed rocket and satellite technology to match the Americans while at the same time moving towards the transoceanic fibre optic net which would render all such space-side devices redundant (Winston 1998: 273–4).

But neo-liberal ideology moved the goalposts during the era of internet development. After the Second World War, Truman's government could correctly declare that, 'the US, almost alone among the nations of the world, relies on privately-owned telecommunications companies' (Oslund 1977: 162). Now the world has followed suit and telecommunications authorities are largely privatized. There is also 'globalization' which the transoceanic satellite and cable system had supported in facilitating a general transfer of manufacturing from First to Third World and the cross-border expansion of financial markets. Privatization and globalization did not, however, mean that the US government abandoned its policy objective of domination. On the contrary. As Vice-President Al Gore told the ITU in 1994: 'We now have at hand the technological breakthroughs and economic means to bring all the communities in the world together ... and it will make possible a global information marketplace, where consumers can buy and sell products' (quoted in Schiller 1995: 17).

The difference this time was that the internet delivered the world's communication system to the US. After nearly a century-and-a-half of effort, the network was at last American – American in the ownership of its central hardware, American in its software and largely American in its international infrastructure. Best of all, in a splendid piece of political manoeuvring, all this was accomplished behind a smoke-screen of anarchic liberty and freedom.

And so to the last anomaly, the actual economic significance of the internet. There is no question that huge sums of money are involved but everywhere one looks one is waiting for a tulip bulb to 'break'. Business is constantly warned to sign up to the e-world or face extinction, yet hard evidence of the value of the internet to most of commerce is yet to be proved. On the contrary, what little is known suggests that the internet might prove to be, literally, counter-productive. For example, one estimate of the internet's impact on the workplace suggested that, on average, UK office workers with access wasted 30 minutes a day playing with it. While only a third of companies were currently running policing software, firms selling such programmes were predicting a 60 per cent increase in business over the first years of the millennium. Even if the workers were not playing, Gallup reported that an interneted office worker received 171 messages a day. Half of these workers could expect to be interrupted at least six times an hour (Aldrige and Doward 1999: 7).

What most resembles the irrationality of a mania is the unproven reliance on the network as an advertising medium. Huge sums are being speculated without any clear evidence that internet advertising 'works'. Unlike other advertising media, the internet is unaudited and its efficacy is almost entirely untested. (I say this without prejudice to the reliability of auditing methodologies used for other media but there is, however much questioned, an independent assessment for them which is largely missing from the internet.) In tulip terms, we are still looking for a 'break' of internet advertising's usefulness. Geocities, for examples, is a company giving users free Web pages, thereby creating a supposedly valuable advertising platform. In 1999, it was bought by Yahoo!, proprietors of the Web's most successful search engine, for $4.6 billion; but this after it reported a fourth-quarter loss of $8.4 million on revenues of $7.5 million.

It is in fact an article of e-faith that a company such as Yahoo! itself is valuable because its search engine is heavily used and therefore, through its hyperlinks, constitutes a viable advertising medium. There is an unaudited claim (from Media Matrix) that its sites were visited by 31.1 million in February 1999 (Schofield 1999a: 3). Yahoo!, reliant on an assumption of the advertising efficiency of such hits, has seen its share price quadruple in a year; and, at least, it managed a strong $18.5 million profit in 1998/99.

In contrast to the portal companies, the service providers had something to sell – access. On this basis there was a far more real subscription business which allowed AOL, the sector's leader with over 15 million subscribers, to produce a profit of $88 million on revenues of $960 million (Caulkin 1998: 5). Subscribers were paying around £17 a month but here again it was thought that advertising revenues could enable the provider to give the service away free. AOL has found itself confronting a host of largely non-communications companies eager to offer free internet access to people who will repay the favour by reading the odd Web site 'banner' and using the link to access the advertisers' sites directly.

Henry Blodget, the Merrill Lynch investment analyst who in 1998 judged that Amazon.com, the cyber-bookstore, would double its share value just before it did just that, was predicting less than a year later that at least 75 per cent of all internet companies would fail to make any money and that only seven to ten would survive to dominate all areas of e-commerce (Martinson 1999: 2). In general, his advice was to avoid all internet companies which dealt with the public and to only invest in those offering online services to other businesses – although it seems to me that many of these were also caught in the advertising nexus. Others suggested that the real money to be made lay with those who produced the actual hardware, the routers, the chip manufacturers and the like (Bannister 1999: 29). This appeared to make better sense.

(This is also certainly true of the computer side of the system. This business continued to flourish. At the millennium's end, IBM was making a daily profit of $24 million; Compaq's sales leapt 48 per cent in the last quarter of the 1998/99 financial year; and Microsoft profits in the same quarter leapt 75 per cent to $2 billion (Schofield 1999b: 4). I will admit that this trade was not an anomaly to the internet exceptionalism thesis – except that the health of these manufacturers translates only tangentially into internet take-up.)

Apart from the dubious nature of businesses based on the internet as an advertising medium and the more solidly based activities of firms selling hard- and software, there was also direct sales – e-commerce, the internet as cyber-mall. In 1998, e-commerce in the US was estimated to have doubled over 1997 and to be about to increase to around $12 billion in 1999. Thirty per cent of these sales were of computers and the software for them. Travel services, CDs and books came next; however, $12 billion, although a tidy sum, is negligible in commercial terms. It represents a mere 0.1 per cent of US retail – around one-third of the cash taken at the tills of America's biggest supermarket chain. Of the seven million British on the net, only one million used it to buy anything in 1998 – that is some £400m of transactions but, similarly, only 0.2 per cent of total UK retail business (Walker 1999: 21).

These are obviously markets worth accessing, just as the old mail-order business was (and is still in some countries) worthwhile; but it is a long way from being transformative. The question mark over this new form of catalogue shopping has to be the extent to which it will replace more conventional retailing. On its face this does not seem too likely a prospect. As a shopping method, the internet offers no more interactivity than does a telephone and its ability to update the catalogues far outpaces the rate at which they might change; also, goods, as ever, require physical delivery. Mail order has been a significant part of retailing for more than a century and it is unlikely that it will fail to transfer to the internet, but it is equally unlikely that the internet will massively increase the mail-order share of shopping in general. The sight of stores which would never take phone orders or install faxes leaping onto the internet bandwagon does not inspire much confidence.

It is significant that the most successful areas of e-commerce are, computing and one exception apart, those which have the least appealing stores outside of cyberspace. There is nothing to bring one to a bank or a travel agent as there is to attract one to the rest of the mall. And there's the rub. Arguments about the advantages of shopping at the computer ignore the centrality of shopping to our economic system and, more specifically, the shopping mall to our culture. They seek to pretend shopping is a chore which the technology can allow us to bypass when, on the contrary, for a vast majority of the citizenry it is almost always one of capitalism's greatest pleasures.

The one e-commerce exception is the cyber-bookstore and here is to be found the most valuable 'bulb' of all: Amazon.com has seen its share price increase tenfold and its sales grow over 300 per cent in a year to $610 million – but it still managed to lose $31 million and filed a report with the US Securities and Exchange Commission promising 'substantial operating losses for the foreseeable future' (Schofield 1999b: 4). The news of the loss caused the share price to rise by another 17 per cent, not least because it was sitting on enough capital to sustain loses at this level for 60 years. As Charles Foster Kane said of his first newspaper, *The Inquirer*: 'I did lose a million dollars last year. I expect to lose a million dollars this year. I expect to lose a million dollars next year. You know, Mr. Thatcher, at the rate of a million dollars a year, I'll have to close this place in ... 60 years.' The difference, of course, is that Kane had his own gold mine; Amazon.com has only the money of its shareholders.

There are considerable anomalies to the received wisdom's view of the internet as an agent of transformation. While its significance and usefulness can be agreed, internet hype can be resisted. The Web is too full of pornography, too firmly part of the West's telecommunication infrastructure, too distracting for workers, too slow in its diffusion, too fulfilling of US foreign policy objectives, too overpriced in the share market, too unproven as an advertising medium, too constrained by culture as an alternative to shopping. Many things can be done by the net and many more will be accomplished when the limitations of Boolean search engines are overcome and the old telephone infrastructure is replaced. But the weight of the anomalies is overwhelming and likely to remain so. I suggest that the internet will never be more transformative than other networks have been in the past – which is not to say that it is no more (and no less) without substantive consequences than was (and are) the telegraph, the telephone, radio, TV, satellite and cable. E-mania, though, can only look forward to sobering up in the face of an inevitable crash in e-shares.

As ever (in my view) Pulitzer Prize-winning humour columnist Dave Barry has it right:

The business community is insanely excited about the Internet. Internet companies are springing up like mushrooms, inspired by such amazing stories as Amazon.com, which started doing business just a few years ago, and is already losing hundreds of millions of dollars a year. A lot of Internet companies are losing money like crazy, yet their stock prices are soaring. In fact the more an Internet company loses, the more desirable it becomes to investors. This seems like a paradox, but there's a very logical economic explanation: Internet investors have the brains of grapefruit. (Barry 1999: 22)

Even the analysts are beginning to smell the flowers. Wall Street maven Henry Blodget, for instance, has noticed: 'There are tons of tulip bulbs out there'.

Indeed, there are.

References

Aldrige, John and Doward, Jamie (1999) 'Internet sheriff threatens high noon for office idlers', *Observer*, 6 July.

Arthur, Charles (1999) 'Web of filth runs out of control', *Independent on Sunday*, 14 November.

Bannister, Nicholas (1999) 'Masters of the e-universe', *Guardian*, 20 May.

Barry, Dave (1999) 'Follow that chocking duck', *International Herald Tribune*, 14–15 August 1999, 22.

Bayley, Stephen (1999) 'There's no accounting for haste', *Observer Review*, 7 November.

Caulkin, Simon (1998) 'Like all bubbles, this will burst', *Observer* (Business Section), 18 April.

CITA (1999) 'Semi-annual wireless industry survey results' http://www.wow-com.com/statsurv

'Communications' (1999) *Britannica Yearbook 1999*. Chicago: Encyclopaedia Britannica.

Cook, Emma, Arthur, Charles and Hughes, Jane (1999) 'So why is the internet so hard to police?', *Independent on Sunday*, 14 November.

Cross, Michael (1999) 'Year of living dangerously', *Guardian* (On Line), 4 February.

EJC (1999) 'UK bans porn made in the USA.' EJC Media News, http://www.ejc.nl/mn/showresultnews.html?3085, 6 July.

Freeman, Shlonn (1999) 'A computer on the doorstep and a toehold inside', *New York Times*, (Business), 8 August.

Graham, Gordon (1999) *The Internet: a Philosophical Inquiry*. London: Routledge.

Hafner, K. and Lyons, M. (1996) *When Wizards Stay Up Late*. New York: Simon & Schuster.

Henwood, Doug (1995) 'Info fetishism', in James Brook and Iain Boal (eds), *Resisting the Virtual Life: The Culture and Politics of Information*. San Francisco: City Lights.

Kuhn, Thomas (1962) *The Structure of Scientific Revolutions*. Chicago: University of Chicago Press.

Licklider, J.C.R and Taylor, Robert (1968) 'The computer as a communication device', *International Science and Technology* (April), reprinted in Paul Mayer (ed.), *Computer Media and Communication*. Oxford: OUP, 1999.

McCrum, Robert (1999) 'The world of books', *Observer Review*, 7 November.

Martinson, Jane (1999) 'Netbubble@burst.com', *Guardian*, 11 October.

Metcalfe, Bob (1999) 'Early signs appear of slowing Internet growth', *Info World Electric*, http://www.infoworld.com, 10 May.

Oslund, J. (1977) 'Open shores to open skies', in J.N. Pelton and M. Snow (eds), *Economic and Policy Problems in Satellite Communications*. New York: Praeger.

Pavord, Anna (1999) *The Tulip*. London: Bloomsbury.

Postumus, N.W. (1929) *Journal of Economic and Business History*, 1(3), May 1929, quoted in Pavord (1999).

Reeves, Richard (1999) 'Police powers to read e-mails "is a breach of rights" ', *Observer*, 24 October.

Schiller, Herb (1995) 'Global information highway: project for an ungovernable world', in James Brook and Iain Boal (eds), *Resisting the Virtual Life: the Culture and Politics of Information*. San Francisco: City Lights.

Schofield, Jack (1999a) 'Portal combat', *Guardian* On Line, 15 April.

Schofield, Jack (1999b) 'Investors roll up for billion dollar bubble', *Guardian* On Line, 4 February.

Snow, M.S. (1976) *International Commercial Satellite Communications*. New York: Praeger.

Thompson, E.P. (1968) *The Making of the English Working Class*. Harmondsworth, Middlesex: Penguin.

Veronhis, Suhler and Associates (1996) *Communications Industry Forecast*. New York: Veronhis, Suhler and Associates

Walker, David (1999) 'Keying in with faith and hope', *Guardian*, 20 May.

Winston, Brian (1986) *Misunderstanding Media*. London: Routledge & Kegan Paul.

Winston, Brian (1998) *Media Technology and Society: a History from the Telegraph to the Internet*. London: Routledge.

Winston, Brian and Walton, Paul (1996) 'Netscape: virtually free', *Index On Censorship* 25(1) 78–83.

and thanks to Collete Snowden for insights into the importance of the telephone and Matthew Winston for audiovisual research.

10
Selling Off Cyberspace

Granville Williams

Introduction

The eminently sensible notion of public space uncluttered by commercialism is now beleaguered on all fronts, and even the theories and political structures which underpinned the concepts of public service in broadcasting, public utilities (gas, water, electricity, telephones) and the provision by a benign state of a range of public services (education, libraries, health services) are discredited or marginalized. Almost daily we are confronted with startling new examples of the forward march of the market and the commercialization of areas of social and community activity previously untouched by its relentless drive. Take, for example, street furniture – the advert-bearing shelters, superloos, drinking fountains, newspaper sellers' kiosks, litter bins and Parisian-style pillars constructed in our city streets – which a French company, J.C. Decaux, has now begun to exploit and dominate internationally. According to Nick Cohen (1999: 178), the benefits of signing such deals to citizens from councils, within whose territorial confines the bulk of these structures exist, are almost non-existent, but they have either seen the painless opportunity to make money through selling the advertising space to Decaux, or, where there has been reluctance, holidays and other hospitality to be lavished on city dignitaries to soften resistance. Whatever reason, the result is that public space becomes a hoarding.

An illuminating study by Susan G. Davis extends the interest which architects, geographers and cultural critics have had in the privatization of public space and makes the important link between scores of urban transformations in the United States and the fact that the urban reshapers are the global media corporations. She asks why are these 'mega media conglomerates moving beyond the construction of literal

179

theme parks and helping to rebuild city centres, reshaping shopping malls and even designing residential and work communities?' Responding to her own question, Davis argues:

> They are in the process of creating public spaces defined by marketing criteria and shaped to the most profitable audiences. These spaces will be devoted to the circulation of well-tested and 'safe' media content and will exclude experimental imagery or oppositional ideas. Privately produced collective spaces based on and filled with familiar mass media content can create a seamless world, one in which the home – currently devoted to extensive consumption of conglomerate culture – is tightly knit to and continuous with the outside. (Davis 1999: 436–7)

Critical attention to the increasing international dominance of giant media, computing and telecommunications groups, and the economic, political and cultural consequences of this trend, is not a recent development. In *Empires and Communications* (1972), Harold Innis first identified the central role of communications in the establishment of imperial power by the Portuguese, Spanish, British, French and Dutch and pointed out that whilst the commodities which formed the economic basis of the empires changed – from spices to precious minerals and oil and on to electronic, media and cultural products – efficient communication was an essential constant in the expansion and maintenance of empire. In the nineteenth century telegraphy played a key role in imperialist consolidation and control (indeed a company like Cable and Wireless has its origins in this first phase of global communications) and as the United States moved into global ascendancy after the Second World War, Herbert Schiller's *Mass Communications and American Empire* (1969) drew attention to the way the United States sought to actively promote its ideology and economic interests through broadcasting, film and other cultural products.

The 1990s saw a dramatic extension in the size and global reach of these huge media corporations, and this has, in turn, stimulated work on both the reasons for this new surge, and the consequences for the democratic process and media policy-making when these companies can deploy enormous lobbying and media power to ensure they get favourable legislative outcomes for their commercial operations at national and international level (Herman and McChesney 1997).

In the 1990s, however, a new, hopeful motif was introduced into the account of what seemed to be the inevitable, irresistible rise to global dominance of a few overweening media conglomerates. Fervent exponents of the liberating powers of the internet saw it as a free space which challenged all the previous assumptions for the development of communication technologies. Cyberspace would be an exclusive domain where the old concerns about media concentration, and the relentless commercialization of new media technologies, would be avoided because of the inherent and distinctive structures of the new system. A potent example of this deeply felt belief appeared in the magazine *Wired* where Jon Katz celebrated in ecstatic terms, 'The netizen: birth of a digital nation'. He asked questions such as: 'Are we a powerful new kind of community or just a mass of people hooked up to machines? Do we share goals and ideals, or are we just another hot market ready for exploitation by American's ravenous corporations?' and responded:

> Where our existing information systems seek to choke the flow of information through taboos, costs, and restrictions, the new digital world celebrates the right of the individual to speak and be heard – one of the cornerstone ideas behind American media and democracy.
>
> Where our existing political institutions are viewed as remote and unresponsive, this online culture offers the means for individuals to have a genuine say in the decisions that affect our lives.
>
> Where conventional politics is suffused with ideology, the digital world is obsessed with facts.
>
> Where our current political system is irrational, awash in hypocritical god-and-values talk, the Digital Nation points the way towards a more rational, less dogmatic approach to politics.
>
> The world's information is being liberated, and so, as a consequence, are we. (Katz 1997: 50)

It is possible to find similar optimistic views scattered through the proliferation of magazines which grew up celebrating the internet around the time of the Katz article, but the sheer power of these ideas also captured the attention of academic magazines like *Media, Culture and Society* which devoted an issue to 'Electronic Democracy' and carried articles, mainly drawing on the US experience, on the impact of the technology on democratic political life. One particular article carries a wealth of examples to develop the argument that computer-mediated communication systems (CMC) challenge some of the old ways of thinking and instead recognize that 'control itself is increasingly exercised through the horizontal extension of network alliances ... As networks become structurally decentralized, ever wider publics gain access to them in ways that lead to an increase in the rate and density of public exchange' (Friedland 1996: 187). His analysis of 'citizen- and community-based information networks' suggest four models: networks that create new information out of advocacy in the service of problem-solving and action; networks in local communities; networks that have grown out of broadly defined government or local planning; and electronic public journalism which is developing out of new network publishing practices. He concludes,

> These findings suggest that access to network tools, which is rapidly widening, is beginning to create public spaces in which new forms of information and relationship building can circulate. This allows for both the practical strengthening of grassroots democratic organizing and its growth and extension to new citizenship groups. (Friedland 1996: 207)

Of course, the internet as a communications and information system has been used very effectively by a range of progressive groups to focus on campaigns and organize activity. From the Web site created during the epic libel trial of two activists in London which detailed the alleged failings of McDonalds brought out at the trial, through the mobilizations against covert attempts to develop a new global corporate reordering of trade involved with the Multilateral Agreement on Investment (MAI), to the dissemination of alternative news and views about the impact and reaction to the NATO bombing of Serbia and the mobilization against the agenda for the World Trade Organization meeting in Seattle. These, and a range of other activities, are an important part of the constant attempts by activist and oppositional groups to convey information and build support for their ideas and activities. However, they have to be placed in perspective, and internet technology, whilst it empowers organizations, giving them the opportunity to organize and communicate globally, does not shift or alter the basic political and economic power structures within and between countries.

There is a good deal of evidence to suggest that the demand for information on the Web is high, but corporate strategy is dominated by the concern to develop lucrative services, and the revenue for these derives from entertainment, pornography, e-commerce and targetting new categories such as 'cyber-tots'.

Any discussion of the future shape and development of the internet, and the creation of new alternative online communities and movements through it, has to take as its starting point the fact that applying the notion of exceptionalism to it is at the very least naïve and misplaced, but also suggests an historical blindness. I want to analyse the basis for the claims that the internet is different and then develop the argument that far from the technology demonstrating a different development path it has, in a relatively short period of time, been subordinated to, and controlled by, the same corporate and commercial imperatives which have influenced the development of other communication technologies, from printing, through radio and television to satellite and cable. Cyberspace is another frontier which has been colonized and claimed in the same way.

Technological determinism

One of the traps which enthusiasts for a new communication technology often fall into is that they proclaim its revolutionary impact and development as if the technology existed in a cocoon and was free to develop uninfluenced by a complex interplay of political, social, economic, technological and commercial factors. The literature demolishing the flawed idea of the immanent transforming powers of a particular technology is extensive, but it still does not stop people from continuing to be seduced by the particular appeal of technological determinism. Frank Webster dealt with some of these issues as the internet was emerging centre stage in discussions about the 'information society' and suggested 'those who envisage a dramatic but asocial information technology revolution and/or radical shifts in technical efficiency, are easily persuaded that these *impact* in such a manner as to bring about an entirely novel form of society' (Webster 1995: 219). With co-author Kevin Robins he returned to these issues and forcefully challenged 'the magical vision of new technologies as the solution to all our social ills – promoting participatory politics, material comfort, improved pedagogy, better communications, restored community, and whatever else you might think of' (Robins and Webster 1999: 5).

Frances Cairncross, who writes for the *Economist* and is the author of *The Death of Distance: How the Communications Revolution Will Change Our Lives* (1997), provides a good example of this tendency to invest wondrous qualities in communication technologies. The opening sentence of her book, in terms of the breathless prose style and the point she makes, echoes the work of numerous other futurist information society writers: 'Describing the electronic miracles of our age in the old fashioned format of ink on wood pulp may strike you as ironic', she asserts, but the response has to be, why ironic? There *is* no alternative format, as she concedes, for a commercial publisher of business books to use, and to speculate on the imminent demise of books (or newspapers and magazines, as others do) because of developments in communications technology is to ignore a range of social, economic and cultural factors which might suggest that rather than ink and wood pulp approaching extinction, the technology of printing will have a certain longevity. Frances Cairncross conveniently lists 30 points which she develops in the course of the book which indicate how the 'death of distance' will shape the future and they demonstrate a perspective on the factors influencing social, political and economic change which is partial, exclusive, elitist and, occasionally, ludicrous (Cairncross 1997: xi–xvi). The communications technologies become almost a panacea for the world's ills so that there will be less need for immigration and emigration (point 23) because 'poor countries with good communication technologies will be able to retain their skilled workers ... they can earn rich-world wages and pay poor-world prices for everyday necessities right at home'. The idea that poor countries have, or will have access to good communication technologies, as a result of economic shifts and structures which have brought about an information society, is one of the myths of globalization. Citing figures from the *UNESCO Statistical Year Book* for 1995, Peter Golding has demonstrated that 'the net consequence of these shifts has been to produce massive global inequities in access to and ownership of communication facilities' and these deficits foreclose 'the communication and democratic potential which information technologies can provide' (Golding 1998a: 78).

Point 28 on the Frances Cairncross list is 'Improved Writing and Reading Skills. Electronic mail will induce young people to express themselves effectively in writing and to admire clear and lively written prose. Dull or muddled communicators will fall by the information wayside.' This is the most breathtaking assertion because it is the sort of statement politicians seize on to assert that everything wrong with education can be fixed by technology. It also ignores a whole range of social and economic factors which have a more direct impact on the educational attainments of children. From experiences in the United States Clifford Stoll reaches much more cautious conclusions about the use of computer networks and the internet in schools: 'They isolate us from one another and cheapen the meaning of actual experience. They work against literacy and creativity. They will undercut our schools and libraries' (Stoll 1995: 3). In an important essay, *The Computer Delusion* (1997), Todd Oppenheimer analysed the enthusiasm of the Clinton Administration for the goal of computers in every classroom (an enthusiasm duplicated in the United Kingdom by the Labour government elected in May 1997) and concluded that it would be better to free the billions of dollars the administration wants to devote to technology and

> make it available for impoverished fundamentals: teaching solid skills in reading, thinking, listening and talking; organizing inventive field trips and other rich hands-on experiences; and, of course, building up the nation's core of knowledgeable, inspiring teachers. These notions are less glamorous than computers are, but their worth is firmly proved through a long history. (Oppenheimer 1997: 62; see also the chapter by Lax in this volume)

The basic critical point about the approach typified in *The Death of Distance* is that it ignores the reality of political and corporate frameworks which are shaping the development of the internet and the information superhighway. We are witnessing, most dramatically in the United States, but also across the industrialized world, a spate of mergers between media, computing and telecommunications companies which indicate that hard-headed business pressures, rather than concerns about education and open global communication, are driving these mergers forward. Frances Cairncross dismisses the irrelevance of size, and suggests (point 14) that small companies will spring up and 'in industries where networks matter, concentration may increase, but often in the form of loose global associations under a banner of brands or quality guarantees.' This viewpoint ignores the clear and powerful trend of cross-media concentration, which extends to the internet and the information superhighway, just a surely as other areas of the media and communications industries.

Media ownership: old issues in new contexts

United States

> Today our world is being remade yet again by an information revolution ... But this revolution has been held back by outdated laws, designed for the time when there was only one phone company, three TV networks, no such thing as a personal computer. Today, with one stroke of a pen, our laws will catch up with our future. We

will help to create an open market place where competition and innovation can move as quick as light. (President Clinton, 8 February
1996. Speech in the Library of Congress on the signing of the
Telecommunications Act)

Governments have legislated and regulated to limit media ownership
in the recent past. The democratic argument was simple: the role of
government was to ensure diversity of voices and to prevent the excessive concentration of media power in the hands of powerful individuals or corporations. In the United States, if a media company owned
TV stations in a city they were precluded from owning newspapers covering that area, and cable companies were established originally to
provide an alternative to the three powerful TV networks – CBS, ABC
and NBC. Clear ownership restrictions also spun off from AT&T, under
anti-trust laws, the 'Baby Bells' which carried the local rather than
long-distance calls.

However, the 1996 Telecommunications Act was to inaugurate irrev-
ocable changes. After intense lobbying, the communications corporations achieved a piece of legislation which permitted a massive wave of
corporate consolidation. The Act removed all numerical limits on television and radio station ownership, and lifted the ban on mergers
between telephone and cable companies. Proponents of the Act
deployed the notion of convergence and the arrival of digital technology to secure the legislative change. The media and telecommunications companies had a powerful lobbying presence in Congress (indeed
there is some evidence that they had a hand in drafting key sections of
the legislation) and argued that deregulation, through the elimination
of barriers to firms moving into other communications areas, would
lead to genuine market competition, and the consumer would get a
better deal through improved services and lower prices. Robert
McChesney has been critical about 'the undemocratic and corrupt
manner in which the core laws and codes regulating communication,
most notably the Telecommunications Act, have been enacted' and
demonstrated how the clear beneficiaries of these changes are the giant
media companies (McChesney 1999: 15).

Changes in the media industry were not, of course, inaugurated
solely because of the 1996 Act. The media industry had been going
through a period of enormous change as a result of deregulation in the
Reagan era. A sense of the scale of the changes can be conveyed by
comparisons over a couple of decades. Ben Bagdikian wrote the first
edition of *The Media Monopoly* in 1983; at the time, the biggest merger

in history was the $340 million purchase by the newspaper company Gannett of Combined Communication Corporation, an owner of broadcast stations, billboards and newspapers. By the time of the fifth edition in 1997 when Disney merged with ABC/Cap Cities, it was a $19 billion deal and, as Bagdikian pointed out,

> This union produced a conglomerate that is powerful in every major mass medium: newspapers, magazines, books, radio, broadcast television, cable systems and programming, movies, recordings, video cassettes, and, through alliances and joint ventures, growing control of the golden wires into the American home – telephone and cable. (Bagdikian 1997: xiii)

In September 1999 the business press strained for the words to describe the scale of a $38 billion merger between Viacom and CBS ('media behemoth', 'juggernaut', 'titan'), but there was no doubt about the near-unanimous endorsement for the merger – it made business sense. The *Economist* commented,

> The merger of Viacom and CBS is part of a five-year long restructuring of the industry, involving all the world's big media companies. They are turning into outfits that produce content and distribute it through as many channels as possible. So 'Rugrats', Viacom's gang of babies with attitude, started life as a cartoon on its Nickelodeon cable channel, has been turned into a film (made by Paramount, Viacom's Hollywood studio), a book (published by Simon & Schuster, Viacom's publisher) and a Web site, and has been sold on chocolates, pyjamas and God-knows-what through Viacom's merchandising arm. These revenue streams make money and also promote the 'Rugrats' brand. (*Economist* 1999: 83)

The same article also pointed to the advertising statistics – $5.5 billion in national television advertising revenue, young audiences on MTV and Nickelodeon complemented by CBS's older audience profile, and CBS's extensive radio and billboard businesses – and concluded, 'No media company's advertising salesmen will be able to offer their customers a wider choice.' The American trade magazine *Variety* also observed that the new giant will have 'a formidable online presence' as both companies have 'expressed interest in spinning out their Internet businesses into separate publicly traded companies' (*Guardian/Editor* 1999: 13).

Some commentators pointed out the fact that the merger was a piece of corporate irony because Viacom as a company was born out of the forced disposal of CBS's distribution businesses thirty years ago to comply with federal rules barring TV networks from owning their own programming. The merger was also seen as an insurance policy as tele-convergence has meant that companies like AT&T and Microsoft wanted to acquire more content to put over their own distribution networks.

The relentless growth of AT&T dramatically illustrates the concept of teleconvergence, and the strategy of dominating the delivery of tele-phony, cable and internet services the 'last mile' into the home. In 1998 AT&T paid $48 billion for Tele-Communications Inc (TCI), America's second largest cable operator, and in May 1999 $62.5 billion for MediaOne so that the company now owns, wholly or partially, more than half of America's cable industry. It also means that AT&T has interests in two high-speed internet service providers (ISPs) – @Home through its purchase of TCI, and Roadrunner, owned mainly by MediaOne and Time Warner. Microsoft paid $5 billion to have a 5 per cent stake in AT&T, and part of the deal is that AT&T will use Microsoft to offer customers e-mail and internet access. AT&T will promote its own services, at the same time charging customers extra for services by other ISPs such as America Online (AOL). This clear attempt by AT&T to block open access flies in the face of industry claims that the 1996 Act would encourage market competition and give the consumer a better deal. The Center for Media Education (CME), a US media pressure group, has challenged this development by AT&T, and argued its case with the chair of the Federal Communications Commission (FCC), William Kennard. The CME states that AT&T is developing sophisticated network controls which discriminate against unaffiliated content so that 'the Internet is being fundamentally reconfigured to serve the cable industry's monopoly business model' and argued that unless the development is challenged it will allow the cable industry to continue its 'well documented history of thwarting competition, program access, and innovation' (CME 1999).

United Kingdom

The effects of the shocks of huge media mergers in the United States are felt in the United Kingdom in two ways. Firstly, it provides a spur to UK media owners to grow bigger, because they appear tiny and vul-nerable in comparison to the power of the top global media owners like Time Warner, News Corporation and Viacom. An insistent lobby by commercial broadcasters urges the government to change the media ownership rules laid down in the 1996 Broadcasting Act, and allow the various regional franchises to merge into a single company. At the same time these commercial broadcasters fire a continuous stream of flak at the public service broadcaster, the BBC, as it develops digital and online services. The commercial broadcasters, including Rupert Murdoch's News International, which has powerful newspaper interests and a dominant (40 per cent) stake in the satellite subscription service, BSkyB, argue that the licence fee which funds the BBC creates an unfair distortion and advantage for the public service broadcaster, whereas commercial broadcasters have to pay for and provide programmes without such financial support. Of course, it makes commercial sense to lobby to limit and contain the activities of the BBC; to the extent that this happens, commercial activities have greater opportunities to expand.

A dramatic example, certainly in terms of UK comparisons, of the push for greater size was the announcement in November 1999 of the planned £8 billion merger of the media groups Carlton and United News and Media. This will give the group control of all the southern and central English ITV franchises (with the exception of the London weekend franchise, LWT, which is owned by Granada), a 29 per cent stake in Channel 5, a 20 per cent stake in the morning television franchise GMTV and a 40 per cent stake in the television news service, ITN, providing news to the ITV franchises, Channel 4 and Channel 5. In addition, the group has a 50 per cent stake in the digital TV company, ONdigital, which it jointly owns with Granada, and owns Express Newspapers, Miller Freeman and the NOP research agency. The merged group, which has a stake in the internet service Line One, is also keen to develop this area of commercial activity.

Whilst the other dominant ITV group, Granada, and BSkyB were critical of the merger because it either thwarted or threatened their own development plans, the interesting aspect was the fact that Chris Smith, the Culture Secretary, whose portfolio includes media, made no direct comment on this merger. Indeed, one report quoted sources close to Chris Smith confirming that, 'He has grown increasingly convinced over the past 18 months that radical consolidation of the ITV sector ... was not only inevitable, but desirable' and cited three reasons: greater size would encourage broadcasters to innovate and invest in programme production, and help television programme exports; mergers would begin to create the scale to compete with rival

European and American media giants; and in terms of the switch to digital, and noting the 70 per cent of British homes who have resisted subscribing to multi-channel television, only a stronger ITV in terms of finance and programming would ensure the success of ONdigital (*Independent* 1999). It seems likely therefore that around 2002 the United Kingdom will see its version of the US 1996 Telecommunications Act, with looser ownership limits, the encouragement of convergence, and streamlining of regulatory authorities covering the different telecommunications and broadcast media.

The second impact of the changes in media ownership in the United States is very directly shown in the narrowing ownership base of the UK cable industry. The planned acquisition of the domestic cable franchises of Cable and Wireless Communications (CWC) by NTL means that only two, American-owned, cable companies will dominate the UK cable industry, and they will have a major impact on the way their subscribers receive programming and a range of other digital services, including access to the internet. The second largest cable company, Telewest, merged with Flextech, which owns channels such as UK Gold, UK Living and Bravo. This example of vertical integration – putting both the content and distribution of the cable channels under the control of the same company – mirrors the pattern of acquisitions which have driven ownership changes in the US. For example, John Malone, the former chief executive of TCI, which merged with AT&T, has a 36 per cent stake in Flextech and a 24 per cent stake in Telewest, and controls Liberty Media in the US. Microsoft also has a 29.9 per cent stake in Telewest, as well as shares worth over £300 million in NTL. If this complex pattern of different ownership stakes in cable seems complicated, the overall picture is strikingly clear: three or four powerful corporations will dominate the global cable and telecommunications industries, and the commercial incorporation of the internet within the aegis of their operations is a strategic priority. The sheer scale and global reach of these companies also raises the important questions: to whom are they accountable?, and how are they regulated?

Cyberspace for sale

The development of the internet in the 1990s, and particularly both the privatization and commercialization of the medium, stand in sharp contrast to the ideas of those university scientists had who originally designed the architecture of the internet. They wanted cyberspace to be a non-commercial, egalitarian preserve. The internet was a development within the public sector, and closely associated with the defence industry, but many observers have pointed out that it could never have been produced by the private sector because 'not only would the long term wait for a payoff have been unacceptable but the open architecture would have made no sense for a capitalist to pursue, since it makes "ownership" of the Internet and profitability much more difficult' (McChesney 1999: 129).

The privatization of the internet's infrastructure, because the net is not a single structure, has been a subtle, unpublicized, even secret process. An invitation-only meeting in 1990 at Harvard University, attended by government officials and representatives of the largest telecommunications and computer firms, first recommended the government should move to privatize the internet. The conference summary report acknowledged that private control of the internet would change the nature of the system, moving it away from public service, with private vendors most interested in providing services to affluent consumers and businesses, but it still recommended privatization. Brian Winston has argued cogently that,

> From the late 80s on, and despite the illusion of independence which had surrounded the enterprise almost from the outset, it was inevitable that this tax-funded and government-managed asset would be handed over to the private sector. ... [In 1995 the US National Science Foundation (NSF)] handed over the backbone and management of the system over to the private telecommunications giants, Sprint, Ameritech and Pacific Bell which became the gatekeepers of the principal access points. Those who seriously believed they were in a brave new world of free and democratic communications were simply ignoring the reality of the situation. (Winston 1998: 333)

The question of who should lay down the operating rules for a privatized internet is also controversial when it comes to consideration of the management of the infrastructure of Web names and address. Network Solutions Inc, NSI, controls the registration of the popular domain name suffixes – .com for commercial organizations, .org for non-profit organizations, and so on. There is no effective system of domain names resolution, so when one company claims that another has violated its trademark or copyright, the system simply defers to US law, which favours US companies. In July 1997 the White House released a report, *A Framework for Global Electronic Commerce*, outlining 'the principles which will guide the US Government's actions as we move forward into the new electronic age of commerce' and explicitly endorsing the commercial exploitation of the internet: 'If we establish an environment in which electronic commerce can grow and flourish, then every computer can be a window open to every business, large and small, everywhere in the world' (White House 1997). The perception of many observers is that the US wants to skew the system's operation towards its interests, in a new variant of imperialism:

> The US claims, in effect, that as it invented the internet (and has 80m of its 120m users) it should be allowed to lay down its operating standards. Many important people in the US are convinced that the internet represents the future of world commerce, and they intend to exploit their competitive advantage ruthlessly. (Bracken 1998: 18)

Eliminating public interest issues

One of the clearest messages from the US Vice-President Al Gore in the months after he proclaimed his vision of the 'National Information Infrastructure' (NII) came when he outlined his key policy objectives at a 'Superhighway Summit' in Los Angeles in January 1994. He proposed legislation to encourage private industry to build the NII by establishing attractive investment opportunities and increased competition and developing a 'more productive relationship based on consensus'. Government, he stressed, would have the responsibility to protect less fortunate and weaker segments of society by guaranteeing a 'universal service' to all sectors of the population.

The proposed legislative package was based on five principles: to encourage private investment; to provide and protect competition; to provide open access to the network; to take action to avoid creating a society of information 'haves' and 'have nots'; and to encourage flexible and responsive government action. The proposals failed, falling victim to political and corporate objections, and whilst broadband communication services began to develop, they were scattered and many of the programmes commercially driven, targeted at finding new revenue and customers rather than serving the public interest (McQuaide 1994/95: 20). One of the reasons for the lack of progress was the mid-term elections of November 1994 – the Republicans were unwilling to give the Clinton Administration any accomplishments which could help the Democratic cause. As it was, the elections dramatically altered the political balance. For the first time since 1954 both houses of Congress came under the control of the Republican Party, and it was in this changed political climate that the 1996 Telecommunications Act was agreed. It stands as a stark example of the way media policy on this key technology, with its interactive decentralized structure, was developed not through public debate, and consideration of public access and social issues, but rather through the involvement of commercial and pro-commercial lobbyists formulating policy in a closed, anti-democratic manner. Sadly, too, any of the public interest aspects which Gore identified in his earlier vision of the NII, such as assuring access to poor and working-class citizens, have been swept aside by rampant commercial internet development. Indeed the Clinton Administration is now an enthusiastic supporter of the emerging electronic market-place, aggressively promoting the commercialization of cyberspace.

Of course, this is not a uniquely American phenomenon. The European Union set up a working group comprising the élite of the European electronics and computing industries, including Siemens, Olivetti and Philips. Chaired by the European Commissioner for Information Technology and Telecommunications, Martin Bangemann, this group produced a report which echoed the US approach – advocating the liberalization of the telecommunications market and moves to allow the private sector free rein to develop the information society. A 1998 Green Paper, *Regulating Communications*, was intent on getting Europe out of the 'slow lane' of the information superhighway, and saw regulation as a barrier to market entry, rather than a framework for supporting public interest objectives like access, public service requirements, or ethical and quality standards (Herman 1998: 4–7).

Information superhighway or information supermarket?

We look at Web sites as eyeball aggregators, trying to bring people in and give them an experience. The aim is to bring in the right people in a very detailed demographic niche. (Jonathan Nelson, CEO of Web site specialists Organic Online)

The future may become a wonderland of opportunity only for the minority among us who are affluent, mobile, and highly educated. And it may at the same time, become a digital dark age for the majority of citizens – the poor, the non-college educated, and the so-called unnecessary.(David Kline, *Hotwired*)

The debate about whether the information superhighway and the internet lead us down the road to greater freedom to communicate and express ideas, or whether the dominant function and purpose is to be an extremely cheap and effective means for global corporate brands to promote themselves, has changed sharply in a relatively short space of time. In part, this is explained by social and economic factors. The internet is not 'free' in the sense that access to it requires a reasonably state-of-the-art computer, a phone line and a modem, the online costs of use and the need for further outlay on maintenance and upgrades. The costs of setting such a system up would be beyond many low-income families in both the US and the UK – food, heat and clothing would all be higher budget priorities. In addition, economic and taxation policies pursued by governments have widened the gap between rich and poor over the past two decades so that the digital divide between the information-rich and information-poor increasingly mirrors an economic divide. Figures for UK family expenditure in 2000 show internet access at 3 per cent amongst the poorest tenth of households, and 48 per cent amongst the richest tenth (Kelso and Adams 2000).

The current and future development of the internet, and the priorities which the media and telecommunications companies have established, also conflict with the hopes and ideals which many invested in it. A few examples illustrate the point. In March 1996 the CME published *Web of Deception: Threats to Children from Online Marketing*, a well-researched report into the techniques used to collect data and compile individual profiles on children. It identified advertising practices where advertising and content were 'seamlessly interwoven in new online "infomercials" for children'. It also cited the way advertising agencies like Saatchi and Saatchi were setting up special units to study children online and develop sophisticated marketing strategies to target them (CME 1996).

When Microsoft pressured computer manufacturers into bundling its Internet Explorer browser with its Windows operating system, and to use it instead of the Netscape Navigator, the result was that Netscape's Navigator dramatically lost market share – falling from more than 80 per cent to less than 50 per cent. Whilst Microsoft was being battered in the Justice Department's anti-trust suit by weeks of damaging testimony about its market power and anti-competitive behaviour, in November 1998 America Online announced it was buying Netscape. It was another example of how the high hopes for independence and competition in the Net arena were being rapidly dissipated. One US commentator pointed out,

The deal certainly confirms a trend in recent months towards consolidation among internet businesses. Successful companies, particularly portal sites that act as gateways to the Net, are 'partnering' with media monoliths like Disney and General/Electric/NBC or are buying one another. All of which may be wholly unsurprising given the broader prevalence of megamergers these days. But are we already resigned to accepting that much of this promising new market, still less than five years old, will be as concentrated and conglomeratized as the rest of the media and communications industry? (Shapiro 1998: 3–4)

Finally, there is the change in the character of the World Wide Web, with the irresistible rise of commercial sites. A January 1996 survey by Network Wizards showed that of 9.4 million host computers connected to the internet '.com' was easily the single largest domain, larger than academic (.edu) and government (.gov) sources combined (quoted in Golding 1998b: 138).

Some conclusions

The perspective and analysis at the heart of this chapter could be criticized for falling into its own kind of determinism. There is the suggestion of an 'iron law' for the development of communication technologies which invests them in the early stage with liberating and democratic qualities, only to see them fall prey to commercialization, access or exclusion based on wealth, and the content of the communications systems determined by marketing criteria to assure lucrative revenue streams. Indeed, one of the key ideas promoting the digital diversity of the multi-channel age is that the viewer is in control, and exercising real choice based on a plenitude of branded channels. However, this view is based on a conception of broadcasting which seeks to attract viewers by securing the rights to sports, films and other content, and persuading the viewer to subscribe to a range of different tiers of programming.

Are we seeing the realization of one of the predictions made by the late cultural critic, Raymond Williams? In *Television: Technology and Cultural Form* (1974) he suggested that:

Under the cover of talk about choice and competition, a few paranational corporations, with their attendant states and agencies, could reach further into our lives, at every level from news to psycho-drama, until individual and collective response to many different kinds of experience and problems became almost limited to choice between programmed possibilities. (Williams 1974: 162)

Two examples provide supporting evidence that we are. In 1999, the *Observer* reported on a company, Future TV, 'which will soon launch a device that monitors what you watch, learns from this, and records programmes which it thinks you will like'. A pamphlet, *Spy TV*, also highlights the unwarranted and unsuspected surveillance to which users of digital television can be subjected. Digital television will bring a huge extension of centralized power into the home, the pamphlet argues, because the profile that is built up of the hours people spend watching television, or the pattern of purchasers using the interactive service Open, can then be sold to and used by advertisers to target particular viewer interests.

What is important, in the face of such seemingly overwhelming powers, is to insist on a different pattern of broadcasting provision and regulation. The huge media corporations invest enormous amounts of time and money to influence politicians and regulatory bodies, and there needs to be an alternative, countervailing force which argues for a different set of priorities to shape media policy, ones based on supporting access, diversity, public service broadcasting, and limiting media concentration. These will have to be argued and campaigned for vigorously and the internet will be one important means of spreading the message, but in the end it will require a powerful, media reform movement of people and organizations to make it happen.

Postscript

This chapter was completed in the weeks before the announcement of the merger between the internet service provider AOL and the US media conglomerate Time Warner on 10 January 2000. The merger, an all-stock transition, involved a $190 billion takeover of Time Warner by AOL, and was greeted with euphoria in the media. From the point of view of the arguments developed in this chapter, however, it is a further dramatic illustration of the speed and scale of the commercialization of the internet.

A report in the *Washington Post* suggested that, 'By spreading its tentacles into content and taking on the Time brand name, AOL will likely be able to expand its global reach' (Dugan and Cha 2000). The director of corporate communications for AOL Europe, Matt Peacock, makes a similar point: 'AOL is a mass market product, the global brand for consumers' (quoted in McIntosh 2000). Clearly, the commercial logic of the deal is impeccable: AOL has access to the massive content resources of the Time publishing empire and the film, music and television of CNN, Warner Bros., Time Warner Cable, and much more, whilst Time Warner gets access to the world's largest online and e-commerce platform.

However, the news of the merger was not universally popular. Bulletin boards on the Web were crammed with complaints from internet users who saw the deal as a blow to the Web's freedom from US corporate dominance. This, as I have argued, is a belated recognition of an aspect of the internet's development which was well under way before the media gave prominence to the latest, and most dramatic, confirmation of the trend.

References

Bagdikian, B. (1997) *The Media Monopoly*, fifth edition. Boston: Beacon Press.
Bracken, M. (1998) 'The Web Wars', *Prospect*, May.
Cairncross, F. (1997) *The Death of Distance: How the Communications Revolution Will Change Our Lives*. London: Orion.
CME (1996) *Web of Deception: Threats to Children from Online Marketing*. http://www.cme.org/children/marketing/deception.pdf. Accessed 19 July 2000.
CME (1999) 'Letter to William Kennard, 29 July 1999', http://www.cme.org/press/Kennard.html. Accessed 19 July 2000.
Cohen, N. (1999) *Cruel Britannia*. London: Verso.
Davis, Susan G. (1999) 'Media conglomerates build the entertainment city', *European Journal of Communication*, 14(1) 435–59.
Dugan, J.I. and Cha, A.E. (2000) 'AOL to acquire Time Warner', *Washington Post*, 11 January.
Economist (1999) 'Two sharks in a fishbowl', 11 September.
Friedland, L.A. (1996) 'Electronic democracy and the new citizenship', *Media, Culture and Society*, 18(2) 185–212.
Golding, P. (1998a) 'Global village or cultural pillage', in R.W. McChesney, E.M. Wood, and J.B. Foster, (eds), *Capitalism and the Information Age*. New York: Monthly Review Press.
Golding, P. (1998b) 'Worldwide wedge: division and contradiction in the global information infrastructure', in D.K. Thussu (ed.), *Electronic Empires: Global Media and Local Resistance*. London: Arnold.
Guardian/Editor (1999) 'Viacom and CBS create a media juggernaut.' 10 September.
Herman, E. and McChesney, R.W. (1997) *The Global Media: the New Missionaries of Corporate Capitalism*. London: Cassell.
Herman, G. (1998) 'Not as green as it's pear-shaped', *Free Press*, no. 103, March–April.

Independent (1999) 'Obstacles multiply for the £8bn media giant merger', 2 December.

Innis, H. (1972) *Empires and Communications*. Toronto: University of Toronto Press. (Originally published in 1960 by Clarendon Press, Oxford.)

Katz, J. (1997) 'The netizen: birth of a digital nation', *Wired*, April 1997: 49.

Kelso, Paul and Adams, Guy (2000) 'As one in four homes go online, the country's digital divide widens', *Guardian*, 11 July, p. 3.

McChesney, R.W. (1999) *Rich Media, Poor Democracy: Communication Politics in Dubious Times*. Urbana and Chicago: University of Illinois Press.

McIntosh, N. (2000) 'Why geeks hate AOL', *Guardian* (G2), 12 January.

McQuaide, T (1994/95) 'The USA's information superstructure falls to the Republicans and the corporate players', *Intermedia*, December/January 1994/95: 20–3.

Observer Business (1999) Article by J. Doward, 'First Hull, then the world', 19 December.

Oppenheimer, T. (1997) 'The computer delusion', *The Atlantic Monthly*, 280(1): 45–62.

Robins, K. and Webster, F. (1999) *Times of the Technoculture*. London: Routledge.

Schiller, H. (1969) *Mass Communications and American Empire*. Chicago: Augustus M. Kelley.

Shapiro, A.L. (1998) 'aol.mergergame.com', editorial, *The Nation*, 21 December.

Stoll, C. (1995) *Silicon Snake Oil: Second Thoughts on the Information Superhighway*. London: Pan.

Webster, F. (1995) *Theories of the Information Society*. London: Routledge.

White House (1997) *A Framework for Global Electronic Commerce*. http://www.iitf. nist.gov/eleccomm/ecomm.htm. Accessed 19 July 2000.

Williams, R. *Television: Technology and Cultural Form*. London: Fontana.

Winston, B. (1998) *Media Technology and Society: a History from the Telegraph to the Internet*. London: Routledge.

11
From Crystal Palaces to Silicon Valleys: Market Imperfection and the Enduring Digital Divide

Anthony Wilhelm

Notwithstanding the current business expansion in the USA, it is unclear on the whole how many Americans, including racial and ethnic minorities, have benefited from the strongest economy in 30 years. While some argue that the working poor have gained from a tight labour market, the middle class is no better off than it was at the peak of the last business cycle (Bernstein et al. 1999). One of the problems is that income inequality endures and indigence remains unabated, as the bulk of wealth expansion occurs across a small segment of the population. Another complication is that despite being lauded as the democratic equalizer, new information and communication technologies (ICTs) gravitate toward the catchment of existing economic power, either bypassing or merely trickling through low-income and minority communities (Wolpert 1999). These inequalities affect both households and whole communities, the former in their ability to purchase and use high-speed internet services and the latter in their capacity to own and control media enterprises.

To give just one example of household gaps in communications technology access, telephone penetration on tribal lands in the Western United States is comparable to computer ownership rates for society as a whole and internet connectivity for households earning above $75 000.[1] Technology stratification reinforces socioeconomic inequalities as well as racial and topographical segregation (Castells 1999). According to December 1998 census data, the gap in home internet access separating ethnic and racial minorities from Whites has actually *grown* in recent years as Native Americans, African Americans and Hispanics have been unable to keep pace with Whites in owning certain online services. What is more, the entry costs are so high to purchase mature media facilities, such as broadcasting stations, that many minority entrepreneurs have staked their claim in new media ventures. Yet even the new media are quickly consolidating and integrating into a generalized broadband infrastructure, with the strategic aim of cross-promoting commercial content to captive audiences (Schiller 1999). These realities pose formidable obstacles to a diversity of ownership and control of telecommunications and new media ventures (Garmer 1998).

Although some communities and strata of society have remained immune to the fortune of surging economic times, we are rapidly becoming dependent solely on the market for solutions to the most intractable of problems and dire of needs. Under the most optimistic of what I am calling *market-exclusive scenarios* – that is, initiatives that depend almost exclusively on market models for success – questions remain regarding the effects of markets on communities with significant human- and social-capital deficits. For example, conservative politicians have put forward school vouchers as an effective avenue for bridging the digital divide, by offering parents the choice to send their children elsewhere rather than investing in salvaging many inner-city schools (Ostrom 1999). With such an exclusive reliance on market solutions and individual choice to mitigate information and technology poverty, even the most modest of public investment and new grant programmes are viewed with suspicion, as the last bastion of 'big government'. For example, one of the Federal government's grant programmes, the Department of Commerce's Telecommunications and Information Infrastructure Assistance Program (TIIAP), has been the subject of political wrangling, despite compelling evidence of its success. An evaluation report from the research firm Westat (1999) documents early grant recipients' success in achieving their implementation goals, such as expanding technology access, establishing community-service networks, and fostering increased collaboration among stakeholders. Despite compelling empirical support underwriting its effectiveness, the programme was budgeted at its lowest level in 2000, $15 million. In the larger scale of a $1.4 trillion dollar Federal budget, this important flagship programme costs the American taxpayer as much as one AH-64 Apache attack helicopter or just over the price of one cruise missile! TIIAP's opponents argue that the programme preempts the development of new markets, a claim that puts poor communities at the mercy of future business ventures to spur investment and innovation.

It is in this unstable environment – in which a flawed market and tepid public investment evade redistributive issues – that deep-seated inequalities and social exclusion are addressed. The latest perspective on inequality and marginalization in a technological society has taken on the label of the 'digital divide'. Described most explicitly as the gap in access to computers and the internet separating various groups in American society, the digital divide can also be theorized in more panoramic terms as the economic and technological forces activating and exacerbating dangerous social fault lines (Wilhelm 2000). These forces hamstring the information and communications underclass, preventing its full participation in the life of the larger community. This chapter will proceed in three sections. The first part explores a new way of thinking about overcoming the digital divide – as the striving for persons to obtain the necessary capabilities to function well in a democratic society. Using the work of Amartya Sen, I argue that technology *development* in the USA is now part and parcel of a larger story about what instrumental means are necessary to participate fully in the life of the community. The second section will explore how market-exclusive solutions now being offered will likely fall short of meeting the needs of the hardest-to-serve communities. I will provide several examples to highlight an alternative, cross-sector mode of addressing the digital divide, one that entails strategic investment in poor communities on the part of non-profit organizations, private foundations, governments and industry. In the third section, I will highlight several policy remedies that take us beyond sole reliance on the market to ensure that persons attain the basic capabilities to achieve their desired ends.

Information technology as essential capability

Amartya Sen (1999) suggests that the primary indicator of quality of life or substantive freedom in a society is the extent to which residents have achieved the capabilities or all-purpose means to participate cooperatively in the life of the community. Rather than looking at development in purely economic terms – for example, as increase in gross domestic product or median family income – Sen suggests that economic facilities are necessary but not sufficient. His more comprehensive approach includes other instrumental freedoms that tend to contribute to the general capability of a person to live more freely, including political freedoms, social opportunities and protective security. Protective securities would include poverty relief and unemployment benefits, while social opportunities refer to such primary goods as universal education and health services. The summation of these instrumental freedoms contributes to the general capability of a person to participate adequately in the life of the larger community. Thinking about capacity in this way encompasses an exploration of what instrumental means are necessary, beyond income, to achieve human freedom. This reckoning will undoubtedly be relative, as basic capabilities in Bangladesh or Benin will be different from those in the USA, both in level and scope (Sen 1999: 89f.).[2] Within a country, moreover, there is uneven community development, in relative human-capital and infrastructure development, what Manuel Castells (1999) has referred to as 'sociospatial segregation'. Addressing these egregious inequalities should involve a conversation about what all-purpose means are necessary to ensure that all persons can achieve their life goals.

One arena where the development gap is yawning in the USA is in unequal access to educational opportunities across communities. In recent years, parents, concerned citizens and advocates have appealed to courts in a slew of states in order to demand fiscal parity and educational 'adequacy' – such as better school facilities, expansion of early childhood programmes, and salary increases to attract and retain high-quality teachers (Gittell 1998). Funded largely by local property taxes, the educational system is severely unequal and places low-income and rural students without a viable opportunity to participate fully in the life of the larger community. Now that internet use in schools is becoming such a magnet for students, the conversation about what facilities are 'adequate' to achieve educational equity and true opportunity is beginning to envelop educational technology issues.

Sen argues that in advanced countries, residents may need access to what in other nations might seem like a luxury, such as internet connections. As the nation with the highest internet connection rates, since the early 1990s American public- and private-sector leaders have made the argument that advanced ICTs are key to one's success in a global information society. The best illustration of this reality in Federal policy-making is the 1996 extension of the universal service policy providing discounted telecommunications services to schools and to libraries, a programme called the e-rate. With this policy firmly in place, America has affirmed the need for advanced telecommunications services as key to success in an advanced, technology-dependent society.

While Sen is right to assume that information technology is a priority to achieve quality of life in advanced countries, his analysis does underplay the value of such investment in the developing world. In Costa Rica, for example, the entire nation is now networked to the last mile with fibre-optic technology, an infrastructure development plan that was fully integrated into and consonant with the nation's human development, economic and environmental goals (Figueres 1999). With its aggressive goal of providing all children access to e-mail by 2001 and in attracting high-technology investment in biotechnology as well as information services and computing, this tiny nation has catapulted itself into the forefront of the information society. Other examples of technology development in Brazil and Bangladesh suggest the potential of these information and communications tools to address other capacity needs, such as economic well-being and educational opportunity.

Since information and communications technologies are becoming so prevalent, a 'network effect' is occurring that has two related effects. First, the use of the internet for e-commerce, distance education and social interaction has become such a boon to the lives of many US residents that it is quickly becoming an acute penalty not to have access. Not having access to the internet, for example, may soon be as pernicious as not having access to transportation or educational opportunity. Related, some services may soon be available only on the Web,[3] which raises the stakes for society as a whole in providing the incentives and infrastructure to attract whole communities to embrace the internet.

The clear and present need for online services has led a variety of policy-makers and industry leaders to suggest that access to the internet may be becoming, almost imperceptibly, a matter of entitlement. While this term is unpopular today in a conservative political climate (particularly bestowing new entitlements on specific classes of residents), the notion that the provision of certain services ought to be guaranteed once they become essential to civic and social life is quite familiar to democratic politics. In a 1995 speech at the opening ceremony of the Seventh World Telecommunications Forum and Exhibition, the former South African president, Nelson Mandela, stated that 'in the 21st century, the capacity to communicate will almost certainly be a key human right'. This sentiment is echoed among senior Federal-level policy-makers, such as former Assistant Secretary of Commerce, Larry Irving, who attested in July 1999 that the digital divide is 'now one of America's leading economic and civil rights issues' (US Department of Commerce 1999: xiii). The cause has even been taken up by industry leaders, such as America Online's CEO, Steve Case. In a speech he gave in May 1999 at the Leadership Conference on Civil Rights policy conference, Case stated that there was merit in viewing access to the internet as a key civil rights issue in the coming years.[4]

Above all, these proclamations support an underlying normative framework in which the internet is perceived as an important instrumental means in society to achieve a certain political conception of the capabilities that persons must possess in order to have a chance to fulfill their rational life plans. At least in the USA, computer facility and internet accessibility are indicators of a conception of development that is steadily gaining currency. To suggest that an internet connection is as necessary as possessing a telephone ratchets up society's interest in establishing the conditions in which such technology is available in the hardest-to-serve communities. Whether the democratic and comprehensive plan of embedding digital divide solutions in a larger context of human and community development will win the day depends on whether policy-makers see beyond market-exclusive solutions to address chronic problems of poverty, social exclusion and underdevelopment.

The market-exclusive framework

The wealth creation and entrepreneurial buzz surrounding the Seattle/Puget Sound community exports a philosophy in which the full potential of high-technology markets has yet to be unleashed to solve pressing social problems. Home to the world's largest corporation, largest private foundation, and, along with Silicon Valley, most active coterie of internet venture capitalists, Seattle is poised at the nexus of world trade and high-technology development, with the research and development budget of Microsoft perhaps larger than that of the whole of the developing world. The attitude and energy typified in Seattle, Silicon Valley, and other high-technology meccas – what I call the 'market-exclusive framework' – personifies a fervent belief that the business potential of the internet is so immense that, if fully realized, it could alleviate social distress, poverty, illiteracy and underdevelopment worldwide. The argument runs that if the proper market-friendly environment is cultivated in societies across the globe, we will witness the mitigation of poverty, illiteracy and disease in this generation, while at the same time making a small class of individuals very wealthy.

Such a vision extends a long legacy of euphoric speculation about the effects of unfettered markets and trade on democratic regimes. At the time of the Great Exhibition of 1851, there was a general sense that the relaxation of tariffs and other barriers to trade would usher in a period of prosperity without end. The construction of the Crystal Palace for the exposition was meant to be an edifice to progress, showcasing the artefacts of international commerce and trade, while displaying the latest conveniences, such as the indoor water closet (Auerbach 1999). Alfred Lord Tennyson wrote a poem to honour the event, called 'Ode Sung at the Opening of the International Exhibition', in which he likened 'growing Commerce' to 'the fair white-wing'd peacemaker' that will bring nations together and outpour the brotherhood of men (Tennyson 1899: 333). The similarities between Tennyson's optimism and the recent euphoric pronouncements about the internet and e-commerce, immersed in the soft glow of international trade and the primacy of markets, reminds us that there is a common thread embedded in Enlightenment thinking during the past two hundred years.[5]

The thrust of the market-exclusive framework is the creation of new markets, particularly at the lower end of the consumer pyramid, where the majority of new business will be generated. As US markets become saturated and the low-hanging fruit is picked, multinational information technology companies look to expand offshore (McChesney 1999). Rather than puzzling over how to serve the last 5 per cent of American households without telephone service, telecommunications companies can find lucrative markets overseas, with millions of new customers eager to access their services. The gap between commerce and democracy is revealed in the information technology sector as the deregulatory, free-market aims of companies pose potential challenges to the democratic, egalitarian values of governments and peoples. With two-thirds of the world's population having yet to make a telephone call, the question remains whether markets alone will begin to deliver these services in abundance. New business models are surfacing to cover the poorest communities, such as the programme Grameen Telecom has instituted in Bangladesh. However, this represents only a trickle, and with financiers demanding such a healthy return on investment, it is unclear what percentage of the world's population will be covered in the foreseeable future.

Market giants have appeased the world's political leaders with the promise of technological advancement and plummeting costs, as regulated by the inexorable Moore's Law. Back in 1965, the founder of Intel Corporation, Gordon Moore, observed that every 18 months we are able to make chips that have twice as many transistors for the same cost. Since there is empirical validity for the truth of Moore's claim, this 'law' has tenaciously captured the imagination of the technology industry. The idea has also spilled into sociology and politics, with the assumptions being no less glorious than Tennyson's pronouncements regarding the Crystal Palace. With one-half of the world's population living on less than $2 a day, will Moore's Law ever deliver these new markets without the strategic intervention of governments, non-profit, and philanthropic institutions?

Articulating the problem of the digital divide in purely market and technology terms ignores the reality of poverty and underdevelopment across the globe – the gap between empirical reality and the normative ideal of the Crystal Palace or Silicon Valley (Derrida 1994). It also side-steps the more holistic and cross-sector solutions that have in the past – and will surely in the future – be key to comprehensive and long-term solutions to the digital divide. I propose an alternative, cross-sector model of collaboration as the necessary corrective to the market-exclusive framework. This cross-sector framework presumes that it will require more than markets for the vast underclass to achieve the threshold level of capacity to participate in a global information society. An advantage of the collaborative approach – assuming groups circulate and share resources, communicate outside of silos, and plug into coordinated, integrated strategies – is that it springs from the unique and diverse experiences of organizations that take as their point of departure local needs, talents, contexts and participation.

The nexus of private and public activity in impoverished communities also presupposes a working knowledge of the varying levels of information poverty. At the bottom of the totem pole are those persons, households and communities that have no concept of telephony and the internet. The next level of disenfranchisement includes persons who say they do not want or need information and communications technology. Finally, many people are eager to participate fully in the larger society, but lack the all-purpose means to operationalize these desires (Wilhelm 2000). Obviously markets will be least responsive to the first of these categories, with poor, rural, and minority communities drawing insufficient attention from enough companies to spark competition for quality, low-cost services. On tribal lands in the USA, for example, there is little economic development and scant telecommunications infrastructure development – due in part to the fact that many companies feel that development of those areas would not generate a sufficient return on their investment.

An alternative, cross-sector approach to building capacity

Implementing a concerted assault on this social problem entails more aggressive strategies on the part of governments, greater strategic investment by private foundations, and expanded hands-on, pragmatic involvement of non-profit organizations. Since there is no 'magic bullet' to resolve the growing digital divide – no one sector or institution can do it all – it is critical to leverage the knowledge and resources across sectors of society in order to address the problem in a coordinated and comprehensive fashion. The notion that markets alone can adequately address deep-seated problems seems wildly out of joint with our experience with poverty alleviation and human-capacity building over the years. Speculations about the limitless potential of new internet business models to address needs hitherto neglected by governments and communities belie the tireless work performed in the public and independent sectors to remedy inequalities wrought by the market. Market-exclusive models also presume that while new markets mature, we ought to defer public investment in the provision of primary goods to our fellow citizens, until such time in the future as we can ascertain where the interests of business and the needs of communities diverge. Restating the problem of information and communications 'haves' and 'have-nots' as one in reality between 'have-nows' and 'have-laters' signifies an unbounded faith in entrepreneurs and technology to deliver a future service to long-neglected communities. While the latest juggernaut takes the form of 'Moore's Law', the sense of earlier nostrums of capitalism, such as Adam Smith's invisible hand, contribute to government inaction on behalf of the poor, forbearing regulation while sheepishly anticipating the ubiquitous deployment of advanced services through the marketplace. Let me examine each sector and the ways in which each is working to resolve the digital divide.

The independent sector – non-profit and philanthropic digital divide efforts

There are at least four distinct roles non-profit and philanthropic organizations are playing to provide more equitable and meaningful technology access in under-served communities. First, non-profits are technology providers. Over the past several years, community technology centres have sprung up around the country, meeting community needs – including the demand for computer training and internet access – in ways not met by existing institutions, such as schools and libraries. Second, non-profit organizations represent information and data nodes, aggregating and facilitating the sharing of information, resources, and 'best practices' across the independent sector, as well as with governments, industry, and the general public. In addition, the independent sector convenes diverse stakeholders, performing an essential role in order to spur connections and spark coordination and integration of efforts across sectors and jurisdictions. Finally, private philanthropy has engaged in smart investments to seed creative applications and to incubate public-interest content on the internet.

Hundreds of community-based organizations have sprouted up in the past few years in order to meet not just technology access needs but also the human-development, social-capital, and social-service needs of community residents. The Community Technology Centers' Network (CTCNet) is an important umbrella organization of over 300 local agencies and programmes that provide access to computers and the internet for peoples of all ages who might otherwise remain outside the information age. Importantly, poor and minority residents are much more likely to use public terminals, located in libraries and community centres, to access the internet. As a recent US Department of Commerce report highlights, 'households with incomes of less than $20 000 and Black households are twice as likely to get Internet access through a public library or community center than are households earning more than $20 000 or White households' (1999: 78).[6]

Non-profit organizations are also providing the data links, information and resources that connect local organizations to the essential tools they need to build their technology capacity. Many organizations, including the National Strategy for Nonprofit Technology Project, the Information Technology Resource Project, and the Benton Foundation, have developed online technology resources for nonprofit groups. The Benton Foundation recently developed a one-stop resource featuring the collective efforts of the non-profit sector on America Online Foundation's e-philanthropy portal, Helping.org. The aim of this service is to provide invaluable information and resources for non-profits, including how to build a Web site, how to get connected, finding online technical assistance, and tips on fund-raising on the internet, as well as publicly available tools and resources for database management.

Another critical role performed by non-profit and philanthropic organizations have played in addressing the digital divide is convening diverse stakeholders so they can meet, network, compare notes, and forge potentially more powerful cross-sector solutions to their problems. In the USA a flurry of conferences and summits on the topic of the digital divide have been convened, in order to promote the sharing of rich experiences and efforts as well as to brainstorm catalytic policy solutions. In October 1999 the Joint Center for Political and Economic

Studies, a non-profit organization in Washington, DC, held a conference called Resolving the Digital Divide, in which leaders from minority groups, nonprofit organizations, policy institutes, academia, industry, and government brainstormed solutions to the digital divide. A set of policy recommendations was to be crafted, to be presented ultimately to the President and to Congress through the channel of the President's Information Technology Advisory Committee (PITAC). In late November 1999, the Technology Alliance in Washington state, in partnership with the Markle Foundation, the Rockefeller Foundation, and the Bill and Melinda Gates Foundation, convened high-level representatives from across sectors to examine the digital divide from an international perspective. Held on the eve of the World Trade Organization meeting, the conference focused on market solutions to the problem – a bent that was resisted by many conference attendees who envisioned a key role for non-profit organizations and governments in attacking these problems.[7]

These conferences are taking place not only on the national and international levels, but also at local and regional levels. In December 1999, to give just one example, the Delaware Community Foundation sponsored a one-day forum on the digital divide in which they invited library, education, government, industry and non-profit leaders from across the small state to share digital divide experiences. During the event, the Delaware Community Foundation announced a grant initiative to spur cross-cutting solutions to broker relationships and to motivate groups to pool their resources and talents.

The common thread woven through all of these conferences, galvanized by nonprofit and philanthropic groups, is the need to partner, collaborate, coordinate existing projects, and share vital information within and across sectors. Of course, the role of foundations is not only to foster collaboration but to strengthen the voice of non-profit organizations and public-interest advocates, who often operate on the fringes of public-policy debates due to limited resources. In 1999 the Ford Foundation funded the Digital Media Forum, a series of meetings and activities of public-interest advocacy organizations and academics, in order to counteract the inordinate power of industry in forming telecommunications policy. In working together rather than alone, these groups can leverage their scarce resources and harness the best progressive academic research to impact important legislative and regulatory decisions.

In another development, private foundations are making strategic investments in research, strengthening the voice of under-served communities, and seeding and incubating innovative online public-service models that address equity and diversity concerns. The Markle Foundation, for example, is leading the way in commissioning research that examines the effects of interactive technology on children's cognitive, emotional, physical and social development. The research, conducted by scholars at the University of Texas at Austin, will be shared with for-profit companies in order to aid the development of interactive products that can improve children's lives. Other foundations, such as Kellogg and Ford, are funding telecommunications policy representation and voice in the Native American community by providing grants to Karen Buller at the National Indian Telecommunications Institute to raise the profile of telecommunications issues among tribal leaders as well as policy-makers.

Finally, foundations are also incubating innovative uses of new communications technology to address the digital divide. The Markle Foundation has provided $35 million to Oxygen Media to improve the quality of internet and cable programming aimed at women. Since many women, particularly single-female householders, find themselves on the wrong side of the digital divide, such an initiative may provide women the relevant content they require to enhance their engagement with the virtual world.

Industry efforts

Virtually all of the major industry players – whether they be telecommunications carriers, computer companies, internet providers or software producers – have made proposals to bridge the digital divide. Some of the companies, particularly the local-exchange carriers and long-distance companies, are required to participate in various universal service programmes, federal and state initiatives to discount the cost of telecommunications connections for poor and rural households, schools and libraries. Many of the larger companies also have foundations in which they address broader human infrastructure and content concerns – examples include AT&T's Learning Network and MCI/WorldCom's Marco Polo project.

Notwithstanding these individual efforts, acrimonious competition has often typified the information technology sector, underscored by the fight between America Online and AT&T over non-discriminatory access to cable customers for independent internet providers. Local-exchange carriers, moreover, have long held that, in the battle for facilities-based competition, cable companies do not experience the same regulatory barriers as local telephone providers, causing competitive asymmetries in the industry. Furthermore, companies have been reticent to share branding on their philanthropic efforts, as evidenced by the duplication in corporate efforts to develop and fund community technology centers, such as AOL's, AT&T's, and Intel's independent efforts. Companies prefer to concentrate on funding efforts in cities in which they have a presence, rather than focusing on coordinating their efforts where needs are the greatest.

In December 1999, information technology companies came together for the first time to commit to share resources and coordinate activities, where appropriate, in the Digital Divide Network. Founded by the Benton Foundation, the Digital Divide Network serves as a catalyst for developing new, innovative digital divide strategies and for making current initiatives more strategic, more partner-based, and more outcome-oriented. The aim is to avoid duplication of effort and to learn from each other's experiences. Companies have partnered to implement these activities, and it remains to be seen how far interest in sharing and collaborating will supersede genuine competitive interests.

Government efforts

Since the mid-1990s the Federal government has placed equitable access to emerging information technology on the front burner of public policy. In 1996 Congress expanded universal service to include discounted telecommunications services for schools and libraries (Benton Foundation 2000), and now the e-rate programme is the largest universal-service programme, larger than the programmes subsidizing telephone connections for low-income and high-cost households. Through grant programmes in the US Departments of Education, Commerce, and Housing and Urban Development, the executive branch has been committed to equalizing access between the rich and poor and to seeding innovative access projects that are fully integrated into education, health-service, and community economic development.

In December 1999 the US Department of Commerce hosted the Digital Divide Summit at which the priorities of the executive branch were made clear. President Clinton issued an executive memorandum, directing several Federal departments to expand the growing network of community technology centres, while at the same time enjoining Commerce Secretary Daley to work with the private sector to develop a national strategy for connecting all Americans to the internet. In addition to these rather sketchy proposals, the President announced another New Markets tour, focused on the digital divide, to encourage private–public partnerships – including providing incentives to companies to invest in traditionally under-served communities.

Some policy prescriptions

Let me provide a few policy prescriptions that might strengthen the concerted role of the independent sector to address the digital divide. The desirable outcome is to resolve the problem of the digital divide within the larger framework of development as freedom, as outlined in the first section of this chapter. Thus public policy must not only address access questions, but also how the internet and sophisticated computer applications will advance educational, health, civic, and other quality of life concerns. If we are collectively determined to view technology development as a necessary means, without which citizens of an advanced society are not equipped to participate fully in the life of the larger community, then it is incumbent upon us to develop inclusive policies and programmes. Let me take each sector in turn and suggest several possible ameliorative strategies.

While non-profit organizations in the USA are delivering a greater share of social and human services, they remain on the whole under-funded and undervalued in our society. When we talk about information and technology 'have-nots', it should be emphasized that most non-profit organizations are small and lack the capacity to utilize information technology effectively to fulfil their diverse missions. It is not only poor and middle-class households that make difficult decisions about whether to purchase a computer. This calculus also occurs among small and medium-sized non-profit organizations for which infrastructure upgrades can be a significant portion of operating budgets. A 1999 report published by the Center for Excellence in Nonprofits found that many Silicon Valley non-profit organizations are still struggling to develop a Web presence. In addition, one-half of all small organizations are not networked. When organizations are asked about software used for enhancing fundraising activities, a majority of respondents remarked that their off-the-shelf software was inadequate for their needs and that cost prohibited them from purchasing a more effective tool. The report arrives at the unremarkable yet previously undocumented conclusion that 'budgetary constraints are a key factor in the full implementation of technology in the nonprofit sector'.

Non-profit organizations and smaller foundations, moreover, will have a harder time building their technology capacity, since they often underestimate the cost of maintaining and supporting equipment as well as the costs of training staff to use the latest software applications effectively. The National Council of Nonprofit Associations' 1997 report, *A Greater Voice: Nonprofit Organizations, Communications Technology and Advocacy*, found that capacity-building was essential among non-profit outfits, many of which were only beginning to scratch the surface of what communications technology enables.

We must begin to address the inadequate funding opportunities afforded to non-profit organizations. As they take on the burden of developing the talents and skills of citizens which schools, governments, and other traditional organizations are unable or unwilling to take on, it is necessary to equip these institutions with the resources required to do the job on more than a shoestring budget. One way to begin to address the paucity of resources in the non-profit sector is to extend telecommunications discounts beyond schools and libraries, to include these community-based organizations. Organizations such as the Boys and Girls Clubs, Computer Clubhouses, and other community technology centres ought to be eligible for discounts. The FCC should begin a proceeding to inquire into extending the e-rate to community-based organizations. If the FCC does not inquire into this matter, then the Federal–State Joint Board, when it reconvenes to discuss the status of universal service, should entertain recommendations to extend e-rate discounts.

The nation's largest foundations, moreover, need to instigate a more coordinated attack on the digital divide. While various foundations have chosen specific components of the digital divide to take on, whether it be the Kellogg Foundation's rural project, the Markle Foundation's international focus, or the Ford Foundation's grant-making in order to strengthen the voice of advocates, these efforts have been, by and large, uncoordinated. A more integrated effort that stems from a common intellectual framework and a shared understanding of how to mitigate inequality and build capacity would be a prerequisite for a more systematic assault on the digital divide. Smart investment is key, and foundations are still figuring out how they can add value in an arena in which information technology and markets are, in many instances, outpacing our ability to make sound investments in organizations and programmes.

Recent executive branch announcements underscore the inertia that has penetrated Federal policy-making. The flagship TIIAP programme continues to get nibbled around the edges, as its funding is gradually eroded. Any new programmes are dead on arrival as the fiscally conservative Congress refuses to preempt the development of new markets by supporting the passage of new government-sponsored grant programmes. The latest lexicon to bolster continued government support for digital divide efforts is that of New Markets, the notion that industry must correct its myopia and see low-income and minority communities as new markets to be exploited rather than as blighted communities to be circumvented. Offering tax incentives and guaranteed loans to potential new investors, the administration hopes to spur economic development in communities that have hitherto been redlined and ignored.

While it is worthwhile to renovate our notions of the purchasing power of traditionally under-served communities, such a behavioural change is necessary but not sufficient to ensure the universal availability of essential telecommunications services. If we agree that a threshold level of information and communications services is required to fulfil citizens' rational life plan, then we must ensure, through vouchers, subsidies, or some other public mechanism, that householders have the capability to purchase such services.

The claims of industry notwithstanding, it seems unlikely that the market alone will ensure that all persons are afforded the threshold capacity to participate fully in the life of the larger community, including engagement in the virtual world. Inequalities in income, educational opportunity, and access to information and communications tools stack the deck against whole communities and classes of people, requiring comprehensive, public solutions. We cannot rely on the unjust reckoning of Moore's Law, with its pitiless calculation that all communities will be served in time, when prices fall enough to envelop the entire population. Industry can and should do more than staff research and development shops with the sharpest scientists and technologists; they should offer a percentage of gross receipts to be set aside for public purposes, including ensuring that the worst-off residents are able to connect to the network.

Just as the Crystal Palace encompassed the aspirations of commerce in the mid-nineteenth century – a symbol for establishing pacific relations among neighbours – so too the silicon transistor and the ceaseless traffic in cyberspace embody the spirit of turn-of-the-century America. Progress should be measured in more capacious terms than wealth creation, however, since a person's capability to function well in an advanced democratic society entails participation in cyberspace, entry to which cannot be guaranteed by market forces alone.

Notes

1. Telephone penetration rates on Indian reservations have been notoriously difficult to ascertain. Based on 1990 data, a US Department of Commerce (1995) report put the figure at 47 per cent, and more recent findings approximate penetration to be between 40 and 55 per cent (Kennard 1999). Computer penetration, according to the US Department of Commerce (1999), is around 42 per cent for all US households, while 60 per cent of households earning over $75 000 can access the internet.

2. While capabilities differ across nations, the leapfrog and transformative potential of information technology cannot be underestimated. In Bangladesh, for example, ICT is reaching rural people via the provision of cellular mobile services by Grameen Telecom. Through a microloan program, village pay phones are leased and made available to villagers for limited purposes.

3. In late 1999 AT&T announced that it would no longer support toll-free information (a service similar to directory enquires in the UK), since the service was available on the Web. While this transition may seem relatively innocuous, it highlights the imperative organizations have toward exploiting the efficiency of the Web, which may make more labor-intensive activities, such as operator-supported information, obsolete. Governments, for example, are heading toward paperless or electronic service delivery, which will have deleterious effect on those who currently do not have meaningful access to the internet.

4. Interestingly, although these leaders talk about access to the prevalent means of communications as a key civil right, there is a wide distance across these public and private leaders' positions regarding what technologies they are describing and the mechanisms to achieve these goals. While regulators in the USA are beginning to examine the next generation of universal service telecommunications technology, what is called broadband service, internet and cable services are not strictly telecommunications services, which complicates what services would count in an evolving conception of universal service. Private-sector leaders, moreover, might refer to the provision of a certain service as a right and still believe that the market is the appropriate mechanism for rolling out these services over time.

5. Kant's famous essay on perpetual peace anticipates Tennyson's remarks and embodies the Enlightenment faith in progress. Kant suggests that 'the *spirit of commerce* sooner or later takes hold of every people, and it cannot exist side by side with war. And of all the powers (or means) at the disposal of the power of the state, *financial power* can probably be relied on most' (1970: 114).

6. Such use patterns justify public policies that support technology centers, such as the US Department of Education's Community Technology Centers program and the 21st Century Community Learning Centers initiative, which funds after-school programs under Title X of the Elementary and Secondary Education Act.

7. The non-profit organization, Digital Partners, is handling a follow-up to the Seattle conference at www.digitaldivide.org.

References

Auerbach, J. (1999) *The Great Exhibition of 1851: a Nation on Display*. New Haven: Yale University Press.

Benton Foundation (2000) *The E-Rate in America: a Tale of Four Cities*. Washington, DC: The Benton Foundation.

Bernstein, J., Rasell, E. Schmitt, J. and Scott, R. (1999) 'Tax cut no cure for middle class economic woes'. Washington, DC: Economic Policy Institute.

Castells, M. (1999) 'The informational city is a dual city: can it be reversed?', in D.A. Schön, B. Sanyal and W.J. Mitchell (eds.), *High Technology and Low-Income Communities: Prospects for the Positive Use of Advanced Information Technology*. Cambridge, MA: MIT Press.

Center for Excellence in Nonprofits (1999) *Technology Survey Final Report*. San Jose: Center for Excellence in Nonprofits.

Derrida, J. (1994) *Specters of Marx: the State of the Debt, the Work of Mourning, and the New International*, trans. P. Kamuf. New York: Routledge.

Figueres, J.M. (1999) Presentation given at the 'Seeking Solutions to the Digital Divide' conference. Seattle, WA: The Technology Alliance, 29 November.

Garmer, A.K. (ed.) (1998) *Investing in Diversity: Advancing Opportunities for Minorities and the Media*. Washington, DC: The Aspen Institute.

Gittell, M.J. (ed.) (1998) *School Equity: Creating Productive Schools in a Just Society*. New Haven: Yale University Press.

Kant, I. (1970) *Perpetual Peace: a Philosophical Sketch*, edited by Hans Reiss. Cambridge: Cambridge University Press.

Kennard, W.E. (1999) Remarks at Public Hearing, 'Overcoming obstacles to telephone service to Indians on reservations.' Washington, DC: Federal Communications Commission.

Mandela, N. (1996) 'Remarks made at the TELECOM 95 conference', *The Trotter Review*, 9 4–6.

McChesney, R.W. (1999) 'The new global media', *The Nation*, 269, 29 November, 11–15.

National Council of Nonprofit Associations (1997) *A Greater Voice: Nonprofit Organizations, Communications Technology and Advocacy*. Washington, DC: National Council of Nonprofit Associations.

Ostrom, M.A. (1999) 'Bush backs charter schools to bridge digital divide', *San Jose Mercury News*, 18 October.

Schiller, D. (1999) 'Deep impact: the Web and the changing media economy', *Info*, 1(1) 35–51.

Sen, A. (1999) *Development as Freedom*. New York: Knopf.

Tennyson, A.L. (1899) *The Poetic and Dramatic Works of Alfred Lord Tennyson*. Boston: Houghton Mifflin and Co.

US Department of Commerce (1995) *Housing of American Indians on Reservations: Equipment and Fuels*. Washington, DC: US Department of Commerce.

US Department of Commerce (1999) *Falling Through the Net: a Report on the Telecommunications and Information Technology Gap in America*. Washington, DC: US Department of Commerce.

Westat (1999) *Evaluation of the Telecommunications and Information Infrastructure Assistance Program for the 1994 and 1995 Grant Years*. Rockville, MD: Westat.

Wilhelm, A. (2000) *Democracy in the Digital Age: Challenges to Political Life in Cyberspace.* New York: Routledge.

Wolpert, J. (1999) 'Center cities as havens and traps for low-income communities: the potential impact of advanced information technology', in D.A. Schön, B. Sanyal and W.J. Mitchell (eds), *High Technology and Low-Income Communities: Prospects for the Positive Use of Advanced Information Technology.* Cambridge, MA: MIT Press.

12
From an Answer to a Question: Globalization in the Information Age

Robin Brown

The driving force behind the third way is globalization. (Blair 1999)

No globalization without representation. (On Line Networking for the Environment 1999)

The adjective 'global' applied to a topic lends it cachet; it seems far more sophisticated to pontificate about global competition or global financial markets than to talk about merely domestic anti-trust or bank regulation. (Krugman 1994: 170–1)

Introduction: globalization and the zeitgeist

If asked to summarize the contemporary age, it is likely that we would focus on the phenomena of information or globalization. The connection between the two is made explicit in the current wave of interest in Marshall McLuhan and, in particular, his hyperbolic claims about the 'global village' (McLuhan and Fiore 1967, 1968). Yet despite the volume of comment that has been written about globalization there is little consensus about what it means or what its implications are.

This chapter seeks to do two things. First, it aims to untangle some of the reasons why the globalization debate exercises such fascination for the contemporary mind. Second, it will argue that only by treating globalization as a topic for investigation rather than a cultural icon can we understand both its possibilities and its limitations for generating inclusion and exclusion. A large part of the problem is that whenever globalization is discussed it is treated as if the phenomenon was already clearly delineated and understood, treated as an answer rather than a poorly formulated question.

I begin by arguing that the fascination that globalization exerts lies in two sources. Its very familiarity and its adoption as a piece of political shorthand.

Cultural roots of globalization

Deeply rooted in Western culture is the idea of an overcoming of the fragmentation of mankind. This can be traced back at least to the biblical story of the tower of Babel and the subsequent linguistic fragmentation of humanity. As early as the fourteenth century, authors such as Dante were bemoaning the fragmentation of the common Christian realm and the conflict that followed and sought ways to overcome this process and restore harmony (Hinsley 1963: 14). Of course, this was to remain just an aspiration but one that was embedded in Western intellectual traditions – not least liberalism and socialism. The drive to reunification was implicit in the belief in progress. Progress implied not so much better weapons as better communications. Better communications would remove sources of misunderstanding between people and bring the countries of the world to enlightenment that would in turn lead them to remove the parasitic rulers who thrived on conflict (Parkinson 1977; Howard 1981; Kubálková and Cruickshank 1989; *Millennium* 1995).

Asa Briggs (1966) identified the existence of successive waves of innovation in communications technologies beginning around 1840 – what he termed the 'communications revolution'. Associated with each wave of innovation we find the same recurring ideas. The world is shrinking, space and time have been overcome – in the 1840s a British anti-slavery campaigner was heartened by the fact that America was now only two weeks away by steamship (quoted in Keck and Sikkink 1998: 46). Reactions to the railway included: 'space has been destroyed', 'I feel as if the mountains and forests of all countries are advancing on Paris', 'frontiers of the races and the states lost their disruptive power' (quoted in Faith 1990: 42,61). Of course, the lessons that were drawn did not stop with simple empirical observations. The next step was to derive general conclusions from them; thus the constructor of the Suez Canal, Ferdinand de Lesseps, saw the construction projects of the nineteenth century – railways, telegraphs and canals – as having an 'identical goal: drawing peoples together, and thereby bringing about an era in which men, by knowing one another, will finally cease fighting' (quoted in Headrick 1991: 3).

Thus, a central reason for the hold of globalization on the contemporary imagination is its *plausibility* not because of any empirical evidence but because of the way that it fits with an important element of the contemporary historical narrative. Given that some of the key defining moments of the new era are the TV pictures of the fall of Ceaucescu and the Berlin Wall and the survival of the Chinese regime following the events in Tiananmen Square, in 1989, it seems highly plausible in everyday discourse to connect communications technologies, the removal of barriers, globalization and progress. At a deep-seated cultural level, we already think we know the answer: globalization serves as a master narrative for making sense of change.

Globalization and political discourse

Although globalization has deep-seated cultural roots, some of its current prominence stems from the idea's usefulness in contemporary political discourse. Globalization serves as a political slogan and a rallying point for three political groupings. The first of these is what might be termed neo-liberals or the liberal right. For them globalization is an unproblematically positive development. Globalization means free trade and free markets that promote economic well-being. These developments are associated with political benefits such as the rule of law and the free flows of information that promote democracy. Further, the tendency of government to act in irresponsible and predatory ways is kept in check by the pressure of international financial flows (McKenzie and Lee 1991). Thus, there is a mutual reinforcement between economic and political developments. For the liberal right, institutionally represented by the International Monetary Fund and the Organization for Economic Cooperation and Development and ideologically represented by the *Economist*, the *International Herald Tribune* and the *Financial Times*, globalization understood as the removal of restrictions to the flows of capital, products, information and people is a positive development.

The second grouping for whom globalization represents a significant issue can loosely be described as the 'opposition'. This in turn may be broken down into two overlapping elements – the internationalists and the nationalists. For the opposition globalization represents the unfettered operation of a capitalist economic system. Different groupings within this opposition take issue with different aspects of it. For environmentalists, globalization represents the subordination of the planet to the needs of capital. Thus, at a global level the discharges of cars and power stations produce global warming and threaten the planet through a failure to internalize the costs of production. Lives are threatened by the construction of unregulated factories that fail to control the discharges of pollution and habitats are swept away in the felling of rainforests. For labour groups the ability of multinational firms to switch production from country to country in pursuit of lower wages produces job insecurity in the developed world and exploitation beyond it (Greider 1997; Teeple 1995; Lang and Hines 1993). These critiques shade into a concern with the loss of control of human society. Mechanisms do not exist that allow control over the operations of global capitalism. One thread of these arguments – the internationalist – is the demand for new mechanisms of global governance but the more important thread is the need for national governments or groups of national governments to reassert control. Indeed what globalization is seen to do is to undermine the sovereignty or capacity of national governments and since these governments are seen as expressions of democratic accountability, the result is that globalization undermines democracy and removes any effective agency from the state. This is a fear that is not simply found on the political left – for instance, international regulation may effectively reduce standards of protection – but also on the right, where the forces of globalization undermine autonomy, identity and culture. Thus many in France see globalization as a capitalist, American plot that will destroy French culture and identity and undermine the welfare state and demand global regulation, while many in America see such regulation as a threat to their constitutional rights or simply their way of doing things. Globalization becomes a threat both in terms of social, cultural and economic flows and in attempts to regulate those flows (Goldsmith 1994).

It is noticeable that globalization is increasingly invoked by a third group, the advocates of the third way. The speeches of Bill Clinton and Tony Blair are regularly peppered with references to globalization or the global economy. For them, the pressures of a global economy are treated as a fact that must be confronted. Governments that fail to adapt to the challenges are failing in their duties. For all three groups globalization serves as a slogan and a symbol as much as analysis of the world. For the neo-liberals globalization is an agenda to be promoted for its positive consequences; for the opposition globalization stands as a symbol of all that is most undesirable; while for the third wayers globalization stands as symbol of modernity.

The many meanings of globalization

To convert globalization from a slogan to an analytically useful concept requires us to convert what we know into questions. The first task is to be more precise in defining what we mean by globalization. Here there are at least four meanings wrapped up in the single term. As David Held puts it globalization is 'the chronic intensification of patterns of interconnectedness' (Held 1993: 38–9). In this sense globalization indicates a pattern of social change where things that have been separate or loosely connected become increasingly integrated. Things in the modern world are more closely linked than they were in the past; consequently, communities are affected by events that happen thousands of miles away. This interconnectedness implies an shift in the nature of social life, an acceleration of change, a growing awareness of the world as a whole and a growing simultaneity of events on a global scale which has caused some social theorists to argue that 'flows' have supplanted 'places' as the appropriate way of characterizing late modernity (Appadurai 1990; Lash and Urry 1994; Castells 1996).

Globalization as a structural change is reflected in the second idea – the way in which a particular object or entity is opened to, or becomes more strongly connected to, the broader world. For instance, in analyzing social change in Southern California Mike Davis (1992: 101) refers to the 'globalization of the regional economy' to indicate a situation in which local economic activity is increasingly tied to that of the entire Pacific region. Alternatively, a company can choose to 'globalize' itself changing its strategy and organization to operate in a more international fashion. In this sense globalization is used synonymously with 'internationalization'.

A third sense of globalization argues that institutions and practices that have previously been confined to particular areas are spreading. Implicit in this is an idea of *globalization as homogenization* – that the parts of the world are becoming more alike. This has both positive and negative elements. From one point of view, the differences that impair communication and produce conflict are being overcome while on the other hand the diversity of the human condition is being steamrollered under the wheels of globalization

The fourth element of globalization that we can cite is that the world is becoming more of a single place. Roland Robertson (1992: 8) defined globalization as the 'compression of the world and the intensification of consciousness of the world as whole'. Robertson emphasizes the idea of the world as whole as one factor in creating 'globality', the world as a single place. In a shrinking world we are more conscious of the world as a single finite place, how it all fits together and our own place in it. For environmentalists the image of 'spaceship earth' facing a threat is both a powerful motivating factor and propaganda tool. Global warming, resource depletion, over-fishing, and the loss of biodiversity each pose a threat to the world as a whole.

Given that a single term stands for all of these ideas it is not surprising that globalization is such a slippery idea.

Theorizing globalization: some assumptions

Any attempt to make sense of large-scale social phenomena requires us to make some assumptions about the nature of the social world. Globalization in all four of the senses outlined above can be seen as largely a product of two sets of developments.[1] The first is the long-run fall in the costs of the movement of information, things and people as a result of the development and deployment of communications technologies. These falling costs allows the use of production strategies, political strategies and market strategies that have previously been unfeasible because of the costs of communication. From this perspective globalization is a long-run process, periodically given a boost by the emergence of new technologies. The current wave of globalization is associated with the development of cheap international telecommunications and the jet airliner. This wave has been sustained by the digitalization and hence convergence of communications technologies. The result is a continuing process of what geographers term 'spatial compression' (Harvey 1989; Brunn and Leinbach 1991).

The second development is the removal of political barriers to communication. Through the twin waves of democratization and liberalization, states have systematically reduced barriers to the movement of capital, goods and information. Over the past two decades the fall of many authoritarian governments and the relative failure of socialist and inward-looking development strategies compared with the apparent success of outward-oriented strategies have encouraged developments that have eased flows and hence encouraged the development of cross-border activities. In many popular accounts of globalization these developments are taken to be causally related – the information revolution produces both democracy and market capitalism. This may be true in a weak sense – political strategies based on denial of information become more difficult to sustain and if there is a natural propensity to 'truck and barter' – as Adam Smith put it, then democracy and capitalism are aided; but the record of postcommunist authoritarianism and crony capitalism suggest that there is no *necessary* connection. Hence the technological and political preconditions of the current wave of globalization are independent factors.

This view of globalization puts a focus on the choices of people and organizations in responding to the possibilities created by political change and new communications technologies. It also suggests that, rather than starting from an assumption that everything is inevitably connected to everything else, the degree of connectedness is a subject for investigation. Thus different areas of human activity – such as finance – may be becoming rapidly connected but others such as politics and industry less so. Similarly, some parts (geographical regions and spheres of activity) of the world are more connected than others.

Inclusion and exclusion

From this perspective we need to ask a set of questions about the consequences of globalization for inclusion and exclusion. Any social order includes some principles of differentiation as fundamental parts of that order – for instance, in a political system based around nation-states the principle of citizenship is a key element. Other forms of exclusion stem from the unintended consequences of the operation of that order – for instance, in the way that poverty denies access to communications resources. Processes of globalization affect existing patterns of inclusion and exclusion as well as possibly generating their own.

In historical perspective exclusion was seen to operate through the division of the world into core and periphery. The core – the Western developed capitalist countries – dominated patterns of economic development, imposed political domination on the Third World and controlled the flow of information and cultural products – including the basic infrastructure of communication, which, through its construction during the era of empire, operated as part of an imperial structure rather than as an element of a national communications system (Mattelart 1994).

In one very important way the globalization optimists are right. Current developments are unleashing a wholesale upgrading of the global communications infrastructure. This stems from the conclusion by national governments and international telecommunications organizations that economic success is closely linked to the existence of a developed communications infrastructure. Hence, communications has become a development priority. This realization has been accompanied by a movement away from state monopoly communications services towards privatization, competition and foreign investment. Given the poor record of investment, maintenance and service by national operators, this is probably a positive development.

Innovation has seen the emergence of improved phone services in most parts of the world and the widespread deployment of cellular phone technology as a way to accelerate the upgrading of wired networks. These tendencies towards the internationalization of the communications industry can be criticized on many grounds. Firstly, the internationalization reduces the responsiveness of communications to national policy goals and priorities. Secondly, the priority of communications development has tended to work to the benefits of elites – urban and able to afford the charges for new telephone services or for using computers at internet cafés. Thirdly, the new developments have tended to promote access to 'global' culture – Americanized, consumerist and capitalist. Finally, the new developments have not resolved the exclusion of the poor and rural from access to communications. However, these criticisms evaluate current developments against an ideal not the reality of the past (OECD 1999; World Bank 1994).

The historical record of communications development suggests that network development is structured by economic patterns and political priorities, but the use made of networks follows a law of unintended consequences (Headrick 1991). The logic of investment in expensive infrastructure projects is to try to maximize use so that costs are reduced and usage spreads to more outlying sections of society. As usage increases, unexpected types of use follow. Here the internet gives an important clue to patterns of exclusion and inclusion. By providing relatively cheap communications via e-mail and relatively cheap information publishing via the net it provides a new tool of political mobilization. It provides a voice and a window for the relatively marginalized – as well as a shop window for mainstream global capitalism. Recent research demonstrates that the leading brands on the net are increasing their dominance. People seeking to use a search engine or find a news source tend to go to the leaders (BBC On-Line 1999). But the fact that higher proportions of Web usage are concentrated on these relatively few sites does not mean that the minority or specialist disappears. For those that seek them, the 'excluded' are still there. For critics the problem is a normative one – the assumption that the marginalized should be the mainstream. Current developments show no signs of producing such an outcome.

The logic of spatial compression operates in favour of what Castells (1996) calls the space of flows. It does imply some logic of incorporation. It implies the incorporation of some previously excluded parts of the world into the global space. It implies the incorporation of chunks of the Third World into the systems of production. Particularly in East

Asia we can trace the spreading tentacles of export-oriented production from Japan to Hong Kong, Taiwan and South Korea, into south east Asia and into southern China (Dicken 1992). For those directly affected by this process, it has meant a movement from the countryside into the cities and the factories and subjection to new forms of discipline as they escape the old forms. Politically speaking, the flows of information relativize political orders – when the situation here can be compared to what happens there alternatives become possible (Nettl and Robertson 1968).

'Globalization' can be conceptualized as a linear process of uneven incorporation into a capitalist mainstream. What this description ignores is a process by which the shock of the new generates its own reaction. Exposure to the 'West' is not a passive process that simply steamrollers difference. Firstly, the products of the West are appropriated into local cultures and take on their own local characteristics. Secondly, the exposure to alien cultural forms increases awareness of the local. One consequence of processes of globalization has been the reassertion of local cultural identities, for instance, in the discourse of 'Asian Values' and through Islamist political movements. Thirdly, this reaction can take an economic form. The explosion in spending in media and broadcasting has not resulted in a domination of American culture but in part has stimulated local production. In Asia exposure to STAR TV forced local broadcasters to compete to develop more dynamic and appealing forms of programming. The emergence of competing broadcasters naturally increased demand for attractive imported programming and as result forced up prices for programming. By doing so it made local production more attractive as an option. Local programming, since it is aimed at the particular audience, tends to be more appealing. Thus one consequence of the globalization of television has been a growth in the diversity of programme production.

Spatial compression does not abolish exclusion/inclusion – indeed it cannot, and why should it? The United States possesses the most sophisticated communications system in the world yet it is still marked by patterns of inclusion and exclusion. Compression changes the patterns in ways that are marked by existing social factors.

Global political change: two examples

I want to take up these themes via a consideration of two concrete cases of the relationship between communications technologies and political change.

The first of these is the emergence of a global ban on anti-personnel landmines. This is usually read as evidence of the emergence of a global pattern of politics – a global movement making use of new communications technologies to produce a global ban. The second of these cases is that of the deposed Malaysian Deputy Prime Minister Anwar Ibrahim. Anwar Ibrahim's arrest and trial was opposed by a campaign that made use of the internet and satellite television, which successfully engaged the support of regional leaders and the American government but which failed to secure his release. If Anwar had been released it would have been hailed as yet more evidence of the way that communications technologies were changing the practice of world politics. In any case it provides an interesting case of the limits to change and the way that we cannot derive conclusions simply from the technology.

In December 1997 122 governments signed a convention prohibiting the use, manufacture, export or stockpiling of anti-personnel landmines. The completion of this treaty can be seen as victory for a new politics of the global in which an alliance of non-governmental organizations acting in pursuit of humanitarian goals networking around new information and communications technologies were able to defeat both apathy and the opposition of national security establishments. Concern with the indiscriminate nature of landmines reached back at least to the 1950s. In 1981 the United Nations agreed a Convention on Prohibitions or Restrictions on the Use of Certain Conventional Weapons which may be Deemed to be Excessively Injurious or to Have Indiscriminate Effects, normally referred to as the Certain Conventional Weapons (CCW) Convention, the second protocol of which imposed restrictions on the use of landmines. In the context of the Cold War few militarily significant states chose to accede to the treaty (Detter De Lupis 1987: 180–95). However, the end of the Cold War allowed a greater prominence for the consequences of proxy conflicts in the Third World. Cambodia and Angola became symbols of the civilian casualties caused by anti-personnel mines. In 1991 the Vietnam Veterans of America Foundation and Medico International decided to create a network of NGOs that would campaign for a total ban on anti-personnel mines. The result was the establishment of a steering group that organized a conference of NGOs. These activities drew in other groups and began to have an impact on governments. France requested the UN to convene a review conference on the CCW and in the run up to the conference a growing number of organizations became involved in what was now known as the International Campaign to Ban Landmines (ICBL). The International

Committee of the Red Cross (ICRC) began to play an active role in promoting the issue. The CCW Review session failed to produce a ban in 1995, but the campaign did not falter. In November 1995 the ICRC launched a media campaign to promote the issue. The ICBL sought to use its 600 member organizations operating in 40 countries to target their local and transnational media. When the CCW Review reconvened in Geneva in late April 1996 30 countries had expressed their support for a comprehensive ban. Despite the growing support there was still resistance to the total ban. At this point Canada took the lead and pushed for what became known as the 'Ottawa process'. Rather than working through the complexities of the UN, states that supported a ban would conclude their own convention in Ottawa in December 1997 – the risk was that so few states would sign as to make the treaty irrelevant. In the intervening period a snowball effect began to emerge as the international campaign continued and some countries began to take unilateral action. In February 1997 South Africa announced that it would abandon the use of landmines. As more countries announced their support for the ban, those that stood outside became more exposed and qualification and reservations were subject to criticism. By the time of the Ottawa Conference outright resistance to the ban was largely confined to Russia, China and the Middle East. While the United States has refused to sign the treaty piecemeal changes in policy have achieved much of the same results (Price 1998).

The emergence of the ban was intimately tied to the use of information and communications technologies on a global basis. Firstly, the ICBL was concerned to use the media to promote awareness of the issue and to exert pressure against recalcitrant governments. Here endorsements of the campaign by high-profile figures such as the Pope and Princess Diana were exploited to advance the cause. Circulation of images of the victims of landmines fed into deeply rooted humanitarian sentiments. Secondly, the campaign was organized as a network that drew in nongovernmental organizations, international organizations and, increasingly, governments. The internet became a valuable tool for the timely circulation of information. The falling costs of circulating information made it easier for the campaign to monitor developments, to identify targets for pressure and to maintain and coordinate its own activities. A final point is that it was the increasing contacts between groups operating locally that convinced those involved of the scale of the problem and the need for global action. One element of the growth of the campaign in the early 1990s was the realization that the threat of mines was not something confined to one country or one region but rather an issue that required global action. Only by working at a global level could the supplies of mines be cut off.

The development of the ICBL and its success provides a case study of a global political practice: ICTs permit the formation of global networks that could generate sufficient political resources to overcome the resistance of many states. The network organization drew in excluded voices. However, the success of the ICBL was also due to the ability to mobilize states on the side of the ban.

At the beginning of September 1998 Anwar Ibrahim, Deputy Prime Minister of Malaysia and heir apparent to the Prime Minister, Mohammed Mahathir, was removed from office. Two-and-a-half weeks later Anwar was arrested and charged with homosexual activity and conspiracy. The conflict between Mahathir and Anwar was played out in the media. State dominance of the media was used to promote accusations against Anwar and to justify his removal from office. In response Anwar addressed crowds of supporters outside his home and travelled around the country to public meetings. Internet sites putting over Anwar's case and counter-accusations sprang up both inside and outside the country (Fuller 1998a). Prior to his arrest Anwar recorded an interview that was beamed back into the country on the transnational satellite channel CNBC (Fuller 1998b). The new media allowed the opposition to sidestep state control of the media in order to mobilize support internally and externally. As protests took place across the country, Anwar Ibrahim's daughter travelled to other countries to engage foreign diplomatic support in particular that of the President of the Philippines Joseph Estrada (*Economist* 1998a, 1998c). Other regional leaders were said to be unhappy with Anwar's arrest but refused to speak out. Despite the weakness of the leadership – the Government used the Internal Security Act to detain leaders without trial – the movement managed to sustain a wave of protests that began to mobilize a broader wave of political disaffection (*Economist* 1998b; Fuller 1998c). The beginning of Anwar's trial in open court served to maintain interest in the case and to ensure that it was reported in the regional media.

At this point the Malaysian government found itself locked in to an externally set timetable, the prior agreement to host the APEC Summit in mid-November. When the date was set the Government would have looked to promote the Summit as evidence of international approval for Malaysia's political and economic success but the effect in November 1998 was to focus media attention on the country and inevitably on the political situation. In the run-up to the meeting the United States and Canada made it clear that they would not hold any bilateral meetings with Malaysian officials as sign of displeasure at the situation (Richardson 1998a). As the meeting opened Madeleine Albright met with Mrs Anwar in a move clearly designed to signal US concern and support for the protesters. More was to follow in a speech to the forum; Al Gore spoke of the 'brave people of Malaysia' pushing for *reformasi* – the slogan of the protesters (Fuller 1998d, 1998e). This statement, presumably designed to build support for the opposition, backfired. Malaysian spokesmen mounted a furious response accusing Gore of interfering in Malaysia's internal affairs. This provided a perfect platform to promote an anti-foreign nationalist line in the domestic media – mobilizing the government's own supporters (Richardson 1998b). The speech was also regarded as going too far by regional governments. An unexpected boost for Mahathir came from the outbreak of violence in Indonesia that was given great prominence in the Malaysian media (and in other available media). Given the history of ethnic conflict in Malaysia, street violence raises the possibility of ethnic violence and hence the government sought to reframe the issue of street protests against the detention of Anwar as one of the threats to domestic stability (Fuller 1998f). Thus, the wave of protests died down especially as the political opposition in Malaysia has always been weakened by divisions along ethnic lines (Jesudason 1996: 136–8).

Conclusion

The central conclusion to be drawn from this chapter is that 'globalization' has to be approached as a question not an answer. The confusion that globalization generates has much to do with the fact that much of the time the conclusion is presumed in the answer. The play of forces at work is too complex to allow simple answers, although this could be taken as a more definite answer: that if we cannot draw these definite conclusions, then globalization is less real that we might hope or fear.

Communications technologies do not operate autonomously to change the nature of the social order. They are part of that order. Underpinning the determinist account is the assertion that communications media are the most important element in any society. Yet for all their importance, they are part of a larger reality that incorporates ideas, institutions, people and habits. The choices that are made about investments in new technologies or in the use of those technologies shape the impacts of those technologies. Much of what is said about the relationship between globalization and technology is actually theoretical discourse – taking a possible relationship as a fact. Empirical investigation always shows that multiple factors are at work that ensure that the 'logic' of the technology does not reveal itself in practice. Thus both the positive and negative possibilities of technologies are mitigated by the social realities.

There has certainly been a growing degree of interconnectedness, partly as a result of the changing political geography of the world. The success of outward-oriented growth strategies in East Asia has encouraged a movement to the market even as the collapse of the Soviet Bloc removed an alternative and encouraged processes of democratization. Yet part of this change lies in the conjunction of a set of political developments that might still be reversed. American exceptionalism and the suspicion of liberalizing trends contains the possibility of pulling the rug from under this globalization. On the other hand, the technological foundation of globalization in the explosive diffusion of digital communications technologies seems unlikely to be significantly slowed. Anti-global politics in a world compressed technologically would provide an interesting situation for exploring the relationship between macrosocial change and technology.

Note

1. It should be noted that this does not exhaust all the relevant factors. For instance, it might be suggested that the development of environmental problems as a result of industrialization is not necessarily connected to the growth of communications. This is true in a scientific sense, but the growing consciousness of the problem is, in practice, a function of the growth of communications.

References

Appadurai, A. (1990) 'Disjuncture and difference in the global cultural economy', in M. Featherstone (ed.), *Global Culture: Nationalism, Globalism and Modernity*. London: Sage.
BBC On-Line (1999) 'Web is Shrinking' 25 August, www.bbc.co.uk/english/ sci/tech/newsid_428000/428999.stm.
Beck, U. (1992) *Risk Society: Towards a New Modernity*, trans. M. Ritter. London: Sage.

Blair, T. (1999) 'Facing the Modern Challenge: The Third Way in Britain and South Africa', Speech, Capetown, South Africa, 8 January.

Briggs, A. (1966) *The Communications Revolution*. Leeds: Leeds University Press.

Brunn, S. and Leinbach T. (eds) (1991) *Collapsing Space and Time: Geographic Aspects of Communications and Information*. London: HarperCollins.

Castells M. (1996) *The Rise of the Network Society*. Oxford: Blackwell.

Davis, M. (1992) *City of Quartz: Excavating the Future in Los Angeles*. London: Vintage.

Detter De Lupis, I. (1987) *The Law of War*. Cambridge: Cambridge University Press.

Dicken, P. (1992) *Global Shift: the Internationalization of Economic Activity*, second edition. London: PCP.

Economist (1998a) 'Malice in Wonderland', 12 September.

Economist (1998b) 'Malaysia's nasty bruising', 3 October.

Economist (1998c) 'Changing the script in the Philippines', 24 October.

Faith, N. (1990) *The World the Railways Made*. London: Bodley Head.

Ferguson, M. (1991) 'Marshall McLuhan revisited: 1960s zeitgeist victim or pioneer postmodernist,' *Media, Culture and Society*, 13(1) 71–90.

Fuller, T. (1998a) 'Mahathir caught in Web of internet awareness', *International Herald Tribune*, 10 September.

Fuller, T. (1998b) 'In videotape ousted deputy blasts Mahathir for corruption', *International Herald Tribune*, 25 September.

Fuller, T. (1998c) 'Malaysia puts Anwar, and itself, in the dock', *International Herald Tribune*, 2 November.

Fuller, T. (1998d) 'Warning aside, Albright meets Anwar's wife', *International Herald Tribune*, 16 November.

Fuller, T. (1998e) 'Gore's speech stuns Malaysia', *International Herald Tribune*, 17 November.

Fuller, T. (1998f) 'Malaysian protests fade after comments by Gore', *International Herald Tribune*, 26 November.

Giddens, A. (1990) *The Consequences of Modernity*. Cambridge: Polity Press.

Goldsmith, J. (1994) *The Trap*. London: Macmillan.

Greider, W. (1997) *One World, Ready or Not*. London: Penguin.

Harvey, D. (1989) *The Condition of Postmodernity*. Oxford: Blackwell.

Headrick, D. (1991) *The Invisible Weapon: Telecommunications and International Politics, 1851–1945*. New York: Oxford University Press.

Held, D. (1993) 'Democracy: from city-states to a cosmopolitan order?', in D. Held (ed.), *Prospects for Democracy: North, South, East, West*. Cambridge: Polity Press.

Hinsley, F. (1963) *Power and the Pursuit of Peace*. Cambridge: Cambridge University Press.

Howard, M. (1981) *War and the Liberal Conscience*. Oxford: OUP.

Jesudason, J. (1996) 'The syncretic state and the structuring of oppositional politics in Malaysia', in Gary Rodan (ed.), *Political Oppositions in Industrializing Asia*. London: Routledge.

Keck, M. and Sikkink S. (1998) *Activists Beyond Borders: Advocacy Networks in International Politics*. Ithaca, NY: Cornell University Press.

Krugman, P. (1994) *Peddling Prosperity: Economic Sense and Nonsense in the Age of Diminished Expectations*. New York: Norton.

Kubálková, V. and Cruickshank, A. (1989) *Marxism and International Relations*. Oxford: Oxford University Press.

Lang, T. and Hines C. (1993) *The New Protectionism: Protecting the Future Against Free Trade*. London: Earthscan.

Lash, S. and Urry, J. (1994) *Economies of Signs and Space*. London: Sage.

Mattelart, A. (1994) *Mapping World Communication: War, Progress and Culture*, trans. S. Emanuel and J. Cohen. Minneapolis, MN: University of Minnesota Press.

McKenzie, R. and Lee, D. (1991) *Quicksilver Capital: How the Rapid Movement of Wealth Has Changed the World*. New York: Free Press.

McLuhan, M. and Fiore Q. (1967) *The Medium is the Massage: an Inventory of Effects*. New York: Bantam.

McLuhan, M. and Fiore Q. (1968) *War and Peace in the Global Village*. New York: Bantam.

Millennium (1995) 'The Globalization of Liberalism', Special Issue, 24(3)(Winter).

Nettl, J. and Robertson, R. (1968) *International Systems and the Modernization of Societies: The Formation of National Goals and Attitudes*. London: Faber.

OECD (1999) *Communications Outlook 1999*. Paris: OECD.

On Line Networking for the Environment (1999) 'Join the People's Rally and March for Fair Trade'. www.seattlewto.org/staging_rally.htm

Parkinson, F. (1977) *The Philosophy of International Relations*. London: Sage.

Price, R. (1998) 'Reversing the gun sights: transnational civil society targets land mines', *International Organization*, 52(3) 613–44.

Richardson, M. (1998a) 'Divided and distracted APEC prepares to meet', *International Herald Tribune*, 14 November.

Richardson, M. (1998b) 'Gore opens APEC rift with praise of reform', *International Herald Tribune*, 18 November

Robertson, R. (1992) *Globalization: Social Theory and Global Culture*. London: Sage.

Stevenson, N. (1995) *Understanding Media Cultures: Social Theory and Mass Communication*. London: Sage.

Teeple, G. (1995) *Globalization and the Decline of Social Reform*. Toronto: Garamond.

Toynbee, A. (1948) *Civilization on Trial*. London: Oxford University Press.

World Bank (1994) *World Development Report 1994: Infrastructure for Development*. Oxford: Oxford University Press.

Index